GERMAN
TANKS AT
WAR

Signal

GERMAN TANKS AT WAR

BOB CARRUTHERS

CASSELL&CO

This book was made possible by the kind assistance of George Parada of the Achtung Panzer Website, an invaluable source for those interested in the story of the German armoured forces in the Second World War. Thanks also to David Fletcher of the Tank Museum at Bovington, a great master of his subject and an even better communicator. Jim Mcdonald of Neidpath Castle and Peter Mooney of the Second Battle Group also made valuable contributions.

Cassell & Co
Wellington House, 125 Strand
London WC2R 0BB

Designed and produced by Cromwell Productions Limited
Copyright © Cromwell Productions Ltd 2000

Additional material by courtesy of Lamancha Productions

First published 2000

British Library Cataloguing-in-Publication Data
A catalogue record for this book is available from the British Library

ISBN 0-304-35394-9

Distributed in the USA by
Sterling Publishing Co. Inc.,
387 Park Avenue South
New York, NY 10016-8810

Printed and bound in Slovenia by DELO tiskarna
by arrangement with Korotan Ljubljana

Half title page: Panzer IIIs loaded down with extra fuel supplies move through Croatia. The problem of fuel supply was to prove an ever present concern for the men of the Panzerwaffe.
Opposite title page: The first glimpse of the Tiger tank in the pages of *Signal* magazine, May 1943, nine months after the tanks had first been deployed in action.
Title page: A Panzer III concealed behind a barn in the long shadows of an early autumn afternoon during the advance into Russia.

CONTENTS

INTRODUCTION

A NEW THREAT

In April 1938, to mark the Fuhrer's birthday, Hitler's magnificent new army marched before him. At the centre of the great parade were the tanks of the new German Panzer Divisions. The event was staged to intimidate the world. True, most of the tanks were small and lightly armed and, unbeknown to the foreign dignitaries, some were allegedly driven past twice, but they served Hitler's grand design. Hitler was a gambler and he gambled upon bluffing his enemies into believing his tank forces were far stronger than they actually were. By a combination of deceit and brinkmanship, Hitler had made a chilling and spectacular assertion of Germany's re-born military might.

Adolf Hitler was the man who provided the impetus to develop the Panzer Divisions of Germany's Wehrmacht, and in the campaigns of the early war years these new tank armies would strike down all before them. The German soldier would become accustomed to fighting against numerical odds but he would also become accustomed to victory. The comparatively few mechanised and armoured units were the only truly modern component of the German Army and they were the key to much of its extraordinary success. The military of many countries were familiar with wireless, with tanks and with war planes, but only in Germany were these elements so effectively combined to form fully integrated fighting units with exceptional striking power. Hitler's Generals had rewritten the rule book of battle. In Poland it took less than a month to dispose of a large but poorly equipped Polish army which had fought along rigidly traditional lines. In France, the German army successfully challenged the largest and most modern army in Europe. In the ensuing 'Blitzkrieg' or 'lightning war' the British forces were completely routed. Only a year later even this achievement was to be eclipsed by Germany's astonishing victories in the war against Stalin's Soviet Union. In June 1941, spearheaded by tank formations, German Armies swept eastward. In a series of huge encirclements, thousands of Soviet tanks were destroyed and millions of Soviet troops killed or captured. For a while it seemed that Hitler would succeed where Napoleon had failed, by conquering the vast eastern power. On the world

Panzer III chassis in the Alkett works during 1941.

stage the tank had become established as a symbol of German invincibility.

It is difficult now to imagine that such small and lightly armoured tanks could spearhead the devastating operation of Blitzkrieg. The secret of their success was speed and co-ordination of effort. In reality, the remarkable string of German successes was due less to superiority of military technology than to the excellence of German methods and training. Many of the German Panzer Division were equipped only with Panzer I and II light tanks. It was the new way of waging war which came as a hammer blow to Germany's opponents, forcing them to radically rethink their own military tactics. Slowly the lessons would be learned and eventually the answer to Blitzkrieg would be found.

Tanks came of age in the Second World War. They also developed quicker and changed more in a six-year period than at any time before or since. The catalyst was the demands of a technological war. Like a crazed version of Darwin's Theory of Evolution, the Second World War accelerated the pace of design. Fast responses to a constantly changing situation were urgently needed and new designs had to be engineered, tested and built in an incredibly short timescale. In the space of three short years, German tank technology progressed from the lightweight and inefficient Panzer I to the mighty Panzer VI - the Tiger, the most complete fighting vehicle of the war. As an example of evolution, the transformation of the Panzer I to the Tiger was an almost unbelievable leap in design terms.

DARWINISM GONE MAD

At the end of the nineteenth century when he proposed his theory of evolution, Charles Darwin noted that there were many branches that led to unsuccessful species and hence to extinction. Of course, Darwin was talking about animals, but tanks, it would seem, followed broadly the same rules of evolution.

In the 20's and 30's, it was understood that tanks in the coming war would need to be able to deal with two major situations. The first were tank-versus-tank actions. Even the lightest tanks were capable of surviving explosions very close to the

vehicle. Faced with the armour of a tank, explosive shell power alone was therefore of little value. To destroy a tank, it was obviously necessary to fire a projectile fast enough to penetrate the armour of the hull and disable the machine, or kill the men inside. Elementary physics tells us that force equals mass times velocity. For the job of destroying other tanks, the tank needs to be able to fire the heaviest practicable shell, at huge speeds. This produces enough force to punch through the armour of an enemy tank. Explosive power alone has little value against the thick armour of a tank. What gives the missile its penetrating power is the enormous velocity which slices through the armour of enemy vehicles. Even today, armour piercing rounds still tend to be solid shot which rely upon a very high velocity, and the enormous pressures and heat created by a round impacting on armour, in order to burn its way or melt its way through the armour to fly around inside, either destroying equipment or killing or injuring the crew.

Tanks of the Panzerwaffe silhouetted against the skyline during the advance to Stalingrad in August 1942.

Kliest's Panzers advancing along a railway line during the early stages of Operation Babarossa. Operating in conjunction with Guderian's forces, these tanks helped to produce some of the largest hauls of prisoners on the Eastern Front.

The armour of most tanks of 1939 and 1940 vintage could be penetrated by relatively small calibre anti-tank weapons, but the armour piercing weapons which fire these high velocity shells were only useful in combat against other tanks. A variety of high explosive anti-tank rounds were therefore developed, which were designed to first penetrate the armour of an enemy tank, then explode inside the vehicle. This fine balancing act was rarely achieved in practice, and it is debatable whether the small amount of explosive contained in the shells was much more effective than the massive kinetic impact of a high velocity round.

In addition to other tanks, tanks needed to be able to deal with infantry and field guns, in these cases they needed to be able to fire a high explosive round. Here, the speed of the shell was less important; what mattered was the weight of explosive packed into the warhead. In simple terms, the bigger the shell, the bigger the explosion. High explosive shells - generally speaking - had a hollow cone into which high explosives were inserted and which were designed to detonate and throw out a lethal stream of metal splinters, which were particularly effective against infantry out in the open. Of course, high explosives

were also useful for destroying non-armoured targets such as lorries and jeeps.

The drive to achieve the combination of destructive power and a tank-killing capability produced two radically different alternatives. Some countries opted for a balanced tank force with some tanks developed for anti-tank duties and others for high explosive capability.

This was the certainly the case with the Wehrmacht: the Germans developed two separate types of tank, each specialised for a particular job. The first were the tank killers equipped with a high velocity anti-tank gun with a longer barrel of smaller calibre.

Most of the Panzer IIIs of 1939 vintage were equipped with the 37mm gun, designed to deal with enemy tanks. By contrast all of the heavier Panzer IV tanks were designed as infantry support tanks. They were equipped with a short barrelled 75mm gun, of lower velocity but higher calibre, ideal for firing high explosives.

As the short-barrelled 75mm gun was designed to fire high explosive in the close support role, the Panzer IV had to be made with heavier armour as this tank was designed to stay close to the infantry, and use the gun to deal with the usual infantry opposition, in the form of machine gun positions, block houses and light artillery. Although it did have an anti-tank capability, the early war 75mm gun was not really to be judged as an anti-tank weapon. The Panzer IV was designed to deal with those targets that a high velocity anti-tank gun could not cope with.

In contrast to the Germans, who developed two different types of tanks to do different jobs, one solution tried by the armies of Britain, France, America and Russia was to house two types of gun in the same tank. This produced the massive multi-turreted tanks like the French Char 2c, the Russian BT-35 and the American Lee-Grant tank.

The dual turret idea was a failure, an evolutionary blind alley which was cruelly exposed on the battlefield. The two turrets made the tank difficult to operate, it was impossible to co-ordinate the guns and the sheer size of the machines presented a huge target that was difficult to miss. With the figure of her commander perched some 15 feet above the ground, it was easy to see why the Lee-Grant tank could not be successfully hidden on the battlefield.

As the war progressed, the same course was ultimately adopted by all sides, which was to combine both an anti-tank capability and an infantry support role in one well armoured vehicle which mounted the largest possible calibre of main gun with the highest practicable velocity. The larger calibre effectively gave it a good high explosive firing capability and the high velocity gave it a deadly killing power against other tanks. The Panther tank of 1944 vintage was considered by many to be the ultimate combination of these two features.

Despite the undoubted promise of machines like the Panther, in 1945, when the war ended, Germany was still developing the super heavy Panzer VII, a huge metal monster, weighing over one hundred tons, massively armoured and sporting a huge 122mm main gun. In an untypically humorous moment, this machine, designed to lead the Nazi war machine, was nicknamed 'Maus' (Mouse). The Maus was never to see action and only four prototypes were built, but it seemed that the crazed minds of the Third Reich would never give up the quest to be the best and the biggest, whatever the cost, but as the humble T-34 had proved, in matters of evolution, sometimes quantity matters as much as quality.

A group of tank men take a well-earned rest from the pressures of life on the move. The strain of constant action can be seen etched into their faces.

Tank Terminology

Some common phrases and terms with their English counterparts might prove helpful.

- **Abteilung (Abt)**
  Detachmant / Battalion
- **Ausfuhrung (Ausf)**
  Variant of Model
- **Begleitwagen**
  Code name for the Panzer I
- **Beobachtungswagen (Beob. Wg)**
  Observation Post Vehicle
- **Bergepanzer**
  Armoured Recovery Vehicle
- **Beutepanzer**
  Captured tanks
- **Fliegerabwehrkanone (Flak)**
  Anti-Aircraft Gun
- **Geschutzwagen (Gw.)**
  Gun vehicle
- **Granatwerfer (Gr.W)**
  Mortar / Rocket Projector
- **Jagdpanzer (Jgd. Pz)**
  Tank destroyer
- **Kampfgruppe (KG)**
  Battle Group
- **Kampfwagenkanone (KwK)**
  Combat Vehicle Gun (Tank Gun)
- **Kanone (K)**
  Gun / Cannon
- **L / (Kaliber / lange)**
  Caliber Length
- **Lastkraftwagen (Lkw)**
  Cargo Truck)
- **leichte (le)**
  Light
- **Lehrtrupp**
  (training company)
- **MK (Maschinengewehr)**
  Machine Gun
- **mittlerer (m)**
  Medium
- **MK (Maschinenkanone)**
  Automatic Cannon / Gun
- **Munitions - Panzerwagen (Mun Pz.)**
  Ammunition Carrier
- **Osketten**
  58mm wide tracks for use in Russia
  (spring of 1944)

- **Panzerabwehrkanone (Pak)**
  Anti-Tank Gun
- **Panzer-Befehlswagen (Pz.BefWg)**
  Command Tank
- **Panzerjager (Pz.Jag)**
  Tank Hunter
- **Panzerjagdkanone (Pjk)**
  Anti-Tank Gun (itself)
- **Panzerkampfwagen (PzKpfw)**
  Battle Tank
- **Panzersphwagen (PSW)**
  Armoured Car
- **Personenkraftwagen (Pzw)**
  Personel Carrier
- **Schurzen**
  Skirts / Aprons (extra protection for
  the suspension and road wheel
  configeration)
- **Schutzenpanzerwagen**
  Half-Tracked Personnel Carrier
- **Schutzenzug (zug)**
  Platoon
- **schwere (s)**
  Heavy
- **Selbstfahrlafette (sf)**
  Self Propelled Gun
- **Sonderkraftfahrzeng (SdKfz)**
  Special Purpose Motar Vehicle
- **Sturmgeschutz (StuG)**
  Assault Gun
- **Sturm-Infanteriegeschütz (SIG)**
  Assault Infantry Gun
- **Sturmpanzerhaubitze (StuK)**
  Assault Howitzer
- **Sturmpanzerkanone (StuK)**
  Assault Gun (itself)
- **Tauchpanzer**
  A submersible tank
- **Waffantrager**
  Weapon Carrier
- **Werkstatt-Kompanie**
  Maintenance company
- **Winterketten**
  560mm wide tracks for use in Russia
  (Fall of 1942)
- **Versuchskonstruktion (VK)**
  Experimental Construction / Prototype
- **Vollkettenfahrzeug (VK)**
  Full-Tracked Vehicle

THE PANZER DIVISIONS

The forerunners of the mighty Panzer Divisions. Forbidden to develop an armoured force, the Wehrmacht had to resort to the humiliating solution of wood and cardboard frames placed over the chassis of conventional automobiles. The first training exercises took place using these bizarre vehicles.

> **"In general, the tanks have proven their worth. The capabilities and overall manoeuvrability of the vehicles is very good. The MG-Kampfwagens are very useful and effective vehicles. However, it should not be overlooked that armour defeating weapons and weapons firing high explosives must be introduced."**
> *General Lutz, Kommando der Panzertrappen, August 1935*

In the wake of the bitter defeat inflicted on Germany in the Great War the allied forces were determined that there should be no repeat of that terrible conflict. The treaty of Versailles imposed draconian limitations on the Germans, strictly limiting the overall size of the army, and, more importantly, limiting the types of weaponry to be allowed. The events of the Great War had clearly identified the powerful effect of the advent of airpower; the result was that Germany was to be denied access to an air force. Despite the fact that the war had seen no major tank-versus-tank battles,

the Allies had seen enough to recognise the potential of the tank as a device capable of achieving major strategic impact in future wars. As a consequence, these new weapons were added to the growing list of items denied to the German forces.

Even in the 20's it was already apparent that, for a modern army, the consequences of entering into battle without tanks could be disastrous. This, of course, was the object of the Versailles treaty, which only permitted Germany a small standing army for the purpose of internal peacekeeping and

A rare image of one of the six Grosstraktor manufactured by Rhinemettal during 1928 and 1929. All six were used in the secret testing programme at Kama.

national defence. However, as the High Command understood all too well, without a tank force the chances of a successful counter attack were slim and for a nation born to the notion of aggressive moves even on the strategic defensive, this was really one step too far. It was this concern which initially shaped the drive for a German tank force. Later these foundations would be usurped by Hitler for his own purposes. Obviously the leaders of the Wehrmacht could not accept the humiliating conditions of the Versailles treaty without demur, and there began a period of covert experimentation which was to lead to the development of a tank capability that would shake the world.

SOVIET CO-OPERATION

Ironically, the roots of the German Panzerwaffe were laid in conjunction with Soviet Russia, the nation that was destined to become Nazi Germany's greatest enemy and ultimately her nemesis. During the 20's the new Soviet Union was an even greater pariah than Germany, and the fledgling soviet state had already withstood the perils of a civil war and foreign intervention,

which had seen British ground troops deployed in an attempt to assist the White Russians. Clearly Moscow could not look to London or Paris for aid, so she turned instead to her former adversary, and German/Soviet tank development began at Kazan, located deep inside Russia where secrecy was relatively easy to maintain.

In April 1926 the first technical specifications had been given for what was eventually to become the Panzer IV. It was given the codename Armeewagen 20 and in March 1927 the first contracts for the design of two experimental machines each were given to Daimler Benz, Krupp and Rheinmetall. These machines were given the codename Grosstraktor and each was to have a 7.5cm gun in a fully traversable turret. The first six Grosstraktor were completed in July 1929 and immediately transported to the secret training grounds at Kama, near Kazan. These machines were the predecessors of the Panzer IV, which was to function effectively throughout the war years.

Although tank design had been exposed to a considerable deal of practical action during the Great War, without a clear indication of how tank-to-tank combat might develop there were a number of competing schools of thought. One favoured large multi-turreted tanks which could perform a number of functions on the battlefield. Others favoured specialist machines for reconnaissance, close support and anti-tank duties. Clearly the Grosstraktor could not fulfil the reconnaissance role. So, in May 1928 the first orders for the design of a lighter tank, code named Leichttraktor were given; this time only Krupp and Rheinmetall were given the order to proceed to complete two prototypes. In May 1930 the two machines were completed and transported secretly to Kazan, where they arrived in June 1930. Very quickly a glaring design fault with the Leichttraktors became apparent. The drive sprocket for the tracks was located at the back of the vehicle, where it was more likely to shed the track. The location of engine at the front of the tank was also considered to be a particularly dangerous proposition. A new design was therefore specified in September 1931 which became known as the Kleintraktor. This machine had the drive at the front and the engine in the rear, an arrangement which was to become the standard in tank design for the next 60 years. The Kleintraktor was to become the forerunner of the Panzerkampfwagen I, and the first experimental machine was completed by Krupp in September 1932. In the secrecy of the tank-proving grounds at Kama the Germans were able to make a great deal of progress on the technical aspects of tank design. At the same time, of course, the crews and officers were receiving practical training in the use of tanks in battle and, crucially, the cooperation between the machines. It was not until 1928, however, that the Reichswehr secretly began to formulate a five-year plan which would lead to the creation of the first tank companies by 1933.

Eventually the first Panzer training unit was born on 1st November 1933, under conditions of extreme secrecy, and was given the code-name Kraftfahrlehrkommando Zossen. It was comprised mainly of officers and men who had taken part in the Russian experiment. At the time of the unit's formation only a very limited number of machines were available. These comprised four Grosstraktor, four Leichttraktor V and six of the Kleintraktor chassis, which had no turrets. Clearly this was not going to be sufficient to develop a tank force; however, the delivery of the first 150 Kleintraktor chassis for driver training commenced in January

1934, from which point the rapid expansion of the tank forces could proceed apace. The first organisation charts for an experimental armoured division were distributed within the army on 12 October 1934, although most of the units were still known by cover names; officially, the Panzer Division were styled as a Cavalry Division.

At the outset the Panzer division was to be composed of two armoured regiments which were supported by a light motorised infantry regiment, a motorcycle battalion, an anti-tank battalion, a reconnaissance battalion, a light artillery regiment, a signals battalion and a light combat engineer company, and there was even a plan for a self-propelled artillery battalion, which was very radical at this time. Already it was obvious that the Panzer division would require an enormous logistical tail, and the first divisions required a strength of 13,000 officers and men, which needed 4,000 field vehicles and 481 tracked vehicles to be able to function effectively. Clearly, the creation and maintenance of a number of Panzer divisions was going to be an enormous undertaking. It was also something which could not be achieved in short timescales as there were limits to the number of tanks which could be manufactured. Unfortunately for Germany, Adolf Hitler was very much a man in a hurry.

DEVELOPMENT OF THE TANK FORCE

The first vehicle to be produced in any numbers was the tiny Panzer I, which at the time was known as the MG Panzerwagen. Delivery of 318 of these had been made by August 1935, along with 15 of the Zugführerwagen, which was later to become the Panzer III. One aspect of tank design which the Germans got absolutely right from the very outset was to identify the importance of radio communications. Although initially only the command tanks were fitted with radios that could both transmit and receive, the other vehicles were at last equipped with receiving radio sets, and this was a major advance upon the thinking of many of the countries which would come to oppose Germany. Throughout 1934 exercises continued with the experimental tank units and a number of other valuable lessons quickly became apparent, particularly the need for close co-operation between the airforces and the tanks on the ground.

At this point the first serious tank tactics which were to bring so much success during the Second World War began to appear. It was soon obvious that the tanks needed to be employed on a relatively narrow front. A divisional front was estimated at about three kilometres, a great change from the wide fronts of the Great War. It was still obvious to the German High Command that the decisions which were being made, were on theory, rather than practice. Germany - and indeed every other nation of the time - had no practical experience to draw on, therefore a number of educated guesses were made. In January 1936 General Beck reported to the High Command, his findings being based on a study of a French organisation. He was also very critical of the slow rise in production capacity which was hampering the development of the tank force. Interestingly, the debate about which tasks tanks were suitable for, and whether specialist machines had to be developed for each task, was already beginning to take shape. Beck's report clearly stated that the three main tasks of the Panzers were supporting infantry, operating in units with other mobile weapons and, finally, combating tanks. Beck himself was unable to come to a decision about whether a single tank should be adapted for each of these purposes or whether a specialist vehicle should be designed for each purpose. Ultimately the decision was that the light tanks would be used in a scouting role and that an infantry support tank would be developed which was ultimately to come in the form of the Panzer IV. This left the Panzer III as the main battle tank. Amazingly the decision was taken that the 3.7cm gun which initially equipped the Panzer III would be sufficient for the battle conditions. The various types of German tank design were to cater for most eventualities on the battlefield. The Panzer I and II were earmarked for the reconnaissance role, the Panzer III was essentially for anti-tank operations and the Panzer IV was designed to provide close support for the infantry. Almost from the outset the limitations of the design for the Panzer I were obvious. The armament, in the form of two machine guns, was inadequate for most purposes on the battlefield. In addition, the very thin armour gave protection only against rifle bullets; almost any battlefield weapon could penetrate the armour. More significant was the fact that the crew was comprised of only two men.

THE CLOSED WORLD

The world of the tank man is a world of very limited vision. With the hatches open, a tank commander can use the height advantage of his vehicle to scan the terrain for miles around. However, once the tank is threatened and the hatches have to be closed, the view of the world is through tiny vision slits, which makes visual recognition extremely difficult. There are a number of tasks which need to be carried out in the tank. Communication, both inwards and outwards, with other vehicles in the formation is absolutely essential and, with the rudimentary radio equipment of the period, this was really a full-time job. In addition to operating the radio, the commander had to be surveying the ground ahead for the driver, and in addition he was expected to operate the machine guns. In simple terms, this was far too many tasks for one man to hope to successfully master during the heat of an engagement. The Panzer I had already shown its limitations, and in fairness it was never really intended as a frontline battle tank. Its purpose, really, was as a training tank, and the numbers ordered were in response to the need to train a large number of men quickly. It was only Hitler's ambitious brinkmanship that would propel the Army into having to press the Panzer I into a service for which it was plainly inadequate; even in 1936 this was obvious for all to see.

The successor to the Panzer I in the reconnaissance role should of course have been the Panzer II. The Panzer II was therefore a slight advance on this sorry state of affairs in that it was a three-man machine which allowed for a driver as well as a gunner and the commander. Although this was some improvement it was still not a great advance on the Panzer I. The 20mm cannon could at least penetrate light tanks, but it really lacked hitting power for serious tank-to-tank engagements. Above all, here were still too few men in the vehicle to conduct all of the tasks satisfactorily. Really, a four-man crew was the absolute minimum and events would quickly demonstrate that five was the number that should be deployed in a modern tank. As early as October 1935 General Liese, head of the Heeres Waffenamt issued a report which gave the limitations of the tanks. He noted that the MG Panzerwagen (Panzer I), although fitted out only with two 7.9mm

The cardboard tanks used to begin the process of training the future Panzerwaffe during the early 20s. The three parts are about to be locked over the car frame to produce the pathetic vehicles seen on page one.

machine guns, could be adapted to attack armoured cars and other light tanks if it was issued with special S.M.P steel core ammunition. In the case of the MG Panzer II, it was noted that the muzzle velocity of the 2cm gun could penetrate up to 10mm of armoured plate at a range of up to 700 metres. It was therefore decided that the Panzer II could engage armoured cars with success, and was also fully functional for combat against tanks with approximately the same armour as itself. Liese noted that the tanks most likely to be encountered in large numbers in a war against the French were the light Renault M17 and M18 tanks, of which there were about three thousand operational in the French forces at the time. It was also thought that the Panzer II would be the equal of the Renault NC37 and NC31 tanks. Against the heavier French tanks, including the Char B, it was noted that the Panzer II was practically worthless. Despite these reservations large-scale delivery of the Panzer II was already in train and was expected to

commence from 1st April 1937. As regards the new Panzer III, which was designed to be the main battle tank, it was obvious that Liese was already beginning to have reservations about the effectiveness of the 37mm gun. Originally the 37mm L/45 had been planned for this vehicle but it was urged that the experimental tanks be upgraded to include the L/65 version, which gave a much higher muzzle velocity and some real prospect of penetrating the 40mm thick armoured plate of the new French medium tanks. With this in mind it was obvious at this stage that a 50mm gun would be a better proposition for the Panzer III; however the addition of the larger gun would demand a significant increase in the diameter of the turret which would in turn mean radical redevelopment of the chassis. Given the pressures of time and the need to equip the formations quickly Liese came to the conclusion that the 37mm L/65 was the favoured route, although it is interesting that the limitations of its design had already been noted.

Panzerkampfwagen I Sd.Kfz.101

In 1931, Major-General Oswald Lutz was appointed "Inspector of Motor Transport" in the German Army (Reichswehr) with Heinz Guderian as his Chief of Staff. Both realised the need for the creation of the German Armoured Forces and a light training tank in which to train future personnel of Panzer Divisions. In 1932, specifications for a light (5-ton) tank were made and issued to Rheinmetall, Krupp, Henschel, MAN and Daimler Benz. The designers' work was based on experiences from co-operation with Swedish Landsverk Company and previous "secret" projects.

In 1933, the Heereswaffenamt ordered the development of the Kleintraktor - an armoured vehicle between 4 and 7 tons in weight. It was designated as the La.S. (Landwirtschaftlicher Schlepper I La.S. - agricultural tractor) to hide its true purpose from the Treaty of Versailles. Rheinmetall, Krupp, Henschel, MAN and Daimler Benz submitted their prototypes which were all similar in design. It was Krupp's design of the LKA I which was selected.

The design of the LKA I was partially based on the British Carden Loyd Mk. IV tankette chassis two of which were secretly purchased from Russia in 1932. Krupp's design was then once again modified and in the summer of 1933, five La.S. chassis were produced and tested at Kummersdorf. It was then decided to mount Krupp's chassis with the Daimler-Benz's superstructure and turret.

In February 1934 further tests were

Armour (mm/angle) Ausf A.
Front Turret: 13/10
Front Upper Hull: 13/22
Front Lower Hull: 13/27
Side Turret: 13/22
Side Upper Hull: 13/22
Side Lower Hull: 13/0
Rear Turret: 13/22
Rear Upper Hull: 13/17
Rear Lower Hull: 13/15
Turret Top / Bottom: 8/82
Upper Hull Top / Bottom: 6/82
Lower Hull Top / Bottom: 6/90
Gun Mantlet: 13/round

Armour (mm/angle) Ausf B.
Front Turret: 13/10
Front Upper Hull: 13/22
Front Lower Hull: 13/27
Side Turret: 13/22
Side Upper Hull: 13/22
Side Lower Hull: 13/0
Rear Turret: 13/22
Rear Upper Hull: 13/0
Rear Lower Hull: 13/19
Turret Top / Bottom: 8/82
Upper Hull Top / Bottom: 6/83
Lower Hull Top / Bottom: 6/90
Gun Mantlet: 13/round

Model:	Panzer I Ausf A.	Panzer I Ausf B.
Weight:	5300 kg	5900 kg
Crew:	2	2
Engine:	Krupp M305 (Boxer), 4-cylinder / 57 hp	Maybach NL38TR 6-cylinder / 100 hp
Speed:	37 km/h	40 km/h
Range:	Road: 200 km Crosscountry: 140 km	Road: 180 km Crosscountry: 130 km
Fuel	144 litres	146 litres
Capacity:	3, 460 cc	3, 790 cc
Length:	4.02 m	4.43 m
Width:	2.06 m	2.06 m
Height:	1.72 m	1.72 m
Armament:	(7.92 mm)	(7.92 mm)
Ammunition Supply:	2250 rounds(MG)	2250 rounds(MG)

Model	Production Period	Number of Chassis Produced	Number of PzKpfw I Produced
Ausf A	1934-1936	1477	818
Ausf B	1935-1939	6023	675
Ausf C (VK 601)	1942-1943	40	40
Ausf D (VK 602)	1942-1943	prototype stage	-
Ausf F (VK 1801)	1942-1943	30	30

performed and in April the improved LKA I (La.S.), known as the MG Panzerwagen - Versuchkraftfahrzeug 617 entered production. On entering production it was renamed the Pz.Kpfw I Ausf A. In April 1934, 15 were produced and all were presented to Adolf Hitler by Heinz Guderian.

The Panzer I was produced in two main very similar variants the Ausf A (1934) and the Ausf B (1935), which both had different suspensions and engines. In 1935/36, the Panzer I Ausf A was experimentally mounted with a Krupp M601 diesel engine, but it could only produce 45hp of power, and the idea of a diesel powered vehicle was rejected.

The debut for the PzKpfw I in a combat situation took place during Spanish Civil War, 1936-38, where both the tank and the tactic of Blitzkrieg were put to the test. Approximately 100 Ausf A, Ausf B and Kleiner Panzer Befehlswagen I tanks saw service with the Condor Legion (Major Ritter von Thomas' Panzer Abteilung 88 also known as Abteilung Drohne) and General Franco's Nationalists. They were, however, outclassed by the Soviet T-26 and BT-5 provided to the Republicans. Some Pz.Kpfw Is which were captured by the Republicans were rearmed with French Hotchkiss 25mm guns mounted in a modified turret.

It was also at this time that the Pz.Kpfw I Ausf B was experimentally armed with 20mm Breda gun mounted in a modified

Panzer I's seen here during the march past Adolf Hitler in front of jubilant crowds in Vienna, March 1938.

turret, in order to increase its combat potential.

The Pz.Kpfw were allocated to two Nationalist tank battalions, the Agrupacion de Carros - 1st and 2nd Tank Battalions.

Following the Spanish Civil War it was obvious that the Panzer I did not have any potential as a combat tank and a further programme development into a fast reconnaissance and light infantry tank was started.

This began with the introduction of the Ausf C, Ausf D and Ausf F, completely new designs sharing only a limited number of components with the standard Panzer I Ausf B. The Panzer I Ausf C - neuer Art (VK 601) was produced by Krauss-Maffei

and Daimler-Benz from late 1942 to early 1943 with only 40(46) being produced. The Ausf D - neuer Art verstarkt (VK 602) was an up-armoured and improved version of the Ausf C which was produced in limited numbers. The Panzer I Ausf F - neuer Art verstarkt (up-armoured new model) (VK 1801) was produced by Daimler-Benz and Krauss-Maffei from April 1942 to January 1943 with only 30 being produced.

In mid 1943, a small number of Ausf C and Ausf F were combat tested with the 1st and 2nd Panzer Division fighting on the Eastern Front and later served in Yugoslavia. A number of Pz.Kpfw I Ausf C ended up in Normandy with LVIII Panzer Corps, where they were lost in 1944. The

VARIANTS OF PANZERKAMPFWAGEN I (SD. KFZ. 101)	
Ausf A (July 1934 - June 1936)	• 2x MG13 Dreyse (7,92mm), • 57hp Krupp M305 (Boxer) engine, • 4 road wheels & 3 return rollers.
Ausf B (August 1935 - June 1937)	• 2 x Mg13 Dreyse (7.92mm), • 100hp Maybach NL 38 TR engine, • 5 road wheels & 4 return rollers, • lengthened and redesigned rear hull.
Ausf A/B (1935 - 1937) Befehlswagen/Command Tank	• 1 x MG 13 Dreyse or MG34 (7.92mm), • 57hp Krupp M305 (Boxer) engine - Ausf A, • 100hp Maybach NL 38 TR engine - Ausf B, • 4 road wheels & 3 return rollers - Ausf A, • 5 road wheels & 4 return rollers - Ausf B.
Ausf C (nA) (July 1942 - December 1942)	• 20mm EW141 gun / MG34 (7.92mm), • 150hp Maybach HL 45 P engine, • fast reconnaissance tank, • airborne tank (Messerschmitt ME 321 Gigant).
Ausf D (nA verst) (1942 -1943)	• 20mm EW141 gun / MG34 (7.92mm), • 150hp Maybach HL 66 P engine, • up-armoured fast reconnaissance/ infantry support tank.
Ausf F (nA verst) (April 1942 - January 1943)	• 2 x MG34 (7.92mm) • 150hp Maybach HL 45 45 P engine, • up-armoured fast reconnaissance/infantry support/ assault tank.

Panzer I Ausf B.

Ausf C, D and F never entered full production. Today, the Pz.Kpfw I Ausf F can be seen in the Museum of Armoured Forces in Kubinka near Moscow in Russia.

The Panzer I was the main tank of the German army during the Polish Campaign with some 1445 in service (as such they provided approximately 50% of all tanks in service). During the African campaign the PzKpfw Is were equipped with larger filters and an improved ventilation system.

In early 1942, Panzer Is were taken out of service and were handed over to the Police and anti-partisan units; those without superstructures were handed over to para-military organizations such as NSKK (National Socialist Motor Corps) for training purposes. A total of 511 PzKpfw I turrets

were used in fortifications of Atlantic Wall, Pomeranian Wall and in the Kostrzyn area.

The PzKpfw I was also used as a propaganda tool being everywhere from military parades to NSDAP rallies. It was a show piece of the Third Reich in the years leading to beginning of WWII.

The lessons learned from the Panzer I provided the German designers and manufacturers with valuable experience in designing and producing the next generation of new panzers that were soon to come. Although the Panzer I was not truly a combat tank, it proved to be an excellent training tank and most of the panzer crews were trained on the Panzer I until the end of the war or operated it in combat as their first armoured vehicle.

Conversions

In 1939/40, 100 PzKpfw I Ausf A/B were converted into Ladungsleger I (Ladungsleger auf Panzerkampfwagen I Ausf A or B / zerstorerpanzer) - a 50kg explosive charge layer vehicle. They were especially designed for engineer units to provide them with the charge carrier for delayed action explosives and saw combat service during the Blitzkrieg in the West with 7th Panzer Division and then in Russia.

During the African campaign, at the Battle of Tobruk, a small number of Panzerkampfwagen I Ausf As were converted in the field by the Africa Korps 5th Light Division into Flammenwerfer auf Panzerkampfwagen I Ausf A. It was armed with light portable infantry Flammenwerfer (flamethrower model) 40 and an MG, in place of right hand machine gun. Some 10 to 12 bursts could be fired with a range of 25 metres.

The most radical conversion based on the modified PzKpfw I Ausf A was the Flakpanzer I (Sd. Kfz. 101) armed with a 20mm Flak 38 L/1 12.5 gun. It was based on the modified Munitionsschlepper 1 Ausf A (Sd.Kfz.1 11) a light ammunition carrier. Approximately 24 were produced in early 1941 by Alkett in Berlin and all went into equipping three batteries of the 614th Flak Abteilung with eight vehicles each. The last of those interesting conversions was lost at Stalingrad in January of 1943. A PzKpfw I was also modified and mounted with 15mm MG 151115 Drilling heavy machine gun. It was captured on the Eastern Front in 1943.

CONVERSIONS

- Munitionsschlepper I Ausf A (Sd.Kfz 111) - light ammunition carrier
- Munitionsschlepper I Ausf A/B - cargo / ammunition carrier
- Kleine Panzer Befahlswagen I (Sd.Kfz. 265) - light command tank
- Sanitatskraftwagen I (Sd.Kfz. 265) - armoured ambulance
- Pionier-Kampfwagen I - engineer tank
- Panzerjager I (Sd.Kfz. 101) - 47mm Pak gun carrier
- Panzerjager I - 37mm Pak gun carrier
- Sturmpanzer I Bison (Sd.Kfz. 101) - 150mm sIG 33 gun carrier
- Leichte Bergepanzer I - light recovery vehicle
- Instandsetzungstrupp I - troop carrier / recovery vehicle
- Fahreschulewagen I - training tank
- Jadungsleger auf PzKpfw I Ausf A/B (zerstorerpanzer) - explosive charge layer
- Minenraumer I Ausf B - mine clearing vehicle (50 produced in 1938)
- Brueckenleger I auf PzKpfw I Ausf A - light bridging vehicle (2 produced in 1939)
- Flakpanzer I Ausf A (Sd.Kfz 101) - 20mm Flak 38 anti-aircraft tank
- Flammeemwerfer auf PzKpfw I Ausf A - flamethrower tank

Inside the German tank works in 1939. In the background are large numbers of Panzer IIIs under construction. The machine in the foreground is an experimental Nebau Panzerkampfwagen, not destined for active service. Its prominence is probably not accidental and may have been designed to confuse enemy intelligence services.

Panzer Is roll through the Uber den Ring, Vienna, March 1938.

Despite the difficult conditions, the fledgling German tank forces had managed to develop some innovations of their own. Influential sections of the officer corps could see the advantages that the tank could bring to the next war and they developed new theories that centred on the use of the tank, theories that would revolutionise the way wars would be fought. Despite the problems of convincing his superiors of the advantages of the tank, Heinz Guderian in particular stuck to his secretive task. With determined persistence, and the help of some impressive demonstration exercises, he finally convinced both the German General Staff and Adolf Hitler that the tank could help to win future wars.

When Hitler precipitated the Second World War with his invasion of Poland in 1939, his tank forces were questionable at best, but the gamble succeeded by the application of a new tactical doctrine - championed by General Heinz Guderian - which was to become known as Blitzkrieg.

Blitzkrieg also evolved at least partially from a re-assessment of war tactics that took place not only in Germany, but in Russia and Britain as well. Two perceptive British military theorists, Major General J.C. Fuller and Captain B. Liddell Hart, understood that the introduction of the tank during the First World War had opened up hitherto undreamed of military possibilities.

As a result of Guderian's efforts, in 1935 the first Panzer Divisions were formed. These revolutionary formations incorporated a Tank

Brigade with 561 tanks to provide the main firepower. A great deal of accurate thought had gone into the development of the Panzer Division, which also included motorised infantry, reconnaissance and artillery. The resulting Panzer Division was a well-balanced force which could call on the support of any or all of the component parts to capture an objective. The purpose of the Panzer Division was to launch a speedy advance, break through into the enemy territory and spread confusion, fear and panic in the enemy command and communication systems. One further innovation was the close link with the Luftwaffe, who could add even more firepower when needed.

THE PANZER DIVISIONS ARE FORMED

On 15 October 1935 the first three Panzer Divisions were formed. General-Colonel Maximilian von Weichs commanded the 1st Panzer Division with its headquarters in Weimar, the 2nd Panzer Division was commanded by Colonel Heinz Guderian and had its headquarters in Wurzburg. General-Colonel Ernst Fessmann commanded the 3rd Panzer Division, with his headquarters in Berlin.

The tank component of the first Panzer divisions was to be a Panzer Brigade, initially composed of two tank regiments. The regiments were, in turn, sub-divided into two Abteilungs (battalions); each Abteilung had four companies with 32 light tanks. The entire brigade strength was 561 tanks including command tanks.

The tank element of the 1st Panzer Division was the 1st Panzer Brigade, which was composed of the 1st Panzer Regiment, stationed in Erfurt, and the 2nd Panzer Regiment, stationed in Eisenach.

The 2nd Panzer Division incorporated the 2nd Panzer Brigade, which was composed of the 3rd Panzer Regiment stationed in Kamenz and the 4th Panzer Regiment stationed in Ohrdruf.

The tank strength of the 3rd Panzer Division, also known as Panzer Brigade 'Berlin', was composed of the 5th Panzer Regiment 'Wundsdorf', stationed in Wunsdorf and the 6th Panzer Regiment (later known as 'Neuruppin') stationed in Zossen.

In 1936 there was a re-shuffle of bases. The 3rd Panzer Regiment was moved to Bamberg, the 4th Panzer Regiment to Schweinfurt and the 6th Panzer Regiment to Neuruppin.

In February and March of 1936 all of the new Panzer units took in extensive training exercises on the proving grounds at Staumuhlen.

Almost from the outset, and while they were still forming and training, the Panzer units had to be prepared for operational service. The first of these emergencies appeared on 7 March 1936, when German infantry units marched into the demilitarised Rhineland. The Panzer regiments were held on alert in the Senna district but were stood down after four weeks. For the remainder of 1936 the units were exposed to a programme of intensive training. Of course, the expansion of the Panzer force was limited by the rate of expansion in the number of available tanks. However, although the process of design and development continued, as many as 3000 light tanks had already been produced by the end of 1936 and the construction of the designs of the Panzer III and IV were well under way when the first baptism of fire arose for the fledgling tank force.

THE SPANISH CIVIL WAR

In 1936 the Spanish Civil War flared into life and the leadership of the Nationalist forces asked the governments of both Italy and Germany for military support. Although Germany itself could not afford to take a formal part in the war, units of volunteers were made available in support of the Nationalists. Among them was a Panzer unit, given the code-name Abteilung Drohne, which was officially named Panzer Abteilung 88. It was commanded by Major Ritter von Thoma and it was drawn from the ranks of the 4th and 6th Panzer regiments. Although the men really were volunteers there was no shortage, and there were sufficient men to form a company and a workshop column. The volunteers were transferred on German passenger ships as civilian members of the trade union travel organisation, which worked under the slogan 'Strength Through Joy'. They took with them Panzer I tanks and were disembarked at Seville. The training role was a real one, and the German troops were responsible for training Spanish National troops equipped with captured T-26 Russian tanks. The volunteers themselves first saw action in October 1936 when a few Panzer I tanks were deployed to support the Nationalists in their drive on Madrid. In early 1937 the unit was reinforced to form three combat companies and a support column. The German tanks were used in numbers for the first time on 11 May 1937 when they took part in a concerted attack on the Spanish Communist positions near Eremita. The volunteers remained in Spain for over two years and were returned to Germany only in February 1939. In his first report of the action in Spain sent back to Germany in December 1936 von Thoma was quick to point out the limitations of the Panzer I. He noted that from the very outset a gun armed tank was far superior to the machine gun armed Panzer I, although the disadvantage could be overcome to an extent by issuing specially hardened ammunition which could cleanly penetrate Russian tanks at ranges of about 120-150 metres.

The Russian tanks, however, quickly adapted their tactics and were able stay out of range, moving to over a thousand metres away where their superior guns made the Panzer I easy prey. The German tanks were particularly vulnerable if the Panzers remained stationary, and von Thoma's orders were to fight constantly on the move. Despite these precautions at least seven Panzers were knocked out by the Russian forces in a single engagement.

The solution to the limitations of the Panzer I in Spain was to attach anti-tank guns to each of the Panzer companies. Once again, with the result of practical experience in the field, von Thoma came to the conclusion that the Panzer I, if it was to be used at all, needed to be accompanied by an infantry support tank which had at least a 7.5cm gun with a range of up to three thousand metres. It was also felt that a better anti-tank gun was needed, with a range of at least 1,500 and not the 900 metres; once again the 37mm gun which was deemed to be inadequate for the task.

Of course the Germans were not the only foreign nationals present in Spain. Both Britain and France had their observers to view the progress of the war. General Fuller wrote an article in the Times on 8 April 1937 which was highly critical of the tanks that were seen in action, particularly the German machines, which Fuller described as 'mobile coffins'. The French went even further and in April 1937 a French newspaper article was particularly critical of the German tanks. It noted that they were a major disappointment because of their slow speed across country and the armour, which was accurately described as almost useless. There was little real defence against enemy anti-tank guns;

from a close range even rifle bullets could penetrate them. The French report concluded that although the French tanks were slower they were much better protected and remained 'king of the battle ground'. Altogether approximately one hundred and fifty one Panzer Is were sent to Spain and all were left behind at the close of hostilities.

In the official Report of the Spanish Civil War which was written in March 1939, it was noted that the light tanks were useful only with flame-throwers since it was impossible to fire the machines guns on the move. Once again it was forcefully noted that the Panzer I was an inferior tank. However, during the time of the Spanish Civil War the expansion of the Panzer forces back in Germany continued relatively smoothly, as did the production of the vehicles.

The harsh evidence from the battlefields of Spain did not go unheeded.

As soon as the Panzer II became available from October 1936, resources were immediately switched and there was no effective increase in Panzer I strength, which remained about 1,400

machines until the outbreak of the war. The number of Panzer IIs rose was rapidly from 115 in May 1937 to 1,200 in September 1939. Additionally the first of the Panzer IIIs came on stream in October 1937 to be followed by the Panzer IV in January 1938. By the outbreak of the Second World War in September 1939 there were 98 Panzer III in service and 211 Panzer IV, the most useful machines therefore still counting for a tiny proportion of the forces available.

BATTLEFIELD TACTICS

In addition to the increase in the numbers of tanks actually available, the practical application of this new force on the battlefield was also being developed. A report on 24 November 1938 gave the guidelines for the planned use of the Panzer Divisions which were to accomplish a number of primary tasks.

1. They were to be used at the most strategically important sectors and employed in mobile operations.

A group of seven Panzer Is serving with Gruppe Thoma in the Spanish campaign during 1937. The many limitations of the Panzer I were clearly demonstrated in the Spanish Civil War, but the lack of a viable alternative meant these machines would see considerable service during the early years of the war.

2. They were to widen and exploit breakthroughs created by infantry reserves.

By now the Army High Command envisaged that nine Panzer Divisions should be available by the Autumn of 1939. The report also made it clear that the Panzertruppen should consist of men that had the highest fighting spirit and that they were to be considered and developed as an elite unit, particularly with regard to their offensive spirit.

Back in Germany, during the autumn of 1936, two new Panzer regiments were formed, 7th Panzer Regiment in Veihingen and 8th Panzer Regiment in Boblingen. The 7th Panzer Regiment was temporarily attached to 1st Panzer Division and the 8th to the 3rd Panzer Division.

From September 14th to 29th 1937, large-scale manoeuvres of the Panzer units took place around Neusterlitz. These were the "Mussolini manoeuvres", named after the Italian dictator who was present. The units involved were the complete 3rd Panzer Division and the 1st Panzer Brigade, from the 1st Panzer Division, who together fielded some 800 Panzer I tanks. On 12 October 1937 a number of new units were formed including the 10th, 11th, 15th and 25th Panzer Regiments, and Panzer Abteilung 65 along with the Panzer Lehr Abteilung. These divisions were earmarked to equip another potentially innovative formation, the Light Division. The habits of the old Cavalry Command died hard and the Light Division was designed to carry out a similar role to the old Cavalry Division in scouting - protecting the flanks of the advance. As such it was equipped with only one tank Abteilung comprising 96 tanks, rather than the two-regiment brigade of a full Panzer Division of 561 tanks.

On 12 March 1938 the Anschluss took Austria into the Reich. The only Panzer unit to take part was the 2nd Panzer Division under the command of General Guderian. In preparation for the operation, SS Regiment Leibstandarte Adolf Hitler, commanded by Sepp Dietrich, was attached to the 2nd Panzer Division. The division covered some seven hundred kilometers in 48 hours, but rather ominously lost a third of its tanks due to breakdowns. Fortunately the 2nd Panzer Division was not involved in any combat. Following the Anschluss, Panzer Abteilung 33 was formed from the sole Austrian Panzer Battalion and other members transferred from German units. This unit was stationed in St. Polten. Panzer Abteilung 33 was assigned to the 4th Light Division and later to the 9th Panzer Division formed in Vienna in January 1940. As a result of the expansion of the Reich, the headquarters of the 2nd Panzer Division were now moved to Vienna, and the 3rd and 4th Panzer Regiments were stationed near the cities of Modling and Korneuburg.

The high command of the Werhmacht join Hitler for the march past of the new tank formations in Vienna. Right from the Füher; Generaloberst Keitel, Reichsführer der SS Himmler, Generalorerst von Brauchitsch, Generaloberst Milch, General Kraub and Reichsstatthalter Dr. Seyss-Inquart.

The Pz.Kpfw (38)t had been designed and tested before the seizure of Czechoslovakia in 1939. The influx of these valuable machines provided the vital extra numbers which made the early campaigns possible. The 7th and 8th Panzer Divisions used the Pz.Kpfw (38)t in place of the Panzer III during the fall of France.

THE AUSTRIAN PRIZE

Throughout the war the German tank forces were to make considerable use of captured enemy material. Although Austrian armoured fighting vehicles cannot be really labelled as captured since they never took part in any combat and were simply handed over to the Germans, their use represented the beginning of a regular pattern. The first pieces of equipment which fell into German hands were the few Austrian fighting vehicles then in service with Bundesheer. Along with 47 armoured cars there were 74 imported Italian Carro Veloce (CV) 33/35 tankettes designated in Austrian service as Kleinkampfwagen M. 1933 / 1935. These were used to temporarily equip the new panzer regiments during formation and training, eventually they were used as ammunition carriers, later some were sold to Hungary.

On 3-4 October 1938 Germany took over the Sudetenland as provided for by the Munich agreement of September 1938. By 10 October the takeover was completed; the only Panzer unit involved this time was the 1st Panzer Division. Once again Hitler breathed a sigh of relief that no armed conflict took place.

In November 1938 Heinz Guderian was promoted to General der Panzertruppen and received his most important assignment, which

well may have changed history - he became Chef der Schnellen Truppen (Chief of the Fast Troops). It meant that Guderian was responsible for the recruiting, training and tactics of all the Wehrmacht's motorised and armoured units.

Under his guidance, six new panzer units were formed. These new units included two new panzer divisions; the 4th Panzer Division (also known as the 7th Panzer Brigade)was formed on 10 October 1938 at Wurzburg and the 5th Panzer Division (also known as the 8th Panzer Brigade) formed on 25 October 1938 at Oppeln. Also formed were the 4th Panzer Brigade at Stuttgart, the 5th Panzer Brigade at Bamberg, the 6th Panzer Brigade at Wurzburg and the 8th Panzer Brigade at Sagan. In addition, the 23rd, 31st, 35th and 36th Panzer Regiments were also formed along with Panzer Abteilungs 65, 66 and 67.

The 4th Panzer Division incorporated the 7th Panzer Brigade, composed of the 35th and 36th Panzer Regiments commanded by General-Major George Hans Reinhardt. The new 5th Panzer Division incorporated the 8th Panzer Brigade, composed of the 15th and 31st Panzer Regiment and was commanded by General-Lieutenant Heinrich Vietinghoff-Scheel. Panzer Abteilung 65, 66 and 67 were respectively assigned to the 1st, 2nd and 3rd Light Divisions.

In March 1939, Germany took over the remaining part of Czechoslovakia. Once again only a single unit was involved in the initial moves - this time the 3rd Panzer Division. Elements of the division reached Prague at 8.20 am on 13 March 1939; they were followed by the 6th Panzer Regiment which rolled in during the afternoon. On 15 March, the first parade of German tanks in Prague took place.

THE CZECH TANKS

Far more significant than the meagre forces obtained from the Anschluss were the armoured fighting vehicles which fell into German hands during the 1938/39 German takeover of the Czechoslovak state. Although, again, they were not strictly 'captured', and were simply handed over to the Germans. The two machines currently under Czech manufacture were to play a very significant role in the evolution of the Panzerwaffe. In due course the famous 8th Panzer Division would be equipped with Czech tanks. The two main Czechoslovak tanks were the Skoda / CKD LT-35 and CKD (also known as Praga and later as the B-LT-38, where the LT stood for Lehky Tank or Light Tank). The 38(t) had just begun its manufacturing cycle but 300 of the 35(t) were already available. Both were quickly pressed into German service as the Panzerkampfwagen 35(t) and 38(t) respectively. Although the LT-35 only remained in production until 1939, the LT-38 was manufactured until June 1942 under German supervision. The PzKpfw 35(t) served principally in the Ist Light Division until October 1939, when all were grouped into the 6th Panzer Division. PzKpfw 38(t) saw service with various Light Divisions and was then were used to equip various Panzer Divisions. By late 1941 the Germans at last had better tanks in production and the PzKpfw 35(t) and 38(t) were relegated to policing and security duties. Some PzKpfw 35(t) were exported and saw service with the Slovak and Bulgarian armies (where some actually served until the 1950s), others were used by the Romanian, Hungarian and Italian armies. The PzKpfw 38(t) was also exported and was in service with German Allies,

including Romania, Slovakia, Bulgaria and Hungary. Both the PzKpfw 35(t) and the 38(t) saw extensive service in Poland, France and Russia. During the fighting in Russia, the need for heavier armour and armament soon made both Czech tanks redundant and they were swiftly relegated to reconnaissance duties. Overall, the Panzerkampfwagen 35(t) and 38(t) were reliable vehicles and served Panzertruppe very well in time of need.

ENTER WITTMANN

Among the new recruits at the time of the Czech takeover was a man who was to acquire legendary status in the ranks of the corps. His name was Michael Wittmann. Michael Wittmann was born in the tiny village of Vogelthal, in the Upper Pfalz, on 22 April 1914. He was the first son of a farmer, Johann Wittmann, and his wife Ursula.

In 1934, at the age of twenty-one, Wittmann joined the German army, signing up for a two-year tour. In the first days of the Nazi regime compulsory military service had not yet been reintroduced, so Wittmann was a volunteer when he reported for military service in Freising, with the 19th Infantry Regiment. As a small standing army, comprised exclusively of volunteers, the inter-war Reichswehr was a high-quality force which expected very high standards. Wittmann met those exacting standards, and on the 1 November 1935, after one year in the service he was promoted to Gefreiter. The following year was the halcyon period for the Nazi party in Germany. The first flushes of economic successes for Hitler's National Socialists impressed the young Wittmann. In the closed world of the military, the fervent Nazi beliefs of many of his colleagues also made an impression. Many of his colleagues planned to join the newly formed Waffen SS and Wittmann decided that he, too, would join the military wing of the Nazi party after his own army service. On 1 November 1936 Wittmann applied for admission to the SS, and was accepted into what was to become one of the most notorious organisations in history.

In the case of many exceptional German soldiers, such as Field Marshal Erwin Rommel, supporters have subsequently tried to play down the enthusiasm they held for Hitler and all he stood for. This is not true of Michael Wittmann. In his case

Michael Wittman was to become the most famous tank commander of World War II. His story is woven into the narrative of this book.

there was to be no redeeming conversion or late change of allegiance. He was a simple man and the seductive allure of the Nazi party drew his unquestioning obedience. Wittmann was given the SS number 311623 and proved to be a model National Socialist. In his free time he participated in sports, recruiting, and took part in the mass political demonstrations and rallies of the period. Thanks to his rigorous military background, Wittmann met the very strict selection criteria and was accepted. He began training with his new unit on 5 April 1937, at the main cadet school in Berlin-Licherfelde. Wittmann was assigned to the 17th Company, which was an armoured scout car platoon. As part of an elite formation, the men of the armoured Scout Company received an intensive training course, which transformed them into expert soldiers.

These skills were later to stand him in good stead, but for the time being the new-found expertise was not needed. Hitler was still achieving his aims by a mixture of bluff and inspired gambles. In October 1938 Wittmann took part in the entry into the Sudetenland. The reception he witnessed as waves of excitement swept through the people made a lasting impression on him. The storm of jubilation eclipsed even the fervent national socialist rallies which he had attended. He was awarded his first of many medals, commemorating the reunification of Austria and the Sudetenland with the German Reich. From now on, medals and decorations would occupy a special place in Wittmann's affections.

TOWARDS THE CONFLAGRATION

The new Nazi regime was clearly not inclined to waste time. In the wake of the Czechoslovakian adventure, on 1 April 1939 the 10th Panzer Division (also known as 4th Panzer Brigade), commanded by General-Major Rudolf Schaal, began forming in Prague. In August/September 1939 an improvised Panzer Division Kempf (also known as Panzerverband Ostpreussen/Kempf) was raised. It was commanded by Werner Kempf. This division was made up of 7th Panzer Regiment along with various other units including SS Regiment 'Deutschland'.

In August 1939 there was a highly significant development. The production of tanks was clearly not keeping pace with the demands of the rapidly

expanding Panzerwaffe, and the only solution was to reduce the number of tanks in a Panzer Division. The strength of the Panzer Regiments within the Panzer Divisions was therefore revised. Each of the two Abteilungs was now composed of two light companies (equipped with the PzKpfw I and II) and one medium company (equipped with the PzKpfw III and IV) along with other units. Each Abteilung now had 71 to 74 tanks including 5 command tanks, and a regiment now boasted only 150 to 156 tanks including 12 command tanks. This meant a reduction in the strength of a Panzer Division from 570 machines to about 300. This was to prove an ominous portent for the future.

Each Panzer Division still had its own infantry, reconnaissance, artillery, transport, communication, medical, technical and general services component but the balance had already begun to shift. At that time, 1st, 2nd and 3rd Panzer Divisions were identical in size and organisation, the 4th Panzer Division still lacked some infantry and anti-tank units, and the 5th Panzer Division had additional infantry and motorcycle units, making it the largest Panzer Division, while the 10th Panzer Division was not yet fully organised.

In 1939 Germany's rearmament was clearly far from complete, but if Hitler delayed his plans any longer Germany's enemies might then be too strong for her. To be successful he needed easy, quick and decisive victories; a great deal would therefore rest on the new Panzer formations. On 17 August 1939 all of the Panzer units were put on alert and prepared to move out. On 25 August, they began moving towards the eastern border of the Reich. On 1 September 1939 the Second World War began.

This photograph demonstrates the building of Sturmgeschütze and Panzer Mark IIIs side by side in the Alkett works in early 1941.

Panzerkampfwagen II Sd.Kfz.121

With suspension developed from the Panzer I, the Panzer II was a larger vehicle but still only intended as a light training tank. It entered service only because the development of the more efficient PzKpfw IIIs and IVs was delayed and a larger, gun armed vehicle was needed. The chassis was designed by MAN and the Panzer II went into production in 1935. The first variants of the Panzer II consisted of Ausf aI, a2 and a3 which had small modifications of the engine and cooling system.

The Ausf C became the main production prototype of the Panzer II. With a new suspension (five separate roadwheels) the Ausf C were thereafter used not only as the lead combat tank, but also as training tanks.

In May 1938 the Ausf D/E, the Schnellkampfwagen, appeared bringing another new suspension: the Famo/Christie-type. However, this proved rather unsuccessful and the Ausf D/E was taken out of service after an unsatisfactory performance. The Ausf C continued to receive modifications and between 1940 and 1943 versions of this -Ausf F and G -were introduced.

The Panzer II was used in large numbers by the Panzertruppe during Polish and French campaigns and later saw extensive service with Erwin Rommel's DAK in North Africa and in the opening stages of the Russian Campaign. One source reports that by the French campaign of 1940, 955 Panzer II were in the hands of the Wehrmacht. Although they were undoubtedly fast vehicles, the PzKpfw II suffered from very thin armour, which offered minimal protection in battle, and an inadequate 20mm gun.

Armour (mm/angle) Ausf A/B/C Sd.Kfz. 121
Front Turret: 14.5/round
Front Upper Hull: 14.5/9
Front Lower Hull: 14.5round
Side Turret: 14.5/22
Side Upper Hull: 14.5/0
Side Lower Hull: 14.5/0
Rear Turret: 14.5/22
Rear Upper Hull: 14.5/9
Rear Lower Hull: 14.5/6
Turret Top / Bottom: 10/86
Upper Hull Top / Bottom: 10/81
Lower Hull Top / Bottom: 14.5/73 / 5/90
Gun Mantlet: 16/round

Armour (mm/angle) Ausf L (Luchs) Sd.Kfz. 123
Front Turret: 30/10
Front Upper Hull: 30/10
Front Lower Hull: 30/22
Side Turret: 20/21
Side Upper Hull: 20/0
Side Lower Hull: 20/0
Rear Turret: 20/21
Rear Upper Hull: 20/28
Rear Lower Hull: 20/28
Turret Top / Bottom: 12/79
Upper Hull Top / Bottom: 10/86
Lower Hull Top / Bottom: 10/90
Gun Mantlet: 30/round

Model:	Ausf A/B/C Sd.Kfz. 121	Ausf L (Luchs) Sd.Kfz. 123
Weight:	9500kg	11800kg
Crew:	3	4
Engine:	Maybach HL 62 TRM, 6-cylinder / 140hp	Maybach HL66 P 6-cylinder / 180hp
Speed:	Road 40km/h	Road 60km/h
Range:	Road: 200km Crosscountry: 125km	Road: 290kh Crosscountry: 175km
Fuel Capacity:	170 litres	235 litres
Length:	4.81 m	4.63 m
Width:	2.28 m	2.48 m
Height:	2.02 m	2.21 m
Armament:	20mm KwK 30 or 38 L/55 & 1x7.92mm MG34 (1xMG-coax)	20mm KwK 38 L/55 & 1x7.92mm MG34 (1xMG-hull)
Ammunition supply:	20mm-180 rounds 7.92mm-3525 rounds	20mm-320 rounds 7.92mm-2280 rounds

Model	Production Period	Number of Chassis Produced*	Number of PzKpfw II Produced
Ausf a1	Late 1935-May 1936	10	75
Ausf a2	May 1936-Febuary 1937	25	
Ausf a3	May 1936-Febuary 1937	50	
Ausf b	Febuary-March 1937	25	25
Ausf c	1937	1900	1113
Ausf A	1938-40	1000	
Ausf B	1938-40	2000	
Ausf C	1938-40	1000	
Ausf D	1938-41	800	43
Ausf E	1938-41	200	
Ausf F	1940-43	1400	524
Ausf G1/G3/G4 (nA) (VK 901)	April 1941-Febuary 1942	75 (12 completed)	12
Ausf H (nA verst) (VK 903)	September 1941	1 prototype	
Ausf J (nA verst) (VK 1601)	April-December 1942	22-25	22
Leopard (VK 1602)	March 1942-January 1943	1 prototype incomplete	
Ausf M (nA verst) (VK 1301)	August 1942	4	4
Ausf L (Luchs) (VK 1303)	September 1943-January 1944	104	104

* Not all of the chassis were used for tank production, large numbers were used for various conversions.

The Panzer II had room for one extra crew man which made the vehicle slightly more efficient, but there were still too few to handle all of the tasks faced by a crew in combat.

The 20mm gun of the Panzer II was patently unsuited to the challenge of a modern battlefield, but delays with the introduction of the Panzer III and IV meant that this training tank would see front line service.

CONVERSIONS

- Marder II (Sd. Kfz. 132)

- Marder II (Sd. Kfz. 131)

- Wespe (Sd. Kfz. 124) 105mm light field howitzer carrier

- Sturmpanzer II Bison - 150mm sIG 33 gun carrier

- Beobachtungswagen II Ausf C - post/command vehicle

- Munitionsschlepper II - ammunition carrier

- PzKfw (Flammpanzer) II Flamingo (Sd. Kfz. 122) (Ausf D/E)

- Brueckenleger auf PzKpfw II Ausf b - light bridging vehicle (1+ produced in 1939)

- PanzerSpahwagen II Ausf L Luchs - reconnaissance tank

- Schwimm Panzer II Ausf. A-C (20mm gun) - amphibious tank (52 converted)

- Bergepanzer II Ausf D/E - recovery vehicle

- Ladungsleger II - explosive charge layer

- Panzer Beobachtungswagen II - artillery observation tank

- Pioner-Kampfwagen II - engineer vehicle

- PzKpfw II Ausf A/B/C armed with 50mm Pak 38 L/60 gun

- Feuerleitpanzer II - fire directing tank

TACTICS AND LOGISTICS

The 'Victory in the West' exhibition staged in Vienna during 1941. This startling achievement was largely due to the efficient employment of the German tank forces. The victory exhibition was designed to underline the effectiveness of the new German military machine.

> **"At the present time, due to our lack of practical experience, any thoughts on the equipping and organisation of Panzer units may only be based on theory. A close study should be made of countries which have practical experience without the encumbrances we have endured in the fifteen years since the war."**
>
> *General Beck Generalstabes des Heeres, 1936*

The training given to the Panzer warriors emphasised speed and independence of thought. When these units were unleashed they offered a very effective weapon that their enemies found impossible to fight against. In Poland this new force had the first opportunity to put its meticulous training into practice; the campaign was a triumph for the Wehrmacht and showed the potential for the tank in battle. Nonetheless, some problems were encountered.

'. . . *in general the bravery and heroism of the*

Polish Army merits great respect.' said Generalfeldmarschall Gerd von Rundstedt

It was here that the ideas of General Heinz Guderian came to appear increasingly attractive. A man of acute intelligence, his plans and tactics were tried out in war games and manoeuvres; once they proved successful in practice they soon convinced Germany's dictator that he had discovered the way to make his dream become a reality. Every detail of the organisation of the Panzer Divisions was explored in meticulous detail so that nothing was left to chance.

MOVEMENT ORDERS

The movement of the Panzer Division was a difficult undertaking and was the subject of scrutiny and careful consideration. For a smooth functioning of the march the Germans stressed: systematic training and practice; attention to detail; care of vehicles and equipment; advanced reconnaissance of routes; precise warning orders; and the issue of detailed march orders. Worked out during the brief adolescence of the Panzer Divisions from 1935-1939, these careful plans were to be rewarded with many successes in the years to come.

In order to secure the march column against enemy attacks, the Germans divided the Panzer column into an Advance Guard (Vorhut), Main Body (Gros), and Rear Guard (Nachhut).

The issue of orders for march and traffic control was the responsibility of the higher command. Movement by road of formations from battalion strength upwards was carried out in the Zone of the Interior at the orders of the Army High Command (OKH) or a headquarters acting on the orders of the Army High Command. In the theatre of war these movements were strictly controlled by Army Headquarters, which issued orders in accordance with instructions from Army High Command or the Army Group. Movements in the areas of military commanders of line-of-communication areas were controlled by orders of the commanders of the relevant areas.

Orders for movement were issued to the formations of fighting troops by the operations group headquarters; those to supply services and units in the line-of-communication area emanated from the supply and administrative group.

The Germans set up a well-organised traffic control service which came under the orders of the operations group. All traffic control services usually wore orange-red brassards. The members of the military police, distinguished by their metal gorgets, also made themselves highly visible to ensure the smooth flow of vehicles.

The Germans allotted to each front line division its own road or sector of advance, usually marked by advance parties. General Headquarters or any other troops directed simultaneously on the same roads were subordinated to the division for the duration of the move. All-weather roads were usually allotted to motorised or armoured divisions, while subsidiary roads were assigned to infantry divisions. Of course Guderian's work was not merely limited to logistics and movement. The real thought was applied to how these new formations could be used in action.

OPERATIONAL PRINCIPLES

In 1945 the US army intelligence section compiled a manual for US troops going to fight in France. This detailed work gives us a fascinating glimpse into the Wehrmacht of 1945 as viewed through allied eyes. One particularly noteworthy section concentrates on German battle tactics. Although the manual was designed for the forces in 1945, these were the same operational principles which were drilled into the Panzertruppen in 1939. It is worth reporting a lengthy sequence here, as the overall objectives of the employment of armoured forces in World War II is well explained:

'*The fundamental principle of German offensive doctrine is to encircle and destroy the enemy. The objective of the combined arms in attack is to bring the armoured forces and the infantry into decisive action against the enemy with sufficient firepower and shock. Superiority in force and firepower, the employment of armoured forces, as well as the surprise element, play a great part in the offensive.*

Co-ordination between the combined arms under a strong unified command is, the Germans emphasise, an absolute requisite to the success of these shock tactics. This has become more and more true as the Allies have developed effective anti-tank weapons and have adopted deeper defences, limiting the self-sufficiency of German tanks. To counter these measures, the Germans have increased the mobility and armour protection of their motor-borne infantry, and have mounted a large proportion of both their direct and indirect heavy support weapons on self-propelled carriages.

In attempting thoroughly to paralyse the defender up to the moment of the tank-infantry assault, the Germans realise that even the most formidable forces are never sufficient for overwhelming superiority on the entire front. They therefore select a point of main effort (Schwerpunkt) for a breakthrough, allotting narrow sectors of attack (Gefechtsstreifen) to the troops committed at the decisive locality. There they also mass the bulk of their heavy weapons and reserves. The other sectors of the front are engaged by weaker, diversionary forces. In selecting the point of main effort, the Germans consider weaknesses in the enemy's defensive position; suitability of the terrain, especially for tanks and for co-operation of all arms; approach routes; and possibilities for supporting fire, especially artillery. Although the Germans select a point of main effort in all attacks, they usually also make plans for shifting their main effort if they meet unexpected success elsewhere. To allow such shifts, sufficient reserves and a strong, unified command are organised.

An attack on a narrow front, according to German doctrine, must have sufficient forces at its disposal to widen the penetration while maintaining its impetus, and to protect the flanks of the penetration. Once the attack is launched, it must drive straight to its objective, regardless of opposition.

MAIN TYPES OF ATTACK

THE FLANK ATTACK (Flankenangriff). The Germans consider that the most effective attack is against the enemy's flank. The flank attack develops either from the approach march - sometimes through a turning movement - or from

flank marches. It attempts to surprise the enemy and permit him no time for countermeasures. Since mobility and the deception of the enemy at other positions are required, the flank attack is most successfully mounted from a distance; the troop movements necessary for the manoeuvre can be executed in close proximity to the enemy only with unusually favourable terrain or at night. Attacks are launched on both flanks only when the Germans consider their forces clearly superior.

ENVELOPMENT (Umfassungsangriff). The envelopment is a combination flank-and-frontal attack especially favoured by the Germans. The envelopment may be directed on either or both the enemy's flanks, and is accompanied by a simultaneous frontal attack to fix the enemy's forces. The deeper the envelopment goes into the enemy's flanks, the greater becomes the danger of being enveloped oneself. The Germans therefore emphasise the necessity of strong reserves and organisation of the enveloping forces in depth. Success of the envelopment depends on the extent to which the enemy is able to dispose his forces in the threatened direction.

ENCIRCLEMENT (Einkreisung). An encirclement, the Germans think, is a particularly decisive form of attack, but usually more difficult

The Panzer IV (F2) with the short barrelled 75mm infantry support gun.

A Panzer II fords a river during the advance in Greece.

PENETRATION AND BREAKTHROUGH (*Einbruch und Durchbruch*). These are not separate forms of attack, but, rather, the exploitation of a successful attack on the enemy's front, wing or flank. The penetration destroys the continuity of the hostile front. The broader the penetration, the deeper the penetration wedge can be driven. Strong reserves throw back enemy counter-attacks against the flanks of the penetration. German units are trained to exploit a penetration to the maximum so that it may develop into a complete breakthrough before hostile counter-measures can be launched on an effective scale. The deeper the attacker penetrates, the more effectively can he envelop and frustrate the attempts of the enemy to close his front again by withdrawal to the rear. The attacking forces attempt to reduce individual enemy positions by encircling and isolating them. The Germans do not consider a breakthrough successful until they overcome the enemy's artillery positions, which is usually the special task of tanks. Reserve units roll up the enemy's front from the newly created flanks.

ATTACKS BY MECHANISED FORCES. In armoured-force operations, the Germans stress the need for the concentrated employment, at the decisive place and time, of the entire combined command of tanks and other arms, less necessary reserves. The tanks constitute the striking force of such a command and normally advance as the first echelon of the attack. Their primary mission is to break through and attack the enemy artillery, rather than to seek out and destroy enemy tanks, which can be more effectively engaged by anti-tank units. The mission of the other arms is to assist the tanks in their advance, and particularly to eliminate anti-tank weapons. The smallest combat unit in such a force of combined arms is the company.

The basic formation for the tank platoon, company, and battalion are file, double file, wedge and blunt wedge. The type of formation used for a specific task depends to a large extent on terrain conditions and the strength of enemy opposition. A German tank platoon normally consists of one command tank and two tank squads of two tanks each.

The tank regiment normally attacks in waves, in either of the following manners.

The tank regiment is echeloned in depth, one tank battalion following the other. The regimental

to execute than a flank attack or an envelopment. In an encirclement, the enemy is not attacked at all in front, or is attacked in front only by light forces, while the main attacking force passes entirely around him, with the objective of manoeuvring him out of position. This requires extreme mobility and deception.

FRONTAL ATTACK (*Frontalangriff*). The Germans consider the frontal attack the most difficult of execution. It strikes the enemy at his strongest point, and therefore requires superiority of men and material. A frontal attack should be made only at a point where the infantry can break through into favourable terrain in the depth of the enemy position. The frontage of the attack should be wider than the actual area (*Schwerpunkt*) chosen for penetration, in order to tie down the enemy on the flanks of the breakthrough. Adequate reserves must be held ready to counter the employment of the enemy's reserves.

WING ATTACK (*Flugelangriff*). An attack directed at one or both of the enemy's wings has, the Germans teach, a better chance of success than a central frontal attack, since only a part of the enemy's weapons are faced, and only one flank of the attacking force or forces is exposed to enemy fire. Bending back one wing may give an opportunity for a flank attack, or for a single or double envelopment.

A powerful study of a Panzer III involved in street fighting for Shitomir during August 1941. The warning not to take tanks into cities was ignored time and time again. Every time they did so the Panzerwaffe paid a high price.

commander's location is between the two battalions. This formation has the advantages of a sufficiently wide front (about one thousand one hundred yards), and close contact by the commander of his units in the conduct of the attack. The normal depth of such a formation is about three thousand yards. This is the usual form of the tank attack. When two tank battalions are attacking, one behind the other, it takes them about half an hour to pass their own infantry.

When the two-battalions-abreast formation is employed, it is almost essential that another tank regiment form the following wave. This formation usually has the disadvantage of being too wide. The regimental commander cannot observe his units, and he has no units of his own behind him which he can commit in a decisive moment. The attack normally proceeds in three waves.

The first wave thrusts to the enemy's anti-tank defence and artillery positions.

The second wave provides covering fire for the first wave, and then attacks the enemy's infantry positions, preceded, accompanied or followed by part of the Panzer grenadiers, who dismount as close as possible to the point where they must engage the enemy. The objectives of the second wave are the remaining anti-tank positions, positions of heavy infantry-support weapons, and machine gun emplacements which hold up the advance of the infantry.

The third wave, accompanied by the remainder of the Panzer grenadiers, mops up.

These three waves are now often telescoped into two, the first wave speeding through the enemy's position as far as his gun positions, the second crushing the enemy's forward positions in detail and mopping up the opposition not dealt with by the first wave or which has revived since the first wave passed through.

A typical attack formation of this type might be divided up among the Panzer division's units as follows: the first wave, on a frontage of about two thousand to three thousand yards, might consist of one tank battalion, two companies forward, supported on the flanks by elements of the assault gun battalion. Close to the rear of the first wave usually follow one or two Panzer grenadier companies in armoured half-tracks. About one hundred and fifty yards to the rear of the first wave moves the second wave, formed of the second tank battalion in the same formation, closely followed by the remainder of the armoured Panzer grenadiers, who are in turn followed at some distance by the motorised Panzer grenadiers. The flanks are protected by anti-tank guns which are normally operated by platoons, moving by bounds. The artillery forward observer travels in his armoured vehicles with the first wave, while the artillery commander of the supporting artillery units usually travels with the tank commander. Assault guns normally also accompany the second wave.

The tanks help each other forward by fire and movement, medium or heavy tanks taking up hull-

down firing positions and giving covering fire while the faster tanks advance to the next commanding feature. Then, the latter give covering fire to the former moving forward to their next bound.

Once the first wave has reached the rear of the enemy's forward defences, it pushes straight on to attack the enemy's artillery. As soon as these positions have been neutralised, the tanks reform beyond the artillery positions and either prepare to exploit the attack or form an all-round defensive position on suitable ground.

The tank unit commander, as the leader of the strongest unit, is in most cases in command of the combat team, and all the other participating arms (Panzer grenadiers, artillery, engineers and anti-tank units) are placed under him. The Germans realise that a strong and unified command is an essential feature of any military operation. For certain missions, however, tank units are attached to another arm, in which case the tank commander is consulted before the final plans for the operations are made.

One of a remarkable sequence of pictures illustrating General Heinz Guderian at the front. It was Guderian's vision which had led to the creation of the Panzerwaffe and he now demonstrated a masterful ability in the field.

Gun and Ammunition Nomenclature

During World War II the Wehrmacht generally described small arms such as pistols and machine guns by the diameter of their bore in millimetres, the most common being 7.92mm and 9mm. Larger calibre guns were usually categorised in centimetres. The practice of most countries was also to use millimetres, for example the American 75mm M3. British tanks and anti-tank guns and some artillery pieces were differentiated by the weight of the projectile they fired, for example the 6-pounder and 17-pounder. However, some older British types retained their identification by the diameter of their bore in inches. 'Calibre' refers to the diameter of the barrel, usually omitting the rifling. We refer to a 7.92mm-calibre MG34 medium machine gun. Small arms ammunition was frequently known by its calibre and cartridge length together, 7.92mm x 57, or by attaching a common name to the calibre, such as Parabellum or ACP. These rules were not applied in any hard or fast manner and variations can be endless.

With the artillery the term calibre was used to describe the diameter of the bore of a gun's barrel in relation to the length of the barrel. The Americans measure this length from the back of the chamber to the muzzle and the Germans measure from the back of the breech to the muzzle, therefore a gun of 56 calibres - often symbolized as L/56 - has a barrel 56 times the length of its nominal bore. In the case of the German KwK 36 8.8cm L/56 gun, this means a total barrel length of 56 x 8.8cm, or 4.93m.

Rifle and machine-gun calibre ammunition came in many shapes, including incendiary and explosive types. The most common were

the jacketed hard point (JHP), jacketed soft point (JSP), tracer and armour-piercing (AP). For the Tiger, three types of 8.8cm ammunition were dispensed - armour-piercing, high explosive (HE) and high-explosive anti-tank (HEAT). The customary variety of armour-piercing was the Pzgr.39, a 10.2kg armour-piercing capped, ballistic-capped round with an explosive centre which left the KwK36's muzzle at a velocity of 773m/sec.

AP rounds usually accounted for half of a Tiger's ammunition supply, the rest taken up with Sprgr. HE rounds for use against soft-skinned vehicles. The hollow-charge Gr.39HL round, which was less productive at short range, was sometimes exchanged for some of the HE load despite being less accurate. The Pzgr.39 APCBC round was capable of piercing 120mm of armour at an angle of 30 degrees within a range of 1000m. The tungsten-cored Pzgr.40 round could easily pierce 170mm of armour at short range and 110mm at 2000m, while the Gr.39HL round could penetrate 90mm of armour up to 2000m.

The gun-aimer and loader at work inside their Panzer III. Something of the claustrophobic nature inside the tank is conveyed by the cramped working space of the gun loader.

The nightmare for every tank crew was to have to dismount the vehicle and change tracks under enemy fire. This was an alarmingly frequent occurrence; nonetheless every effort had to be made to salvage an immobilised vehicle. (Propaganda drawing for *Signal* magazine).

INFANTRY TANK CO-OPERATION

When the enemy has well prepared positions with natural or constructed tank obstacles, the German infantry attacks before the tanks and clears the way. The objective of the infantry is to penetrate into the enemy position and destroy enemy anti-tank weapons to the limit of its strength and the fire power of its own support weapons, augmented by additional support and covering fire from the tanks and self-propelled weapons sited in their rear.

Only after the destruction of the enemy anti-tank defence can the tanks be employed on the battle line to the fullest advantage.

When the tank obstacles in front of the enemy position are already destroyed, and no additional tank obstacles are expected in the depth of the enemy's main defensive position, the infantry breaks through simultaneously with the tank unit. The infantry attack is conducted in the same manner as it would be without the co-operation of tanks. Heavy infantry weapons are kept in readiness to fire at possible newly discovered anti-tank positions. Of particular importance is protection of the open flanks by echeloning the flank units and employing heavy weapons at the flanks.

In most cases, the infantry follows the tanks closely, taking advantage of the firepower and paralysing effect of the tanks upon the enemy's defence. The Germans normally transport the infantry to the line of departure on tanks or troop-carrying vehicles in order to protect the infantry and to increase its speed. The infantry leaves the vehicles at the last possible moment, and goes into action mainly with light automatic weapons.

The tanks advance by bounds from cover to cover, reconnoitring the terrain ahead and providing protective fire for the dismounted Panzer grenadiers. The tanks do not slow their advance to enable the infantry to keep continuous pace with them, but advance alone and wait under cover until the infantry catches up with the advance. Terrain that does not offer sufficient cover is crossed with the greatest possible speed.

The infantry attacks in small formations also by bounds under the fire cover of its own heavy weapons and of the tanks, staying away from individual tanks because they draw the strongest enemy fire.

When a tank company attacks with infantry, there are normally two platoons on the line, one platoon back, and the fourth platoon in reserve. The interval between tanks is usually 100 to 120 yards.

The tank's machine guns usually engage infantry targets at about one thousand yards range and under, while the tank guns engage targets at 2000-2500 yards.

The co-ordination between tanks and Panzer grenadiers moving into combat on armoured half-tracks is similar to the technique employed in a purely armoured formation, since the armoured half-tracks are not only troop-carrying vehicles but also combat vehicles. When the terrain is favourable for tank warfare, the Panzer grenadiers in their armoured half-tracks follow immediately with the second wave, after the first tank wave has overrun the opponent's position. A deep and narrow formation is employed. After the penetration, the main mission of the Panzer grenadiers is to overcome the enemy positions which survived the first wave.

In attacking enemy pillboxes the Germans use combat groups consisting of tanks, infantry and engineers, assisted by artillery. The normal composition of a combat group attacking one bunker is one platoon of tanks and one platoon of infantry reinforced by one squad of engineers. Before the combat group is committed against the enemy pillbox, artillery fires high explosives and smoke shells at the neighbouring pillboxes to isolate them, shells the terrain between pillboxes, and conducts counter-battery fire. Under the protection of this fire, the combat group advances close to the pillbox while other infantry units attack the enemy in the terrain between the pillboxes.

One tank squad covers the advances of the other tank squads and the infantry platoon by direct fire against the pillbox, particularly against the observation and weapons' openings. The first tank squad halts under cover whenever possible and covers the advance of the second tank squad.

When the combat group reaches a barbed wire obstacle surrounding the pillbox, the two tank squads have different missions. One tank squad remains in front of the pillbox, and its tanks are driven into a position from which they can overlook the terrain, and watch out for anti-tank guns and machine gun emplacements, while the other tank squad (the pillbox tank squad) rolls across the obstacle to enable the infantry and engineers to get close to the pillbox. The pillbox tank squad then fires on the pillbox at close range. The infantry squad meanwhile takes the surrounding terrain and covers the engineers who blast the entrance of the pillbox with TNT.

ARTILLERY-TANK CO-ORDINATION

Artillery support is of decisive importance for the preparation and the successful conduct of a tank attack. A unified command for the entire artillery controls the artillery fire as long as the infantry and tank units are fighting on the same line. When the tanks break through the enemy forward defence lines, the self-propelled artillery or any other artillery battalion designated for the support of the tank unit is placed under the command of the tank unit commander.

The Germans believe that the artillery fire must not check the momentum of the attack. Consequently the heaviest fire must fall well ahead of the tanks or outside their sector.

The mission of the artillery preparation before the attack is to destroy, or at least to neutralise, the opponent's anti-tank defence in the area between the line of contact and the regimental reserve line. Continuous counter-battery fire prevents the enemy from shelling the tank assembly area and from breaking up the preparation of the tank attack.

The artillery has the following missions before the tank attack:

Counter-battery fire on enemy artillery located in positions which command the ground over which the tank attack is to be made.

Concentrations on enemy tanks in assembly areas:

Harassing fire on all areas in which the anti-tank units are located or suspected. Fire is heaviest on areas in which tanks cannot operate but from which they can be engaged effectively.

Adjusting fire with high explosives on probable enemy observation posts commanding the sector to be attacked. These observation posts are blinded with smoke as soon as the attack begins.

Experience has taught the Germans that the flanks of a tank attack are vulnerable. Therefore they assign to the artillery and the rocket projector units the task of protecting flanks by barrages using high explosives and smoke shells.

The artillery has the following missions during the tank attack:

Counter-battery fire.

Blinding enemy observation posts.

As the attack progresses, engaging successive

lines of anti-tank defence, especially areas to the rear and flanks of the sector attacked.

Screening the flanks of the attack with smoke and neutralising the enemy's infantry and rear areas.

Delaying the movement and deployment of enemy reserves, particularly tanks.

The Germans stress that this wide variety of tasks must not lead to the wholesale dispersal of effort. The main task of the artillery is at all times the destruction of the enemy's anti-tank weapons, tanks, and artillery.

Liaison between artillery and tanks during the attack is established by the commanding officers and the artillery liaison group, which normally moves with the first wave. Artillery forward observers, if possible in armoured observation posts, ride with the most forward elements. A German field expedient is for the tank unit to take along a forward observer in one of its tanks. It often happens that the tank man himself has to take over the observation for the artillery. He himself can request artillery fire and shift concentrations when the situation requires such changes.

INSIDE THE PANZERS

To the infantrymen, crouched in their foxholes, even the smallest tanks project an aura of invincibility. Rolling relentlessly onwards, they can seem like an unstoppable armoured juggernaut,

the very essence of armoured might. Tanks appear from the outside to be so invulnerable and impersonal, it's easy to forget that, inside the vehicle, there are men just the same as any others, with the same fears and emotions which run through every soldier on the battlefield.

In many respects, these emotions are heightened because the tank gives the protection of its armour, but imposes a host of other restrictions on its crew.

Inside the tank, visibility is severely limited. The interior is cramped and noisy. The crew are acutely aware that their vehicle is a prime target for every enemy weapon on the battlefield. With their own stocks of fuel and ammunition aboard, they know that one hit can turn the tank into a blazing inferno. There is also the danger that infantrymen might get close enough to attack with anti-tank weapons, from unseen hiding places.

The main sources of danger for tank crews in battle during the Second World War stemmed chiefly from the lack of visibility from inside the tank. The crew relied on a series of narrow vision slits that allowed them to see a very small area directly in front of that slit; the early Panzers had a number of those around the vehicles but there were always blind spots. Most armour on the battlefield at that time didn't move much quicker than a man running; in consequence a man running with a hand-held anti-tank device was frequently able to out-manoeuvre tanks.

Assembly workers hard at work producing Sturmgeschtze in January 1942. These machines are equipped with the short-barrelled 75mm which had already proven to be ineffective for many of the tasks faced by the Stug.

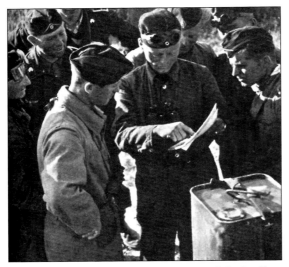

A hurried field conference, as the men of the leading tanks in a German formation threatening Dubno are briefed on their next mission.

Shortly after the Second World War Basil Liddel-Hart conducted a highly impressive series of interviews with leading German officers which formed the basis for a masterful study entitled *The Other Side of the Hill*. From the ranks of the Panzerwaffe Liddell personally interviewed Guderian, von Thoma and Manteuffel - who was to rise to prominence later in the war.

One factor which emerged very clearly from those discussions was the reliance on the speed of armour as opposed to the heaviness of its ordnance or armour plate. Manteufell went as far as to stress that the speed of manoeuvrability of a tank was by far the most important attribute. Von Thoma confirmed this view when he asserted that, given the choice between a thick skin or a fast runner, he would choose the fast runner every time. This view made for an interesting departure from the commonly held view that the German High Command valued heavy tanks above all else.

Under favourable circumstances, placed in good positions, with their strong frontal armour facing the enemy, the crews of the German tanks of the Second World War had good cause for confidence. The Panthers and Tigers of the later war years could withstand most guns on the battlefield from all but the closest ranges. Once infantry tank-hunting teams got close to the tanks, or enemy tanks were able to manoeuvre into a position to fire at the weaker sides or rear of the tank, the picture changed dramatically. The all conquering

armoured hull could just as soon turn into a steel coffin.

For tank commanders to have a good field of vision, it was necessary for them to stand with their heads fully exposed outside the vehicle. But when the bullets started to fly, the commander and driver had to retreat inside the vehicle, closing their hatches behind them. Once the tank was battened down, the crew had only a very limited view of the outside world. With their diesel engines roaring and weapons firing, the heat generated inside the tanks was oppressive. In battle, the noise, the smell of sweat, smoke, fear and cordite, was an ever-present ingredient to life in the Panzers. Not only was it a claustrophobic world, unbearably noisy and uncomfortably cramped, but the severely restricted view made it difficult to spot targets or to defend against enemy tank-hunting teams.

Once the tank was battened down for better protection it became difficult to see anything at all, especially for the driver, who only had very small slots to look through and he could see very little. He had to rely on the commander to a great deal, who was sitting higher up in the tank, to advise him if there was any trouble ahead. In the Second World War tank-hunting teams were trained to move up close to enemy tanks to disable them. Occasionally they would climb onto vehicles themselves and set anti-tank mines or drop grenades into exhaust outlets and any open hatches.

As it was designed to fire over long ranges, the main gun of the tank was useless at close quarters. For combat against infantrymen who got too near the vehicle, tanks were equipped with grenade dischargers which could be operated from inside. The turret of a tank is very much like a mobile pillbox, with only the minimal openings for weapons. The armour gives protection, but severely limits visibility. In desperate situations there was the option of a small opening called a pistol port. When teams of infantry got close enough to climb onto the vehicles themselves, the crew of the tank had to either clamber out and engage the enemy with small arms, or rely on supporting infantry and other tanks in the unit to spray their vehicle with machine gun fire to kill any infantry clambering aboard.

Tanks of all nations tended to mount at least one or two machine guns for close quarter defence. Some tanks in fact mounted as many as six. But in addition to these, smoke projectors which could lay a smoke screen, mine layers, grenade launchers and even light mortars could be built on to tanks for close quarter protection against infantry or anti-tank gun crews. Later in the war the Germans used a cement-like paste called Zimmerit which coated the sides of the vehicles that were reachable by anyone attacking the tank; its purpose being to stop magnetic mines being attached. At longer ranges, there were other dangers. Concealed anti-tank guns were the chief menace. One well-placed shot could blast a tank to fragments. These guns were difficult to spot and could be camouflaged very easily.

In order to give the tanks protection against enemy guns they need as much armour as possible. Ideally, every inch would be covered in thick steel plate. However, the crew need to be able to see out of a tank, so vision slits and hatches had to be allowed for. The engines need air intakes, and exhaust pipes to allow the fumes to escape from the engine. These weakly armoured parts of the tank are where it is most vulnerable, and they were the favourite aiming points for lurking anti-tank guns. From the confines of a tank, anti-tank guns were often impossible to find until it was too late.

COMMUNICATIONS

With the high levels of noise inside a Panzer communication was very difficult. To communicate with other vehicles, other than by radio, was almost impossible.

The German engineers solved the problem of internal communications by an internal intercom which linked the crew and allowed them to communicate via headphones and microphones. The German practice at the time was to use a throat microphone which had two small microphones against the side of the throat; these would be pressed to speak to the rest of the crew. The radio set over that also allowed for broadcasts to the rest of the unit. The headset had a pair of headphones to muffle the sound of the engine but it generally was a very, very loud engine anyway. For communications between the tanks themselves, all German machines were equipped with radios. In the early war years, there were no such refinements on the Russian side.

In the famous T-34 for example, as good as the tank was, the communication was very poor. Early models had no radio at all so the commander had to get out of his turret and wave two flags about, one red and one green, and give signals like a ship on the high seas. This primitive system had initially been used by the Panzerwaffe, who of course discovered that it did not work very well. It was only much later that the T-34/85 had a proper radio for contact with each crew member and of course to Headquarters.

AMMUNITION

With the space taken up by the main gun, the crew and the engines, there was surprisingly little room in a tank for the ammunition which was vital to survival on the battlefield. Most tanks could hold enough shells for around ninety shots, tightly packed into every conceivable space. Most commanders favoured a mix of 40 per cent high explosive and 60 per cent armour piercing, but it was often a matter of a personal assessment of the likeliest target to be faced on a given mission. Getting the balance right was a crucial decision. Armour piercing rounds were useless against infantry and high explosive would not penetrate tank armour. Having a large stock of the wrong kind of ammunition effectively left the tank impotent.

In battle, many experienced crews could fire one round every five seconds, so not surprisingly, ammunition supplies could quickly become exhausted, rendering the tank helpless. At this delicate juncture, the tank commander was faced with a crucial choice: either leave the field to re-arm and re-fuel, or await re-supply in the field.

The bulky tank ammunition could not be transported on foot and required a vehicle to re-supply the tanks. Trucks were too vulnerable to be sent into the fighting area, so the Germans developed a special turretless tank called a Munition-schlepper to carry out the dangerous job of ammunition re-supply on the battlefield.

To ensure that ammunition supplies were used wisely, German tanks were forbidden from firing on the move. The prescribed tactic was to strictly engage enemy targets from a static position. This made aiming much easier, giving the gunner the best chance as he lined up his target on the middle triangle of his gun sight. To help him in aiming his shells, they were equipped with a tracer element, which produced a trail of bright light to help pinpoint the path of the shell as it flew towards its target.

Panzerkampfwagen III Sd.Kfz.141

The PzKpfw III was designed to be the Wehrmacht's main combat machine and was developed by Daimler-Benz in the mid 1930s under the pseudonym Zugfuhrerwagen, which means platoon commanders' truck. The first prototype of the PzKpfw III was produced by Daimler-Benz in Berlin 1936. As the introduction of a 50mm gun would have meant a considerable re-design, the 37mm gun was used instead.

Following numerous modifications, the Ausf A (1-Serie) appeared in May 1937 and by the end of 1937, 15 were produced. Only 8 of the Ausf As were fully armed and the unarmed machines were used for further testing and modification.

Daimler-Benz produced 15 Ausf Bs (2-Serie) in 1937, 15 Ausf Cs (3a-Serie) by the beginning of 1938; it continued by introducing the next variant the Ausf D (3b-Serie), 55 of which were produced in 1939. Of the entire Ausf Ds production run, only 30 were armed.

All early models of the Panzer III, including the Ausf A/B/C/D were pre-prototypes of the whole series and were unsuitable for large scale production. Every new prototype was a marginal improvement on the last. Each model featured a different type of suspension, a variation on the Maybach DSO -such as the HL 108 TR engine. Only a relatively few vehicles saw combat in the early stages of the war; the Ausf D saw service during fighting in Denmark and Norway in May 1940 and in Finland in 1941/42. In February 1940, remaining Panzer IIIs Ausf D were handed over to NSKK for training purposes.

Armour (mm/angle) Ausf H
Front Turret: 30/13
Front Upper Hull: 30+30/90
Front Lower Hull: 30+30/23
Side Turret: 30/25
Side Upper Hull: 30/0
Side Lower Hull: 30/0
Rear Turret: 30/13
Rear Upper Hull: 30/30
Rear Lower Hull: 30+30/8
Turret Top / Bottom: 10/89
Upper Hull Top / Bottom: 17/77
Lower Hull Top / Bottom: 16/90
Gun Mantlet: 37/0

Armour (mm/angle) Ausf L/M
Front Turret: 57/15
Front Upper Hull: 50+20/9
Front Lower Hull: 50/21
Side Turret: 30/25
Side Upper Hull: 30/0
Side Lower Hull: 30/0
Rear Turret: 30/12
Rear Upper Hull: 50/17
Rear Lower Hull: 50/9
Turret Top / Bottom: 10/83
Upper Hull Top / Bottom: 18/79
Lower Hull Top / Bottom: 16/90
Gun Mantlet: 50+20/0

Model:	Ausf H	Ausf L/M
Weight:	21800kg	22700kg
Crew:	5	5
Engine:	Maybach HL 120 TRM 12 cylinder / 265hp	Maybach HL 120 TRM 12 cylinder / 265hp
Speed:	Road: 40km/h Crosscountry: 20km/h	Road: 40km/h Crosscountry 20km/h
Range:	Road: 165km Crosscountry: 105km	Road: 155kh Crosscountry: 95km
Fuel Capacity:	320 litres	320 litres
Length:	5.52 m (with the gun)	6.41m (with the gun) 5.56m (with the gun)
Width:	2.95 m	2.95 m
Height:	2.50 m	2.50 m
Armament:	50mm KwK 38 L/42 2 x 7.92mm MG34 (1 x MG - hull) (1 x MG - coax)	50mm KwK 39 L/60 2 x 7.92mm MG34 (1 x MG - hull) (1 x MG - coax)
Ammunition supply:	50mm - 99 rounds 7.92mm - 2700 rounds	50mm - 92 rounds 7.92mm - 3750 rounds

The first Panzer III model to go into anything like full-scale production was the Ausf E of which 96 were produced. With a thicker 30mm frontal armour, a Maybach HL 120TR engine and new suspension and gearbox putting its weight up to 19.5 tonnes, the Ausf E was the best machine so far.

By 1940, and during the 'E' model production, it was decided to fit all models with a 50mm gun as standard. The L/42 gun was fitted on Ausf E, F, G and H. From 1941, Hitler insisted that the more powerful L/60 (50mm) gun was fitted on Ausf J-1. In 1942, 104 Ausf J's were converted to Panzerbefehlswagen III and in April 1943, 100 Ausf M's were converted by Wegmann into the Flammpanzer (Flamethrower Tank); designed to fight in urban areas such as Stalingrad. Although the models produced never actually reached Stalingrad they did see service on the Eastern Front. Additionally, many Ausf Ms were converted into the Sturmgeschutz III or the Ausf N.

The Panzer III provided the main battle tank for the Panzer Divisions in the early years of the war. Yet its production was slow and stopped altogether in August 1943.

However, in 1943/44, the Panzer III prototypes were fitted with dozers and were used to clean up the streets of war-torn cities.

Raw Materials Used in Production of PzKpfw III	
Steel:	39000.00kg
Tin:	1.40kg
Copper:	60.10kg
Aluminium:	90.40kg
Lead:	71.10kg
Zinc:	49.10kg
Rubber:	125.00kg

The early version of the Panzer III was equipped with a 37mm main gun. Even before they saw combat these guns were already known to be unsuitable for most tanks.

A pair of Panzer III tanks stand guard in a recently captured French town.

CONVERSIONS

- PzKfw III (Flamm) Ausf. M (Sd. Kfz 141/3) - flame-thrower
- Befehlswagen III Ausf. D1 (Sd. Kfz 267-268) - command tank
- Befehlswagen III Ausf. E (Sd. Kfz 267-268) - command tank
- Befehlswagen III Ausf. H (Sd. Kfz 266-268) - command tank
- Befehlswagen III Ausf. K - command tank
- Beobachtungswagen III - observation vehicle (Sd. Kfz 143)

INTO BATTLE

A war artist provides a vivid impression of the co-operation between the Panzer Grenadiers and the tanks in action in Russia during 1942.

"Teamwork between the Panzers and the infantry was exemplary. They quickly began to work together without apparent difficulty. The place of the armour leader is at the head of the formation. He can only command his unit properly from the front"

After action report, Poland 1939

The first moves in Hitler's master plan had been achieved without bloodshed, but as tensions rose, Adolf Hitler's crooked path led only downwards into chaos. The conquest of Poland heralded the coming of the Second World War.

On Friday, 1 September 1939, the tactical principles of the Panzerwaffe still had to be put to the test. The German attack began at 4:45 am, when the Battleship *Schleswig-Holstein* on a so-called 'goodwill visit' opened fire on a Polish naval depot and garrison at Westeplatte. An hour later the first German units crossed the border. On 3 September 1939 Great Britain and France declared war on Germany.

Originally, Germany was to invade Poland in the early hours of 26 August 1939, but at 8:00pm on 25

August, Hitler postponed the attack. The final order was transmitted at 4:00pm on 31 August, but was only given to the troops at 4.45am on 1 September 1939. The invasion was preceded by numerous German border provocations and diversions including the notorious incident at the radio station at Gliwice staged by German troops in Polish uniforms.

Hitler was about to plunge Europe into years of barbarity and turmoil on an unprecedented scale. Although the Polish campaign was predominantly a conventional war, the German battle plan did include some elements of what was to become known as 'Blitzkrieg'. Hitler made no declaration of war for example, a fact which, unbelievably, caught his victims off guard every time it occurred during the war and which gave him the vital advantage of surprise.

Attacks by the Luftwaffe preceded the invasion. Screaming over Poland ahead of the main armies, their task was to destroy the Polish air force and then to act as airborne artillery for the ground forces. Spreading terror among the civilians was also an important part of their mission. The attempt to destroy the Polish air force on the ground was only partially successful, since many of their warplanes were moved to new locations. Nonetheless, air superiority was quickly established, and by day three the Polish air force had been virtually annihilated.

From the start, the Germans engaged in an innovative new form of mobile warfare. At vital stages during the attack, Stukas hurtled earthwards to place their bombs almost to within centimetres of the centre of their targets. Co-ordination between the air force, the motorised and armoured formations was exemplary, providing enormous flexibility, especially in the absence of artillery support.

THE GERMAN FORCES

The German invading force was divided into five armies and reserves, all under command of General Walther von Brauchitsch. The Germans attacked from three directions - Silesia/Moravia and Slovakia, Western Pomerania and East Prussia. Colonel General Gerd von Rundstedt's Army Group South, which was composed of the 8th, 10th and 14th Armies, attacked from Silesia/Moravia and Slovakia and had the strongest complement of armoured formations, with over 2,000 tanks and 800 armoured cars, in four Panzer Divisions, four Light Divisions and two Motorised Divisions.

General Gunther von Kluge's 4th Army, part of Colonel General Fedor von Bock's Army Group North, attacked from Western Pomerania, with eight Infantry Divisions, two Motorised Divisions and one Panzer Division. General George von Kuechler's 3rd Army, also part of Army Group North, attacked from East Prussia with two Infantry Divisions and one Panzer Division. Altogether Army Group North boasted 600 tanks and 200 armoured cars. All three attacks were designed to converge on Warsaw. In total, German forces included 1,850,000 infantry, supported by over 3,000 tanks and 10,000 artillery pieces. The Luftwaffe deployed 2,085 aeroplanes grouped in two air fleets. Additionally the attacking force held advantage by being able to attack Poland from three directions at once. The Germans also had a well-established spy network and could count on the help of many ethnic Germans living in Poland; the Germans also knew the Polish rail and road network very well as German firms had built it.

Panzers IIIs and IVs of the 14th Panzer Division move through a Russian village in the months prior to the attack on Stalingrad.

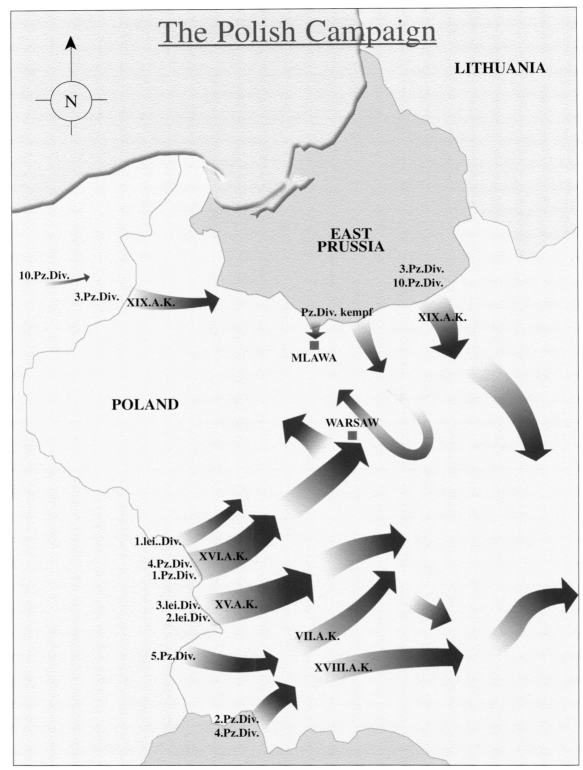

The Polish Campaign

LITHUANIA

EAST PRUSSIA

3.Pz.Div.
10.Pz.Div.

10.Pz.Div.

3.Pz.Div. XIX.A.K.

XIX.A.K.

Pz.Div. kempf

MLAWA

POLAND

WARSAW

1.lei..Div.

XVI.A.K.

4.Pz.Div.
1.Pz.Div.

3.lei.Div. XV.A.K.
2.lei.Div.

VII.A.K.

5.Pz.Div.

XVIII.A.K.

2.Pz.Div.
4.Pz.Div.

The light divisions deployed alongside the Panzer Divisions for this campaign were deemed to have been a failure.

Units of the Panzerwaffe were equipped with four types of tanks: 1445 PzKpfw I, 1226 PzKpfw II light tanks and around 100 PzKpfw III and 211 PzKpfw IV medium tanks. In addition, there were 215 command tanks and other armoured vehicles including the Czech PzKpfw 35(t) and a few 38(t). Each of the Panzer Divisions fielded around 300 tanks. Along with the tanks, there were some 308 heavy armoured cars and 718 light armoured cars; the few lucky Panzer Grenadiers were transported in one of 68 armoured personnel carriers.

The Polish Army fielded 39 Infantry, 11 Elite Cavalry Brigades, three Mountain Brigades and two Armoured Motorised Brigades along with various support units. The Army Groups, 'Lodz', 'Krakow' and 'Karpaty' between them had 241 tanks and 32 armoured cars. Army groups 'Pomorze', 'Poznan' and 'Modlin' deployed some 234 tanks and 52 armoured cars. The Reserve formations had some 185 tanks between them. The Polish Army was not yet fully mobilised or prepared for war, as according to the Polish defence plan - Z. Nonetheless, the Poles responded to German attacks on all fronts, attempting to contain the invading force in order to counter-attack. Polish planners correctly predicted directions of German attacks but knew that they could only delay them in order to allow their Allies time to act. In total, the Polish forces fielded some one million infantry, approximately 900 tanks and 4,300 artillery pieces supported by 400 aeroplanes. Only a small percentage of all Polish equipment was modern, the rest largely obsolete, as Poland had only begun the process of reorganisation and modernisation in 1936. The Polish army lacked motorised transport and relied on infantry and horse-drawn transport. In addition the Polish army was surrounded by the enemy on three sides along a 3,000-kilometer-long frontier.

On September 1st and 2nd, the Polish forces were was already involved in heavy fighting in the Battles of Mlawa, in Pomerania, while retreating eastwards in attempt to establish a line of defence and delay the invaders. Polish forces made up of infantry on foot were unable to fall back and establish defensive lines as they were constantly pursued and outpaced by German motorised and Panzer units. Many Polish units and even armies were surrounded and destroyed, while attempting to either defend or withdraw. The Polish High Command realised as early as 5 September that the

situation was critical and there was no hope without immediate assistance from its Allies. Many units were cut off but continued fighting. After heavy fighting and desperate defence, on 8 September the Germans reached Warsaw.

On 9 September the bloodiest and most bitter battle of the entire campaign began. The Battle of Bzura was a Polish counteroffensive designed to relieve Warsaw. It was executed by Army groups 'Pomorze' and 'Poznan', both of which were in danger of being surrounded themselves. At first the Poles were successful and inflicted heavy losses on the German forces principally due to the element of surprise. Again, the speed of the German units made further operations impossible and by 16 September Germans began pushing the Polish Army towards Warsaw.

When Hitler visited the tank corps soon after the invasion, it was the destruction that the panzer divisions had caused which astonished him most. The Blitzkrieg elements were falling smoothly into place.

Although brilliantly conceived and executed, the overall German strategy was still based on the classic German tradition of encirclement and envelopment carried out mainly by conventional forces.

By September Poland's situation was already beyond hope. Despite the obvious hopelessness of the situation, on 18 September the largest tank-versus-tank engagement of the campaign took place near Tomaszow Lubelski. The battle ended on 20 September with the total destruction of Polish forces under General Tadeusz Kutrzeba. Although it delayed the capitulation of Warsaw, the battle was fought in a lost cause.

The first German attack on Warsaw took place on 9 September, but from then until 24 September Polish defenders successfully resisted all attacks. On 25 September the Germans began a ground and aerial bombardment of the city, and from 25-27 September unsuccessfully attempted to storm the city. Many tanks were lost in the street fighting, which again underlined the flaws in the Panzer I. On 28 September, Warsaw capitulated because of the extreme conditions and lack of supplies. At the same time, from 10 September, Fortress Modlin (under General Wiktor Thommee) was also unsuccessfully attacked by the Germans, until its capitulation on 29 September.

A Pz.Kpfw 35(t) lies abandoned in a tank graveyard. This particular example has been gutted by fire and has lost its turret-mounted machine gun. This Czech-made tank provided an important stop-gap during the early campaigns.

Stalin had been unpleasantly surprised by the speed of the German advance. Even with the supposed security of a non-aggression pact with Hitler in his pocket, Stalin did not want to see Germany control the whole of Poland.

On Sunday 17 September the Red Army invaded Poland from the east to 'liberate' and 'protect' Belorussians and Ukrainians living in Eastern Poland. This came as a shock to the Poles and made regrouping of remaining Polish forces an impossible task. The Soviet invasion force was made up of two fronts - Timoszenko's Ukrainian and Kowalow's Belorussian. Both fronts consisted of 1.5 million soldiers, 6,191 tanks, 1,800 aeroplanes and 9,140 artillery pieces. After heavy fighting, on 18 September, the Soviets captured Wilno, followed by Grodno and Lwow on 22 September, reaching River Bug on 23 September.

On the night of 18 September the Polish President and High Command along with a single armoured battalion equipped with French Renault R-35 tanks entered Romania, where they were interned. On 18 September Germans and Soviets met in Bresc and Bugiem and exchanged 'greetings'. On 2 October Polish defenders of Hel (under Rear Admiral Unrug) capitulated. The last battle of the Polish campaign took place on 2-5 October - the Battle of Kock. On Friday, 6 October 1939 the last Polish troops capitulated.

The Polish Army of 1939 used a variety of vehicles. Those included: 574 TK and TKS tankettes (light reconnaissance tanks), 102 obsolete Renault FT-17 light tanks, 160 7TP light tanks and 50 British Vickers 6-ton tanks, along with approximately one hundred armoured cars. The Polish Army's tanks were grouped in light tank battalions and light tank companies, but they were scattered throughout the army. Tankettes served with infantry divisions, cavalry brigades and independent units attached to larger units. In addition, Poland had a single Mechanised Brigade.

The Polish light tanks and tankettes were the first opponents for the German Panzers. Patriotic but outnumbered Polish tank crews with their mostly outclassed equipment fought bravely and managed to destroy a number of German vehicles, as they simultaneously defended their homeland from both the Germans and the Soviets. The Polish Campaign is surrounded by numerous myths such as the destruction of the Polish airforce in the opening hours of the invasion and vain cavalry charges against German armoured units. Both stories were creations of German and some Italian propaganda, and are very far from the truth. The Polish airforce was deployed at numerous airfields and, although numerically inferior and partially obsolete, was very active during the course of the campaign up to and including the battle for Warsaw. Polish cavalry brigades never charged tanks with their sabres or lances. They were conventionally equipped with weapons such as 37mm Bofors wz.36 (model 1936) anti-tank guns. At the time of the battles the cavalry brigades were in the process of being reorganised into motorised brigades so the men in the ranks were well aware of the realities of modern warfare.

THE COST OF VICTORY

German casualties in the campaign amounted to around 10,000 killed and 30,000 wounded. Although significant, those losses were very low compared to Polish casualties of which 66,000 were killed, 133,000 wounded and 420,000 taken prisoner. In addition, the Germans had 1,000 armoured fighting vehicles knocked out during the campaign, mainly disabled by anti-tank guns. According to German sources only 89 PzKpfw I, 83 PzKpfw II, 26 PzKpfw III, 19 PzKpfw IV, 7 PzKpfw 35(t) and 7 PzKpfw 38(t) were complete write-offs. That aside, it should be noted that the Polish campaign proved to be the most costly and challenging campaign for the Germans, until the invasion of the Soviet Union in June of 1941.

Some 70,000 Polish soldiers escaped to Hungary and Romania, 20,000 to Latvia and Lithuania, the majority eventually making their way west to continue fighting. On 30 September the Polish Government in Exile was established in Paris.

WITTMANN IN BATTLE

In the ranks of the Leibstandarte Adolf Hitler was the fledgling tank ace Michael Wittmann. The Leibstandarte Motorised Regiment fought hard in Poland from the first day of the campaign. On that day the armoured scout platoon was soon in action, and Wittmann had received his baptism of fire. The campaign in Poland was brief (only 30 days in duration) but, nonetheless, his experiences had whetted his appetite for combat. In the following year Wittmann and his armoured car again saw action in the rapid campaign that led to the fall of France.

The Polish campaign demonstrated the speed and power possessed by Panzers and the excellence of the Panzer Divisions. It also demonstrated that the time of large armies made up of infantry marching on foot and cavalry was over. At the same time, it provided the Germans with real experience of using armour in combat conditions.

Above all the Germans learned that tanks were not suited for combat in built up areas; heavy losses had been suffered in the direct assault on Warsaw. They also discovered that well organised anti-tank defences are very costly for tank forces to assault in the absence of proper preparation. What the Polish Campaign also proved beyond doubt

A war artist's impression of German tanks moving through a burning Russian village published in the April 1942 edition of *Signal*, the propaganda magazine.

was that PzKpfw I and II were unsuitable to be used as front-line combat tanks and should be completely replaced with the heavier PzKpfw III and IV. The other sobering lesson was that during the course of the campaign the Light Divisions had proved to be unsuccessful, being too weak to perform the tasks of either Cavalry or motorised infantry.

THE DANGEROUS WORLD

The tank was the catalyst for success and gave the Nazi regime a stunning propaganda coup. The reality of battle, however, had been a sobering experience for many crews. In tank-versus-tank contests the crews prayed that their first shot would hit, turning the enemy vehicle into a flaming mass, as the fuel and ammunition exploded. A miss could mean their own destruction by return.

The prospect of the awful death of men trapped in a burning tank haunted the tank crews. In the footage from all of the major tank battles of the Second World War, from Poland through North Africa, and into Russia, the black columns of smoke from burning vehicles can be seen hanging on the horizon like gathering storm clouds. All too often they marked the funeral pyres for their hapless crews.

Death or injury could come to the tank crews from a myriad of sources. It was not always necessary to even damage the vehicle. One other ever-present danger for tank crews were metal splinters caused by direct hits on the outside of a tank. As the outside velocity of the impact was converted into violent internal energy, these deadly fragments were blown from the inside of the turret, where they would fly around the inside of the tank slicing through the bodies of the crewmen packed together in their claustrophobic world. Riveted tanks in particular were most susceptible to this unpleasant phenomenon, which made the 35(t) and 38(t) deeply unpopular with the crews.

CAPTURED POLISH ARMOUR

On a more positive note, the Polish Campaign provided Germans with a supply of captured Polish armoured fighting vehicles, including the 7TP three-man light tank and the TK series of two-man tankettes for light reconnaissance. These were locally produced versions of the British Vickers tanks and tankettes. The 7TP light tank was the Polish army's main battle tank and some 170 were in service as of September 1939.

On 11 September 1939 Adolf Hitler's order stated that military equipment was to be collected from the battlefields and moved to special collection points. Captured 7TPs were designated as Panzerkampfwagen 7TP 731(p), while TK-3s were designated as Leichte Panzerkampfwagen TK(p), TKS as Leichte Panzerkampfwagen TKS(p) and C2P as Artillerie Schlepper C2P(p).

During the course of campaign the 5th Panzer Division had actually pressed captured TK series tankettes into service, while the 1st Panzer Division also used a few captured 7TP tanks. The Ist Panzer Regiment's 4th Company's commander, Second Lieutenant Fritz Kraemer, is known to have used one of them after his own machine was disabled. It remained in the original Polish camouflage scheme hastily painted with white crosses on the sides of the turret along with the number '400' representing command tank of 4th Company.

On 5 October 1939 a grand Victory Parade took place in Warsaw and a small number (probably eighteen) captured 7TPs now belonging to the 203rd Panzer Abteilung stationed in Spala were presented to Adolf Hitler. A single captured 7TP, with its frontal armour plate penetrated by a 20mm anti-tank projectile, was displayed during the Leipzig International Fair in March 1940.

Following the Polish campaign, captured tankettes were repaired in the workshops in Warsaw and then pressed into service by Wehrmacht units stationed in the General Government of Poland. In 1940 two platoons of TKS tankettes were certainly part of a light Panzer company. In Warsaw a number of captured 7TPs were used as headquarters tanks in 1939/40, probably with 203rd Panzer Abteilung. In 1940 this unit was moved to Norway and later to France. A number of 7TPs and TKS tankettes took part in the 1st anniversary of the General Government parade in Warsaw on 6 October 1940. Afterwards 7TPs were used for internal policing duties and later on as artillery tractors.

In Germany there was jubilation and a sense of restored national pride. The nation's virile leader acquired new prestige and laurels from the fatherland, and the Third Reich felt that it was entering into a glorious new world of its own making.

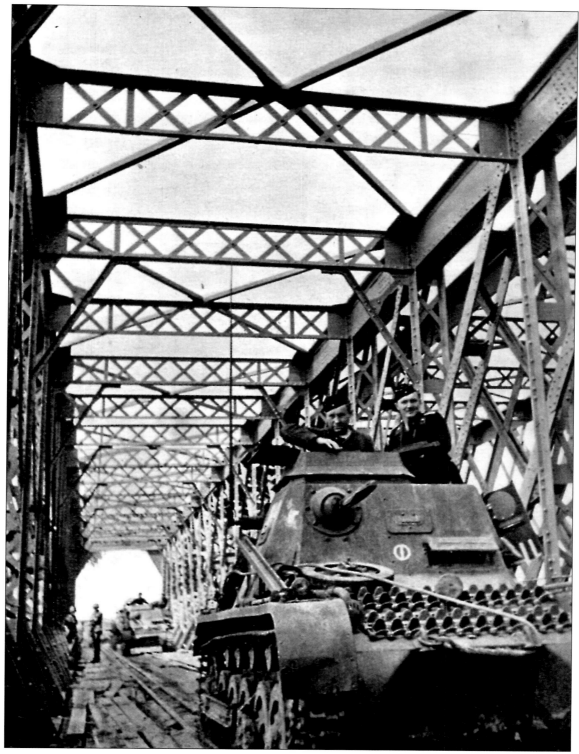

A command version of the Panzer I photographed in August 1941. These vehicles were clearly redundant at the time of the Spanish Civil War. Only Hitler's brinkmanship forced an unwelcome and unexpected war on the Panzerwaffe which meant these unsuitable machines would see action in the Russian campaign.

Panzerkampfwagen IV Sd.Kfz.161

Originally designed as an infantry support tank with a unique tactical role. Although the Panzer IV had thin armour, it carried a powerful 75mm gun and could match any other tank at that time. The prototype of the Panzer IV was given the code name Bataillonfuhrerwagen. The Panzer IV was ordered by Hitler from Krupp, MAN and Rheinmetall Borsig to weigh in at 18 tonnes with a top speed of 35 km/hr. The Krupp design -the VK 200 1 (K) -was eventually selected to enter into full-scale production in 1935. Along with the Panther, it was to become the main combat tank of the Third Reich.

The PzKpfw IV was perceived as the 'workhorse' of all the Panzer divisions and more were produced than any other variant in the 1933-1945 period. The Ausf A was built as a pre-production vehicle and only 35 were produced. The modifications from this gave rise to the Ausf B which emerged in 1938 with an increased frontal armour thickness and a six-speed gearbox, which enhanced its cross-country performance. That same year Krupp-Gruson produced the Ausf C and 134 of this model were in production until 1939.

The Ausf D/E saw an upgrading of its armour thickness and improved vision blocks for the driver. The Ausf E was the first of the Panzer IV fitted with turret mounted stowage bins. The Ausf F 1, produced between 1941-1942 was the last Panzer IV to be based on the short version chassis. 25 of the F Is were converted into Ausf F2s (it had the British nickname of "Mark IV Special" because it

Armour (mm/angle) Ausf D		
Front Turret: 30/10		
Front Upper Hull: 30/7		
Front Lower Hull: 30/12		
Side Turret: 20/25		
Side Upper Hull: 20/0		
Side Lower Hull: 20/0		
Rear Turret: 20/0		
Rear Upper Hull: 20/9		
Rear Lower Hull: 20/10		
Turret Top / Bottom: 10/83		
Upper Hull Top / Bottom: 12/84		
Lower Hull Top / Bottom: 10/90		
Gun Mantlet: 35/0		

Armour (mm/angle) Ausf G		
Front Turret: 50/11		
Front Upper Hull: 50 or 50+30/10		
Front Lower Hull: 50 or 50+30/12		
Side Turret: 30/26		
Side Upper Hull: 30/0		
Side Lower Hull: 30/0		
Rear Turret: 30/10		
Rear Upper Hull: 20/12		
Rear Lower Hull: 20/9		
Turret Top / Bottom: 10/83		
Upper Hull Top / Bottom: 12/85		
Lower Hull Top / Bottom: 10/90		
Gun Mantlet: 50/0		

Model:	Ausf A	Ausf B	Ausf C/D	Ausf E	Ausf F1	Ausf F2/G	Ausf H/J
Weight: (tonnes)	17.3	17.7	20	21	22.3	23.6	25
Crew:	5	5	5	5	5	5	5
Engine:	Maybach HL108 TR V-12 250 bhp	Maybach HL120, TRM V-12 300 bhp	Maybach HL120, TRM V-12 300 bhp	Maybach HL120, TRM V-12 300 bhp	Maybach HL120, TRM V-12 300 bhp	Maybach HL120, TRM V-12 300 bhp	Maybach HL120, TRM V-12 300 bhp
Speed:	32 km/h	40 km/h	40 km/h	40 km/h	40 km/h	40 km/h	38 km/h
Range: (road)	250 km	260 km	230 km	220 km	200 km	190 km	Ausf H = 180 km +Ausf J= 270 km
Fuel Capacity:	443 litres	470 litres	470 litres	470 litres	470 litres	470 litres	470 litres Ausf J = 680 litres
Length:	5.6m	5.87m	5.87m Ausf D = 5.92m	5.92m	5.93m	6.63m	6.63m
Width:	2.75m	2.75m	2.75m Ausf D = 2.86m	2.86m	2.88m	2.88m	2.88m
Height:	2.65m	2.65m	2.65m Ausf D = 2.68m	2.68m	2.68m	2.68m	2.68m
Armament:	L/24 & 2 x 7.92mm MG	L/24 & 1 x 7.92mm MG	L/24 & 1 x 7.92mm MG	L/24 & 1 x 7.92mm MG	L/24 & 1 x 7.92mm MG	L/43 & 2 x 7.92mm MG	L/48 & 2 x 7.92mm MG

was far superior to any other tank at the time). It was followed by the modified version of the Ausf G in May 1942.

The Ausf H, introduced in April 1943, was exclusively armed with a newer version of the 75mm KwK 40 L/48 gun and was fitted with steel/wire armour skirts. Over 3,770 of the PzKpfw IV Ausf H were made and saw action. Even in 1945 the last model, the Ausf J, was an effective weapon given the right crew. A selected number of the Ausf H and J were also converted into command tanks or observation tanks towards the end of the war period.

To its ultimate credit, the PzKpfw IV was the only German tank to stay in production throughout all the war hostilities. It was spacious inside and preferred by crews over the Panther, Tiger and King Tiger as it was more technically reliable.

CONVERSIONS

Flakpanzers (Air Defence)

- Mobelwagen - Sd. Kfz. 161/3
- Wirbelwind
- Ostwind

Panzerjagers / Sturmpanzers (Tank Destroyers and Assault Guns)

- Hornisse/Nashorn - Sd. Kfz. 164
- Hummel - Sd. Kfz. 165
- Jagdpanzer IV - Sd. Kfz. 162 / 162/1
- Sturmgeschutz IV - Sd. Kfz. 163 / 167
- Sturmpanzer IV Brummbar - Sd. Kfz. 166

Prototypes / Projects

- Geschutzwagen IV (Sd. Kfz. 165/1) - 105mm L/28 howitzer carrier
- Geschutzwagen IV (Sd. Kfz. 165/1) - 75mm Pak 39 L/48 gun carrier
- Geschutzwagen IV - 105mm L/28 howitzer carrier - (Rh) prototype
- Heuschrecke 10 / Gw IVb - 105mm L/28 - 3 prototypes built
- Panzerjager 105 - 105mm K18 L/52 gun - 2 prototypes built
- Panzerkampwagen IV mit hydrostatischen Antrieb
- Ostwind II
- Zerstorer 45
- Kugelblitz
- Panzer IV with 2 x 75mm rifles and 20/30mm target gun (planned)
- PzKpfw IV Ausf C/D/E mounted with rocket projetors (experimental)
- PzKpfw IV Ausf F2/H mit 75mm KwK 42 L/70 (experimental)
- PzKpfw IV Ausf D mit 50mm KwK 39 L/60 (experimental)
- Pzkpfw IV Ausf H with Schmallturm turret (project)
- Sturmpanzer IV - 305mm Morser M 16 carrier (planned)
- PzKpfw IV Ausf C mit Minenrollen - PzKpfw IV with mine roller

Other

- Befehlswagen IV Ausf H/J - command tank
- Beobachtungswagen IV Ausf J - observation vehicle
- Munitionspanzerwagen IV - ammunition carrier
- Panzer IV Ausf D (75mm L/24 gun) - submersible tank
- Bruckenleger IV - bridging vehicle Ausf C/D
- Infanterie Sturmsteg auf PzKpfw IV - assault bridge
- Panzerfahre - amphibious armoured ferry
- Munitionsschlepper fur Karlgerat - Ausf D/F - ammunition carrier
- Bergepanzer IV - recovery vehicle

HITLER TURNS WEST

Grenadiers advance past a knocked-out allied tank. The unpopular riveted construction of many of the early war tanks can clearly be seen in this example.

> "The confident feelings among the Panzertruppen are based chiefly upon our superior combat elan and only secondly on our fire power. The total of gun armed Panzers is less than those allocated to the French forces. Improvement is necessary in these areas."
>
> *Oberst Kuehn, 3rd Panzer Brigade, June 6 1940*

Among Germany's enemies dismay and apprehension reigned. Their disquiet was well founded. The next display of German military expertise, code-named 'Exercise Weser', was to be equally ruthless. Norway and Denmark were both neutral countries. Their strategic importance became crystal clear, however, when Hitler realised that Germany's supplies of iron ore from Sweden could easily be severed by an allied invasion. On 7 April German forces launched their invasion of Denmark and Norway by land, sea and air, to grant those countries the euphemistically

phrased 'Protection of the Third Reich'. The Wermacht swept over the border into Denmark, and as troops landed at Copenhagen the Luftwaffe circled ominously overhead. Denmark had no choice but to accept an ultimatum and surrendered early on 9 April to its mighty neighbour. Norway had last seen a war in 1814 and was totally unprepared for the invasion.

Destroyers protected by the *Scharnhorst* and the *Gneisenau* transported mountain troops to Trondheim and Narvik, where they were landed by amphibious craft, and similar landings took place at Oslo, Kristiansand and Bergen. Once again the speed of German activity had rendered the plans of her enemies ineffective. Three of the experimental heavy tanks, Neubau-Panzerkampfwagen IV, were deployed during the short campaign in Norway, but although they did see some action, the real purpose was the propaganda value. This was to be the one and only deployment of the Neubau-Panzerkampfwagen IV in action. From now on only the Panzer IV would be deployed in the infantry support role.

The door to Scandinavia was now slammed in Britain's face and, buoyed with success, the Führer confidently focused on a more glorious prize than any he had yet attained - France.

France was Germany's ancient enemy and had been her humiliator at Versailles. Hitler initiated planning for 'Fall Gelb' - Case Yellow.

Case Yellow was repeatedly postponed. The delay was put to good use, as an intensive study of the Polish campaign was undertaken. The role of the armoured divisions and the other Blitzkrieg components came under particular scrutiny. One of the men eager to discover what improvements could be introduced was Heinz Guderian.

Since the Great War Guderian had worked extensively with wireless, and gained invaluable experience in the deployment of infantry, artillery and aircraft. He had a clear vision of the force he wished to create. He had won the battle to ensure that his tanks would be concentrated in armoured divisions, not dispersed in small numbers. They would be spearheads of a single, large military formation, also encompassing aircraft, artillery and mechanised infantry. The commander would not be stationed far in the rear, but would operate near the front, responding instantly to changing situations and issuing orders by wireless directly to his units.

Making the most efficient use possible of available technology was only part of Guderian's work. He also had a clear understanding of the value of proper training, and knew that it was vital to encourage drive and initiative even in the lowest ranks. The German army as a whole had incomparable standards; the men of the tank arm were trained to an even higher pitch.

By the early months of 1940 Guderian was moving steadily closer to realising his ideal of a highly mobile, integrated striking force. In Poland the tanks had rarely driven more than ten miles a day. Now Guderian disposed of larger, far more

modern forces, to be used in the first full-scale experiment in Blitzkrieg tactics. Early in the morning of 10 May 1940 Fall Gelb was activated. German forces swung down into the Low Countries and the term 'Blitzkrieg' a synonym for terror and death, was burned into the pages of history.

As the tide of Hitler's conquests now turned to the west the Germans would be fighting more modern armies equipped with at least equal and sometimes superior equipment. The British and French forces also had superiority in numbers and were much better prepared than the Poles. By a combination of careful planning, surprise and some very daring innovations, the Germans were able to make the victory against Poland seem like a side-show. New tactics, such as the German Paratroopers who were dropped on top of the major Belgian fortification of Eben Emael in gliders, made their first appearance on the modern battlefield during this campaign. The Maginot Line that stretched along the majority of the French border to the east was easily bypassed when German Panzers advanced through the Ardennes region in Belgium. Once past here they advanced all the way to the coast with little in their way to stop them. What had proved impossible in four years of trench warfare during the First World War was to be accomplished in the space of six weeks. In France the value of the tank in modern warfare would be well and truly established.

THE BRITISH TANKS

Without the restrictions which had been placed on Germany, the main allied countries of Britain and France had also been engaged in developing their weapons during the '20s and '30s. They did, however, take different routes. The other major nations had not always recognised the full potential of the tank and therefore design and innovation in this aspect were rather more limited. France had relegated the tank to the role of an infantry support weapon. Britain had seen the potential of this new machine and set about developing new designs. By the outbreak of the Second World War they had come up with four main designs.

The Matilda Mk I was designated a light tank and weighed 11 tons. It was crewed by two men. The main armament was provided by a Vickers machine gun. Like the Panzer I this tank was little more than an armoured machine gun carrier. However, unlike the Panzer I, this vehicle had very good armour protection 60mm thick. This was double the thickness of the best German tank at the time. For a light tank it had a very low top speed of 8mph. The Matilda I's limitations were cruelly exposed in the French campaign. Although it protected its crew well, it was no match for the determined German Panzer crews. The one-man turret was also a major drawback. Over one hundred and forty of these machines were sent to France, but all of them were lost in that campaign.

The Cruiser Mk IV was an improved design that weighed in slightly heavier at 15 tons. It had a four-man crew that allowed for better results in battle. The main armament was the two-pound gun backed up with a Vickers machine gun. The armour was not as thick as the Matilda I, but was still good at 38mm. The top speed of this tank was 30mph. It had excellent suspension but the engine suffered from reliability problems. Over three hundred of them saw action in the French campaign.

The A9 Mk I Cruiser weighed in at 13 tons and was crewed by six men. The main firepower was the two-pounder gun, but this time it was backed up with three Vickers machine guns. It was thinly armoured at 14mm but had a good top speed of 25mph. Like the Cruiser Mk IV, the structural design consisted of many angles that trapped the armour-piercing enemy shells. This, coupled with the thin armour, resulted in many of them being lost in the French campaign.

The best of the British machines, the Matilda II, was an infantry support tank. The Matilda II weighed 27 tons and had a crew of four. It was armed with a two-pounder gun backed up with a Vickers machine gun. It was very well protected with 78mm thick armour. The speed was a maximum 15mph. This tank performed reasonably well and remained in service after the fall of France.

THE FRENCH TANKS

French thinking in tank use was influential in the design of their new machines. Like the British, they had four main designs available at the start of the French campaign.

The Char Somua S-35 was a medium tank weighing 20 tons, manned by a crew of three. A 47mm main gun, backed up with a 7.5mm machine

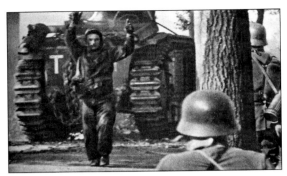

A French tank man surrenders to German grenadiers. Although better armed and armoured than the German machines, the French tank forces were hampered by inferior organisation and tactics.

gun, provided the armament. The armour protection was very good, at 55mm. It had a top speed of 25mph. This tank was more than capable of tackling the Panzers of 1940 vintage and was well designed. This was one of the few captured French tanks which the Germans made use of in the army after the campaign was over.

The Char B1 was the heaviest tank in use by the French, weighing 32 tons. It was manned by a crew of four, which was too few. The main firepower consisted of one 75mm gun, situated in the hull. This was backed up by a 47mm gun located in the turret. In addition there were two 7.5mm machine guns on board. The armour protection was an excellent 60mm but the speed was limited to 17mph. Despite the glaring flaws, this tank was to give a good account of itself in the fight against the Germans. The Germans found that this beast could be easily knocked out by a well-placed shell in the ventilation grill. At the start of the French campaign this was probably the most formidable tank in use.

Also facing the powerful forces was the Hotchkiss H.35 - one of the two light tanks in use by the French. It weighed in at 12 tons and had a two-man crew. The weapons that were fitted to this tank were a 37mm main gun backed up with a 7.5mm machine gun. The armour on this tank was a very respectable 40mm, and the top speed was also good at 22mph.

The Renault R35 was another one of the French light tanks. It weighed 10 tons and was manned by a crew of two. It also had a 37mm main gun backed up with one 7.5mm machine gun. The armour protection was 45mm thick. However, top speed was only 12mph.

On balance, the allied machines, and in particular the French tanks, outclassed the Germans in armour protection and main armament. The Germans were surprised to find that their 37mm anti-tank gun was ineffective against the thick armour of these tanks. The downfall of the allied tanks was the way in which they were employed tactically, and also some of their design faults, like the one-man turrets used in the French machines.

CASE YELLOW

The invasion of France was code-named 'Case Yellow'. The plan had been devised by von Manstein, but had been credited to Hitler. It was a variation of the Schlieffen Plan from the First World War. The Schlieffen plan had the objective of drawing the allies into the Low Countries. They would follow this by swinging through behind the allies and ending up in Paris, thereby encircling the allied forces. The plan had just failed in the First World War, but the Germans were confident that it would bring them victory this time. However, the plans for Operation Yellow had fallen into the hands of the allies through an unfortunate accident. This meant that the German staff had to rethink their plan of attack. This time von Manstein envisaged a spoiling attack in the Low Countries, like the original plan. The main change was the direction of the main thrust. It would be delivered through the Ardennes region which was thought to be tank-proof. For the attack the Germans split their forces into three Army Groups. Army Group B would advance through Holland and Belgium, thereby providing the bait for the allies. Army Group A would move through the Ardennes and would provide the main thrust. Army Group C would be opposite the Maginot Line and would keep the French defenders busy. The main thrust had the objective of racing through the enemy positions and on towards the French coast near Bolougne and Calais.

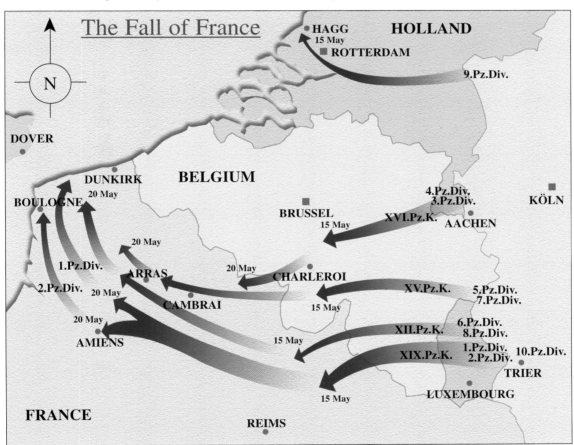

The deployment of German armour during the initial stages of the fall of France from May to June 1940.

Panzerkampfwagen 35(t)

Armour (mm/angle) 35(t)
Front Turret: 25/10
Front Upper Hull: 25/17
Front Lower Hull: 25/30
Side Turret: 15/14
Side Upper Hull: 16/0
Side Lower Hull: 16/0
Rear Turret: 15/15
Rear Upper Hull: 15/60
Rear Lower Hull: 16/0
Turret Top / Bottom: 8/81
Upper Hull Top / Bottom: 8/85
Lower Hull Top / Bottom: 8/90
Gun Mantlet: 25/round

Between the wars the new Czech nation maintained an advanced defence industry with a production capability extending to light and medium tanks. In 1935/36, Skoda's LT(Light Tank) vz.(model) 35 entered service. It was designed to rival a range of foreign vehicles in service at the time such as the Polish 7TP, the British Vickers 6 ton, the Soviet T-26, the Italian Carro Armato M 11139 and M13/40 and the German PzKpfw III tanks. The LT-35 equipped four fast divisions of the Czech Army as of 1938. During its service with the Czech Army, the LT-35 gained a reputation as an unreliable vehicle and it was only considered to be a "interim solution" before the LT-38, (later PzKpfw 38(t)) could be fully developed and ready for production. The LT-35's unreliable reputation was due to its untested but advanced technical design. By 1938 most of its teething problems were solved and overall the LT-35 proved to be a reasonably good tank. LT-35s were produced in different variants and were also known under different designations such as R-2 and T-II. Before the war the LT-35 was also sold to other countries including Bulgaria and Rumania. The 1938/39 German take-over of the Czechoslovak state meant that in March of 1939 219 LT-35s were confiscated from the Czech Army and most were incorporated into the German Army. A small number remained in service with the Slovak Army. In German service, the LT vz.35s were designated as Panzerkampfwagen 35(t)(t for Tschechisch - Czech). The LT-35 was comparable to German PzKpfw III and in 1939 was a vital addition to the Panzerwaffe. Despite a Czech

decision to phase the LT-35 out of production after 1938, it was extended until 1939, under German supervision at the CKD (Ceskomoravska Kolben Danek) Works in Prague and the Skoda Works in Pilsen (after 1938 both became part of Reichswerke Hermann Goring).

Overall 424 were produced between 1935 and 1939 by Skoda (approx. 340) and CKD (approx. 84). PzKpfw 35(t) formed the bulk of the 1st Leichte (Light) Division during the Polish Campaign and then the 6th Panzer Division (formerly the 1st Leichte Division) during the French Campaign and the Invasion of Russia.

PzKpfw 35(t)s took part in the Polish (1939) and French campaign (1940) and in the early

Model:	35(t)
Weight:	10500kg
Crew:	4
Engine:	Skoda T 11/6-cylinder 120hp
Speed:	35km/h
Range:	Road: 190km
	Crosscountry: 120km
Length:	4.90m
Width:	2.10m
Height:	2.35m
Armament:	37mm KwK 34(t) L/40 (Skoda 37mm A3 vz.34)
	2 x 7.92mm MG34 or MG35/37 (t)
Ammunition Supply:	37mm - 72 to 90 rounds
	7.92mm - 1800 to 2550 rounds

37mm KwK 34(t) L/40 Penetration of Armor Plate at 30 degrees from Vertical					
Ammunition:	100m	500m	1000m	1500m	2000m
Panzergranate 39	37mm	31mm	26mm	22mm	0mm
Pzgr. 39 (APCBC) - Armour Piercing Composite Ballistic Cap					
Pzgr. 40 (APCR) - Armour Piercing Composite Rigid (Tungsten Core)					

stages of the invasion of Russia (1941). During Operation Barbarossa the PzKpfw 35(t) was seen to be badly outclassed and of little value under combat conditions. Under winter conditions, the PzKpfw 35(t)'s mechanical components proved to be once again unreliable particularly as the clutch, brake and steering were all operated by compressed air. The LT-35(t)'s construction was riveted and a direct hit on its armour plate could sheer rivet heads off which would fly around inside the vehicle and kill or wound the crew. In late 1941, Germans had better tanks in production and the PzKpfw 35(t) was relocated to second line duties such as policing and antipartisan units. Some PzKpfw 35(t) were handed over to the Slovak, Bulgarian (where they served until 1950s), Romanian, Hungarian and Italian armies or were used by the German Police and the anti-partisan units.

Following the introduction of PzKpfw 35(t) into German service, it became a base for a few conversions. In September of 1940, Skoda produced the design for T-13 tank based on LT-35 but it never entered production. In 1941, tests were carried out to convert PzKpfw 35(t) into a tropical version but were never concluded. Also from March of 1942 to 1943, 49 PzKpfw 35(t)s were converted into Morser Zugmittel 1 Artillerie Schlepper 35(t) - artillery tractors by removing the turret and upper part of the hull

and fitting a canvas cover in their place. Some were also mounted with 12,000kg towing hook in the rear. Others were canibalised and saw service with coastal batteries. In 1939/40, designers tried to utilize the LT-35 chassis as the basis for a Panzerjager 35(t), armed with the Skoda 47mm Pak 36(t) U43 (Skoda 47mm A5 gun) gun. This design never entered production and only two prototypes based on Morser Zugmittel 35(t) were produced and were in service until late 1943. Some 20 were converted to Befehlswagen 35(t) - command tanks fitted with additional radio equipment. A few other support or auxiliary vehicles were based on the LT-35 chassis and were produced in limited numbers. Most of the PzKpfw 35(t)'s turrets were used for fixed fortifications on the Danish coast and in Corsica.

In mid 1943, a team directed by Lt.Col. Constantin Ghiulai designed a self-propelled anti-tank gun designated 'T.A.C.A.M Skoda R-2' for the Romanian army. A small series was produced at Leonida factory. Some sources state that as many as 40 were made. It was armed with captured Soviet ZIS-3 and F-22 UWS 76.2mm L/42 gun based on the modified PzKpfw 35 design. The gun was mounted in an open at the top and rear lightly armoured superstructure (made using armour plates from captured vehicles). The superstructure was mounted in the frontal part of the hull (in the place of the turret), while other components and characteristics

The 35(t) provided a valuable influx of strength at a time when the German Panzer forces desperately needed extra machines to match the ambitious expansion programme.

remained unchanged. Overall the design of T.A.C.A.M was similar to that of the German Marder series mirroring its high profile and light protection. Only 30 rounds were carried along with two machine guns for local defence for the crew of three men. The vehicle weighted 11500kg, had a range of 190km/h on the road and maximum speed of 34km/h. Due to the difficulties with 76.2mm ammunition, plans were made to utilize the German 88mm Pak 43 L/70 or Romanian 75mm Resita model 1943 gun but were never realized. T.A.C.A.Ms never saw service when Romania was Germany's ally and were only used against the Germans. Today, one 'T.A.C.A.M Skoda R-2' can be seen in the museum in Bucharest, Romania. In addition, to T.A.C.A.M Skoda R-2", there was also variant based on captured Soviet T-60 light tank, designated 'T.A.C.A.M T-60", of which some 35 were produced.

In 1940, Hungary purchased two examples and the licence from Skoda to produce S-IIc:

(T-22) medium tank - an improved model of the LT-35 light tank. From 1942 to 1944, Hungarians produced Turan I (40M) medium tank, which was a modified version of T-22. It was then followed by Turan II (41 M) produced from 1943 to 1944 and prototype of Turan III in 1944. In addition, Zrinyi (40/43M assault guns based on the Turan were produced in 1943. The Turan I was armed with a 40mm L/51 gun, the Turan II with a 75mm U25 gun and the Zrinyi with a 105mm L/20.5 howitzer. The prototype of Turan III was armed with a 75mm U43 gun, while there were also plans to arm the Zrinyi with the same gun. All designs were used by the Hungarian Army.

Overall, Panzerkampfwagen 35(t)s were reliable vehicles and served Panzertruppe very well in the time of need. Today, PzKpfw 35(t)s can be seen in the museums in Belgrade (Serbia), Bucharest (Romania.), Sofia (Bulgaria), Aberdeen (USA), while the LT vz.35 can be seen in Slovakia.

CONVERSIONS

• Zugkraftwagen 35(t) - light artillery tractor

• Munitionsschlepper 35(t) - ammunition carrier

• Morser Zugmittel / Artillerie Schlepper 35(t) - artillery tractor

• Panzerjager 35(t) - 47 mm Pak 36(t) L/43 carrier

• Befehlswagen 35(t) - command tank

A German tank crew perch on the hulk of a knocked out French tank during the early phases of the French campaign.

The allies anticipated a re-run of the First World War plan and they distributed their forces accordingly. The bulk of them were positioned north in readiness for the expected attack through the Low Countries. They had two further lines of reserves; one of these was positioned in the Ardennes region. The allies grossly overestimated the tank strength of the Germans and thought that they had over seven thousand tanks.

The reality was that, although the Panzerwaffe had now been expanded to ten Panzer Divisions, the Germans had just over 2,400 tanks for the attack. In the form of the Panzer I, over 1,400 of these were no more than armoured machine gun carriers. The allies had over 3,300 tanks to field against the Germans. In the important areas of main gun and armour protection, the allied machines outclassed the German tanks.

When the attack began in the early hours of 10 May it caught the allies by surprise. The Germans made quick gains and good advances. This was helped considerably as the allied strength was in the north, whereas the bulk of the German strength would smash through the Ardennes, further south. The allied thinking had lulled them into a false sense of security and they felt confident that they would destroy the Germans easily. Although the

Germans lacked numerical superiority in machines, they had been training hard on their new concepts and had tested the coordination of their forces. The concept was fairly simple, but very effective and advanced for the time.

A point of impact would be chosen that was small in width. The armour would concentrate on this central point and the weight of firepower would be used to overwhelm the enemy. Once a breech had been made the rest of the Division would rush through the gap and into the rear enemy areas. The tanks would continue to race deep inside the enemy lines, whilst the infantry and artillery would deal with any pockets of resistance and capture key objectives. The anti-tank gunners would set up a defensive screen to protect the areas already captured. Under this well coordinated attack, the allies fell back in confusion and panic. They were still thinking of the last war and were prepared for a defensive battle. The Germans had proved that a rapid deep advance into the enemy lines provided its own defence.

The strategy that had eventually been settled upon for the attack was of breath taking audacity.

A surprise offensive was launched through Holland and Belgium which it was hoped would draw the allied forces northwards away from their entrenched defensive positions in France. Then a powerful concentration of German armour would crash through the weakly defended Ardennes region. Without real opposition, this arm of the attack would thrust into France to tear the allied armies in half.

FALL GELB ACTIVATED

Soon after the attack was launched it was obvious that the great stratagem was working immaculately and it was reported that when Hitler was told, he almost wept for joy.

To the south, the seven armoured German divisions leading the principal offensive were feeling their way through the Ardennes.

Believing a passage to be impossible here, and, relying on the massive fortifications of the Maginot Line, the French had largely neglected this region, and the Germans had to contend with little more than a bemused Belgian horse soldier, peering uncomprehendingly through the trees.

Although the French airmen observed the German movement, their reports were ignored, so the vast assemblage edged on unhampered towards the river Meuse and France.

The river Meuse was the one great obstacle confronting the invaders. It was reached on the morning of 13 May. Despite skirmishes, the defenders still remained in ignorance of the scale of the impending onslaught. Away to the north a large clash of French and German armour confirmed the allied command in their mistaken analysis of German intentions.

The Meuse was to be crossed at three points. Exploiting German air superiority, the defenders at Sedan were subjected to an intensive bombardment lasting six hours. It was a murderous onslaught, and Guderian's engineers crossed the river swiftly afterwards, followed by the first infantry.

By evening, the Germans had smashed their way across and were on the other side in strength, having at last broken the shattered French forces. The two other crossings had also been successfully forced, a crippling blow to the whole allied defence.

In front of the Germans lay long stretches of ideal tank country held mainly by poorly-trained, ill-equipped and elderly reservists. The flying artillery of the dive bombers was already at work wreaking

wholesale destruction and inspiring widespread terror. Behind the spearheads extending back from the Meuse nearly to the Rhine itself, crowded the 25 divisions of the supporting infantry.

That same day, 15 May 1940, Holland surrendered.

On the following day, as the breach ripped in the southern French defences widened dramatically, it was belatedly apparent to the allied command that a potential catastrophe was in the making. The slow, clumsy bombers sent against German targets were sharply repulsed. The armies, attempting to make a hasty retreat from the Lowlands, found the roads choked with panic-stricken refugees.

For transmission of orders and reports, the allied command relied heavily on despatch riders and on the telephone network. Except that now, neither could be relied upon. In the aftermath of invasion, hundreds of French aircraft had been hurriedly removed to safe locations, and no one could find them. The skies were becoming the unchallenged domain of the Luftwaffe.

In many allied units morale and discipline were evaporating. The twin German spearheads thrust on, piercing deeper into France.

The most significant advance was made by the 7th Panzer Division commanded by General Erwin Rommel. His tank force advanced quickly through the lightly defended areas in Belgium. When they ran into heavier defended areas in France, they used their speed, surprise and weight of fire to overwhelm the enemy. This unit became the first to cross the river Meuse. Once across, they continued their advance towards Arras. The 7th Panzer Division was advancing so fast that they were given the unofficial nickname of the 'Ghost Division'. The 'Ghost Division' had good reason to celebrate Hitler's Czechoslovakian adventure. They were mostly equipped with 38(t) tanks.

THE COUNTERATTACK AT ARRAS

When the 7th Panzer Division advanced further they came into the area held by a mixed British and French force. The British, who were to the north of the German advance, decided to mount a counter-attack from the direction of Arras. They were under the impression that the French, who were south of the German advance, would also attack. On 21 May the British launched their attack into the flank of the Germans.

The allied force was small in comparison to the German forces, but they put up a good fight and actually caused a panic in the German High Command. Elements of the 7th Panzer Division were redirected back towards Arras to meet the threat. The Germans had estimated the attacking allied force to number hundreds of tanks when, in fact, it was considerably less than this. Although the British attack was determined, a French thrust from the south failed to materialise and the battle could not halt the advance of the enemy. It did, however, give the Germans a bloody nose and cause them considerable concern. This attack had showed what could be achieved if the allies had been better coordinated.

Guderian's amazing sweep from the Meuse to the sea exemplified Blitzkrieg in its purest and most lethally efficient form. Urged on by their impetuous commander and to the increasing alarm of some his superiors, his tanks drove onward to the coast, frequently covering 50 miles a day and far outstripping the supporting infantry. Often the mere sight and sound of the thundering tanks was sufficient to disperse any opposition.

The disaster at Sedan caused consternation among the French High Command. Astute French officers had read correctly the lessons of Poland. Tragically, their Generals suffered from the military equivalent of myopia and blithely ignored them. New technology had been accepted only grudgingly, new ideas, never. In the long, cumbrous chains of command, it could easily take two days for an order to reach the front, by which time the battle situation was usually completely transformed.

A Panzer III rumbles by a dispirited British soldier in the wake of the allied collapse in Greece.

Guderian's tanks drove relentlessly on. All over France wild rumours abounded; of fifth-columnists and saboteurs, of bizarrely-disguised German paratroopers, of imminent new disasters. The already prevalent mood of defeatism deepened further.

Yet the French had more troops than the Germans and a superiority in nearly all types of armaments. They even had more tanks than the Germans, and the best of them, such as the heavily armed Chars and Somuas, were formidable vehicles of war.

What were missing were the will and the perception to use all of these advantages in a concentrated approach to modern warfare. It would have required an impossibly drastic shift in the thinking of the past 50 years. Quarrels between French and British, inter-service rivalries and other dangerous pettiness combined further to make an effective military response impossible.

On 20 May Guderian reached Amiens. The last link between the allied forces to the north and south was severed, adding still further to the already dire confusion in the chain of command.

On the 24th Hitler issued one of the most controversial orders of the war. For two days the tanks were halted. This respite prevented a massacre taking place during the subsequent evacuation of the BEF from Dunkirk. This has been one of the most hotly debated actions of the war and numerous possible reasons have been ascribed to Hitler's curious order. One very plausible explanation is that Hitler, from his studies of the rates of attrition of the tank forces, had become concerned that his armoured forces would be too worn down to continue the battle against France.

Throughout his military career Hitler was inclined to dabble in every aspect of detail, even to the point of inspecting the daily strength returns for the Panzer Divisions. There is a strong possibility that he may have confused the numbers of unserviceable machines, which could be repaired in the very short term, with those that were complete write-offs. The lessons from the street fighting in Warsaw may also have had an impact. With the withdrawal of the BEF, France now faced the mighty German forces alone. They were unable to hold back the tide of men and weapons.

Once Dunkirk was secured the Germans surveyed the mayhem that had been left behind by the retreating BEF. The British had been forced to abandon all of their equipment and the majority of this lay in ruin around the port. The German victory was not yet complete and the next phase required them to turn south and concentrate on the remaining French and British forces that still numbered some 66 Divisions. This part of the advance began on 5 June 1940. Less than 3 weeks later the enemy was completely defeated.

By 10 June, with the Germans outside the French capital, the government abandoned Paris. Widespread fighting continued but there was no place for illusions. A full-scale rout was taking place.

On 20 June, after just six weeks of war, France agreed to sign a demeaning armistice.

Hitler was overjoyed at this astounding vindication of the methods of Blitzkrieg. Germany rejoiced with him and with the glorious euphoria of victory mingled a deeper, more human desire. For the German population the war was surely over. The nation's honour had been restored, German prosperity assured by the new order in Europe. The ignominy of Versailles was lost in the past. Under their revered leader this transformation had been achieved at a cost far below all expectation.

The Armistice was signed by the leaders of the destroyed French forces in the same railway carriage that they themselves had used at the end of the First World War. This was the perfect end to what was almost a perfect victory for Hitler and his new Panzer army.

The part played by the German tanks in the victory had been crucial. In a few weeks they had destroyed the armies of Holland, Belgium, France and Britain. The confidence of the Germans was at an all time high. They had complete faith in their men and machines. The close support of the Luftwaffe had also been a deciding factor and helped to instil terror upon the fleeing enemy soldiers. Hitler now regarded the war as almost won. New weapons development was restricted after this time due to the strains on the economy and resources were routed to anti-tank weapons and the more economical assault guns. The deficiencies that were apparent with regard to armour protection and main armament in these early campaigns were to resurface in later campaigns, but with greater consequences. The best that Germany could offer in 1941 would be severely outclassed by the Russian tanks.

With a sense of invincibility in everyone's mind, a complacency and lack of urgency set in. Although Hitler was already looking to undertake the biggest gamble yet, the equipment of the tank forces did not undergo any serious redesign. It is true to say that an expansion programme was undertaken that was to add many new units to Germany's armed forces, but there was no real thought given to improving the existing tools of destruction. Minor modifications were made to the Panzer III which had the main gun upgraded to a 50mm weapon and a slight increase in armour thickness. The Panzer IV also had the armour increased slightly, to 50mm. The expansion programme also had to cater for the units that needed their battle losses replaced. German tanks required hundreds of man-hours to complete; this meant they were comparatively slow to come off the production line compared to the Russian T-34s that were simple and cheap to produce.

Other experiments were conducted in preparation for the proposed invasion of England, code named Operation Sea Lion. One of the most interesting was the development of a submersible Panzer III. Although the planned invasion did not materialise, this development would be used in the early stages of Operation Barbarossa. Hitler, although annoyed at the failure of the Luftwaffe to deliver victory against England, plunged ahead with the planning for the mighty invasion of the Soviet Union. He was confident that his army would deliver victory once more. The men on the front line would quickly discover just how inadequate their tanks would be against the enemy. The puny 37mm gun was still used to equip many of the Panzer IIIs, which were then Germany's main battle tanks. The same 37mm gun was also carried by all of the Czech made 38(t) tanks which, in 1940, were Germany's most numerous battle tanks. These guns were insufficient to penetrate at all but the shortest range, and even the upgrade to a 50mm gun carried by some Panzer IIIs by 1941 was still not really sufficient.

Only the 75mm gun of the Panzer IV and Sturmgeschutze battalions were really suited to the demands of the modern battlefield, but even then it had its limitations. The short barrel of the 75mm gave the shells only a limited velocity, which was effective against the thinly armoured tanks of the early war years but proved to be totally inadequate when the Germans met the superior Russian tanks during 1941.

Panzerkampfwagen 38(t) Sd.Kfz.140

The LT (Light Tank) vz. (model) 38 was destined to become one of the most widely used Czechoslovak tanks, although not in Czechoslovak hands. Ordered into production in 1938, the LT-38 drew on the experience of many countries and gained an excellent reputation among its foreign users such as Sweden (THN Sv), Iran / Persia (TNH), Peru (LTP), Switzerland (LTH - Pz39) and Lithuania (LTL).

The 1938/39 German take-over of the Czechoslovak state meant that in March 1939, 150 LT-38s in production were confiscated and CKD/Praga was ordered to complete them. All of these machines were incorporated into the German Army as PzKpfw 38(t) Ausf A - Sd.Kfz. 140. After the German take-over of the Czechoslovakia, the LT-38 became one of the most important tanks used by the Panzertruppe and was retained in production as a battle tank until June of 1942. During the war, PzKpfw 38(t) were exported and saw service with German allies including: Romania (50), Slovakia (90), Bulgaria (10) and Hungary (102). The PzKpfw 38(t) also saw service with the allies. A single tank was captured by British and French troops in May / June 1940, another example (turret number-543) was captured either during the Italian Campaign in 1943 or Normandy in 1944 and was tested in England. Numbers of PzKpfw 38(t)s were captured and pressed into service by the Red Army. Finally, in May of 1945, PzKpfw 38(t) now known as LT-38137 (37 standing for 37mm gun) was back in service with the Czechoslovak Army as a training tank until the early 1950s.

Armour (mm/angle) Ausfuhrung A
Front Turret: 25/10
Front Upper Hull: 25/17
Front Lower Hull: 25/16
Side Turret: 15/10
Side Upper Hull: 15/0
Side Lower Hull: 15/0
Rear Turret: 15/10
Rear Upper Hull: 10/60
Rear Lower Hull: 15/12
Turret Top / Bottom: 10/90
Upper Hull Top / Bottom: 8/90
Lower Hull Top / Bottom: 8/90
Gun Mantlet: 25/round

Armour (mm/angle) Ausfuhrung G
Front Turret: 50/10
Front Upper Hull: 50/17
Front Lower Hull: 50/16
Side Turret: 30/10
Side Upper Hull: 15+15/0
Side Lower Hull: 15/0
Rear Turret: 22/10
Rear Upper Hull: 10/60
Rear Lower Hull: 15/12
Turret Top / Bottom: 15/90
Upper Hull Top / Bottom: 8/90
Lower Hull Top / Bottom: 8/90
Gun Mantlet: 25/round

Model:	Ausfuhrung A	Ausfuhrung G
Weight:	9400kg	9850kg
Crew:	4	4
Engine:	Praga EPA, 6-cylinder / 125hp	Praga EPA, 6-cylinder / 125hp
Speed:	Road 42km/h Crosscountry 15km/h	Road 42km/h Crosscountry 15km/h
Range:	Road: 250km Crosscountry: 160km	Road: 250kh Crosscountry: 160km
Length:	4.60 m	4.61 m
Width:	2.12 m	2.14 m
Height:	2.40 m	2.40 m
Armament:	37mm KwK 38(t) L/47.8 2 x 7.92mm MG37(t)	37mm KwK 38(t) L/47.8 2 x 7.92mm MG37(t)
Ammunition Supply:	37mm-72 rounds 7.92mm-2400 rounds	37mm-42 rounds 7.92mm-2400 rounds

37mm KwK 38(t) L/47.8 Penetration of Armour Plate at 30 degrees from Vertical					
Ammunition:	100m	500m	1000m	1500m	2000m
Panzergranate 39	41mm	35mm	29mm	24mm	0mm
Panzergranate 40	64mm	34mm	0mm	0mm	0mm
Pzgr. 39 (APCBC) - Armour Piercing Composite Ballistic Cap					
Pzgr. 40 (APCR) - Armour Piercing Composite Rigid (Tungsten Core)					

Approximately 1,400 PzKpfw 38(t)s were produced in 8 different variants (Ausf A/B/C/D/E/F/S/G) with various modifications and improved armour protection. All were armed with Czech made 37mm Skoda A7 vz.38 guns designated by the Germans as 37mm KwK 38(t) U48 (L/47.8). In early models construction was riveted, and a direct hit on its armour plate could sheer off rivet heads which would kill or wound the crew. Later model construction was largely welded. Late models were further up-armoured and few were possibly rearmed with German made 37mm KwK 35/36 L/46.5 gun. A number were also converted to flamethrower tanks by replacing the hull machine gun with a flamethrower, with fuel supplied from a towed single-axle trailer carrying 200 liters of fuel linked by a flexible hose. There was also a PzKpfW 38(t) swimming tank with a prototype AP-1 float but it never entered production. Further production of the PzKpfw 38(t) chassis continued with improved models of Ausf H/K/L/M, which were used as a base for various vehicles (such as the Marder III Ausf H/M, Bison/Grille Ausf H/K/M and Hetzer). In addition, older models returned for repairs were often also used as a base for a conversion.

PzKpfw 38(t)s were built under German supervision and they saw extensive service in Poland (3rd Leichte Division), Norway (XXXI Armee Korps), France (6th, 7th and 8th Panzer Divisions), Balkans (8th Panzer Division) and Russia (6th, 7th, 8th, 12th, 19th and 20th Panzer Divisions). During the fighting in Russia, the need for heavier armour and armament rendered the PzKpfw 38(t) inadequate and in 1942 it was relegated to second line duties (e.g. reconnaissance and service in armoured trains).

In September of 1939 plans were laid for the development of a fast/light reconnaissance tank. 15 PzKpfw 38(t) nA (neuer Art) were produced by BMM (Praga/CKD) in early 1942, but its design was not accepted for production. In 1942, the usual German process of adapting the chassis for other purposes commenced with the Marder III and Flakpanzer 38(t). In 1942 and 1943 a number of PzKpfw 38(t) had their turrets removed and were converted to driver training vehicles; late in the war they were mounted with wood burning generators. Training vehicles based on turretless tanks were designated as PzKpfw 38(t) Schulfahrwanne and were used by school units of the Wehrmacht and NSKK. Some 351 PzKpfw 38(t) turrets were used for German fortifications in Norway (75), Denmark (20), the Western Atlantic shore (9), Italy (25), Southwest Europe (150) and Eastern Europe (78).

The 38(t) was to prove an acceptable stop-gap which gave the Panzerwaffe an alternative to the Panzer III which was slow in arriving in good numbers.

CONVERSIONS

• Bison (Grille) Ausf. H/M - 15cm s.IG. (Sd. Kfz. 138/1) - howitzer carrier

• Munitionspanzer 38(t) Ausf M - ammunition carrier

• Schutzenpanzerwagen 38(t) Ausf M - armoured personal carrier (planned)

• Marder III (Sd. Kfz. 139) - 76.2mm Pak 36 (Russian) gun

• Marder III Ausf. H/K/M (Sd. Kfz. 138) 75mm Pak 40 gun

• Befehlswagen 38(t) - command tank

• Munitionsschlepper 38(t) - ammunition carrier

• Panzerjä ger 38(t) / Jagedpanzer 38(t) Hetzer

• PzKpfw 38(t) nA - fast/light reconnaissance tank

CAPTURED TANKS

As we have seen, during the Second World War the German Army utilised large numbers of captured tanks; the trend had already been established after the Polish campaign. The German Armed Forces now captured and confiscated a far more significant haul of armoured fighting vehicles, many of which were pressed into service by the Wehrmacht, Waffen-SS, Luftwaffe and Police units. These Beute Panzerkampfwagen (captured Panzers) were gathered at special collection points, where they were examined for any potential benefits to the new owners. If possible, useful tanks were returned to the factories where they had been built and repaired, modified and painted in German colours and markings.

As of October 1940 the German Army Office requested that, if possible, two examples of every captured vehicle were to be provided for evaluation at the Kummersdorf (Motor Vehicle Test Centre of the Army Weapons Office's Test Section) and Berka (tank school) facilities. Eventually, after all tests had been concluded, they were moved to the Tank Museum of the Army Vehicle Office in Stettin-Altdamm (now Szczecin).

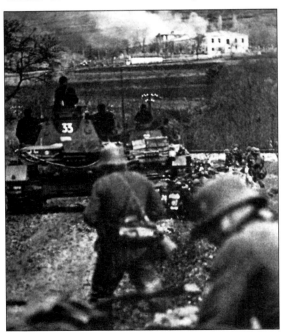

On campaign with the "flying ghost" Division. A shot from *Signal* magazine displaying the daily life of the 11th Panzer Division on campaign in France and the Balkans.

These tests determined the combat value of various tanks and provided information on their general characteristics, along with shooting tests that were summarised in firing tables. In the desperate days of March 1945, the High Command of the Army Group Vistula authorised the captured tanks from the museum to be used in the defence of Stettin. Some of the foreign captured tanks were put in the active service with special captured tank units (formed from May 1940), others were allocated to Panzer or Infantry Divisions in various roles, such as reconnaissance. Some units, for example Panzer Abteilung 216 in the Channel Islands and the 7th SS-Freiwilligen-Gebirgs-Division 'Prinz Eugen' in the Balkans were totally equipped with captured equipment.

According to original German captured tank inventories as of 10 April 1945, there were still 424 captured tanks in German service, 71 on the Eastern Front, 172 in Italy, 74 in the Balkans and 107 in Norway and Denmark; of these 310 were operational. In general, the most common practice was the conversion of foreign tanks into various weapon carriers. Some tanks were also converted into other supplementary vehicles, such as artillery tractors. Foreign tanks were mainly used for training purposes, while some were used for internal policing duties in occupied territories (Polizei-Panzerkampfwagen). Field modifications were very common and totally non-standard. The most common modification to tanks was the replacement of the original cupola top with split hatch covers and the installation of radio equipment.

In order to identify and classify captured and foreign equipment, Foreign Equipment Listing (D.50) series - Kennblaetter Fremdengerat - was published. It consisted of 14 volumes (updated during the course of war) and captured motor vehicles were listed in the twelfth volume (D.50/12). All vehicles were divided into seven numerical block categories:

200 for armoured cars;
300 for half-tracked (semi-tracked) vehicles;
400 for armoured half-tracked (semi-tracked) vehicles;
600 for fully-tracked artillery tractors;
630 for armoured artillery tractors;
700 for tanks (including British armoured carriers);

A column of Panzer II tanks halts for a well-earned rest during the Balkan campaign. The movement of armoured formations by road was an extremely complex logistical undertaking.

800 for gun carriers and self-propelled guns.

In addition, letters followed numbers. Letters were used to recognise the previous user (not producer) of a certain piece of the equipment. For example Soviet T-34 was designated as Panzerkampfwagen T-34 747(r).

(a) amerikanisch - American
(b) belgisch - Belgium
(e) englisch - English and Canadian
(f) franzosisch - French
(h) hollandisch - Dutch
(i) italienisch - Italian
(j) jugoslawisch - Yugoslavian
(o) osterreichisch - Austrian
(p) polnisch - Polish
(r) russisch - Russian
(t) tschechisch - Czechoslovakian

CAPTURED TANKS IN GERMAN HANDS

After their victory in Western Europe, Germans pressed captured British equipment into service, and some examples remained as late as 1945.

The Belgian Army had some one hundred and fifty Vickers Carden-Loyd Mark I 'Dragon' (export version) light tanks designated as Char Leger Modele T.

In addition, there were some seventy-five Renault FT-17/18 two-man light tanks, but there is no evidence of them being used by the Germans, although it is possible that they were classified as Dutch or French FT series tanks.

The main haul of captured enemy tanks to fall into German hands came after the fall of France. During the course of the French Campaign the Germans captured approximately 2,400 out of the 3,500 French tanks in service as of 10 May 1940. On 30 August 1941 Hitler issued an order that all captured equipment was to be used to equip Panzer Divisions newly formed in France. Captured tanks were issued to the four Panzer Regiments numbered from 201 to 204; these regiments were equipped entirely with captured tanks, additional machines were transferred to Panzer Abteilung z.b.V. (special employment units), which included Panzer Regiments 100, 202 to 205, 211 to 214 and 223 Panzer Abteilung. In addition there were numerous captured tank platoons. The majority of those units operated in occupied territories, especially the Balkans, where they performed internal policing and security duties.

CAPTURED FRENCH TANKS

The oldest captured tank in German service was the Renault FT-17/18 (FT - Faible Tonnage - Light Weight) two-man light tank, designated by the victorious Germans as Panzerkampfwagen 17R/ 1 8R 730(f). The French Army still had some eight hundred examples of this antiquated machine which dated in its design back to early 1917. It was produced in numerous versions and widely exported to Belgium, Czechoslovakia, Finland, Holland, Yugoslavia and Poland. It was recognised as having no front line combat value upon its capture by the Germans and many of the captured tanks badly needed repairs. Nonetheless, some were still used for training, policing and security duties in the Channel Islands, Germany, Norway and Serbia. Others were used as command and artillery posts. Some were converted to artillery tractors by having the upper part of the hull, along with the turret removed.

The remaining FT-17/18s were used in armoured

trains or were handed over to the Luftwaffe to be used for security duties and as snow ploughs for their airfields. Some were still in use as late as 1945. According to original German captured tank inventories as of July 1943, there were still1 12 FT-17/18 tanks in active service in the West, mainly France. Some tanks took part in the Paris rising of August 1944, being used both by the Germans and the uprisers.

The Renault VM/AMR 33 (1933) and Renault ZT/AMR 35 (1935) were two-man light cavalry tanks. Again, they had little combat value and were mainly used for police duties in occupied territories. In German service, AMR 33 was designated as Panzerspahwagen VM 701(f).

The Renault Char Leger R-35 two-man light tanks were the most numerous French tanks as of May 1940, and approximately eight hundred and forty (out of 1,035 in service) were captured by the Germans. The Renault R-35 was designated as Panzerkampfwagen 35R 731(f).

The R-35 was a reasonable design. Some R-35s in France were even pressed into German service during the course of the campaign in France. After the campaign, repaired vehicles were modified to German standards by replacing the original cupola top with split hatch covers and the addition or replacement of radio equipment.

Although R-35s and R-40s were not obsolete vehicles, their characteristics made them unsuitable for front line service and only a small number were used as infantry support tanks. The majority were relegated to second line duties in Western Europe. Some twenty-five Renault R-35s served with the Panzer Abteilung z.b.V. 12 (special employment unit) and were used in an anti-partisan role in the Balkans; another 30 were handed over to the SS and were used for policing duties in occupied territories.

In late 1941 46 R-35s were also used to equip the 100th Panzerbrigade, which was the basis of the newly formed 21st Panzer Division of North Africa fame. The R-35s were not taken to Africa and after the debacle in Tunisia the same machines were used for training the nucleus of the new division again in late 1943. Panzer Abteilung 206, which operated in the Cherbourg peninsula in June 1944, is known to have used two R-35s in action. A Number of R-35s also saw service with 100th Panzer Ersatz und Ausbildung Abteilung (Reserve Tank Battalion), which was supporting the 96th Infantry Division in the St. Lô - Caretan area in June 1944. In addition, some were also used by units stationed in the Channel Islands along with the garrison in Paris. Some unmodified tanks were also used in armoured trains.

The Germans felt they had little to gain from the employment of many of the French tanks captured in the wake of the fall of France. These light tanks are being employed for ploughing duties, a purpose to which many were better suited than combat.

In 1940 Germans handed over 109 R-35s to Italy, where they equipped two reserve tank battalions but proved to be useless due to the lack of spare parts. Undeterred, in 1941 the Germans sold some forty R-35s to their Bulgarian allies, where they equipped the Ist Armoured Brigade that performed security duties in Serbia until September 1944, although the Bulgarians must surely have encountered similar difficulties to the Italians.

From May to October 1941, Alkett in Berlin converted 174 R-35s to anti-tank hunters. Designated as '4.7cm PaK(t) auf Panzerkampfwagen 35R(f) ohne Turm' or Panzerjäger 35R 731(f), it was intended to replace the inefficient Panzerjäger I. These machines equipped the second-string tank destroyer units of Infantry Divisions. Interestingly, there were still some one hundred and ten in service in France as of early 1944, and 20 remained in service as late as May 1945 in the Channel Islands.

A number of R-35s escaped the conversion process and remained in service with garrison infantry units, and in 1945 there were still a few Panzerkampfwagen 35R 73 1 (f) in German service. According to original German captured tank inventories, as of July 1943 there were 58 R-35s in service in the West.

The Renault Char D-1 infantry (medium) tanks were designated by the Germans as Panzerkampfwagen D-1 732(f). Although the Germans captured a number there is no evidence of them being pressed into service. As of 10 May 1940 the French Army had some seventy-five D-2s in service, although it can be assumed that few were used for security duties or as mobile fortifications. It is most likely the majority were scrapped and their turrets were handed over to Croatia, where they were mounted on armoured trains.

A total of 1,188 Hotchkiss tanks were in service with the French Army as of 10 May 1940; of these, the Germans captured approximately six hundred. Generally, all Hotchkiss tanks were referred to as Panzerkampfwagen 38H 735(f).

The Germans modified Hotchkiss tanks to their standards by replacing the original cupola top with split hatch covers and by the addition or replacement of radio equipment. Hotchkiss tanks were issued to captured tank Panzer Regiments of various Panzer Divisions (including the 7th and 8th in late 1940) as battle tanks, and saw service in

France, Norway, Crete, the Balkans, Finland and Russia. The first unit to be equipped with Hotchkiss tanks and which saw combat in Finland in the summer of 1941 was Panzer Abteilung 211. Some Hotchkiss tanks also equipped the 100th and 101st Beute-Panzer-Brigades. Hotchkiss tanks were also used in a reconnaissance role, as command tanks. Some tanks, including some sixty in service with the SS, were used for internal policing and security duties. The Germans also handed over 15 Hotchkiss tanks to Hungary in 1943 and sold 19 to Bulgaria in 1944. Two H-39s were handed over to Croatia. As of 20 May 1942 there were 15 Hotchkiss tanks with Panzer Abteilung 212 stationed on Crete.

Twenty-four Hotchkiss tanks were converted to communication and command tanks designated as Ein Grosser Funk und Befehlswagen 38H 735(f), also known as Artillerie-Panzer-Beobachtung 38H 735(f), artillery observation vehicles. All 24 were issued to 21st Panzer Division's 155th Panzerartillerie Abteilung stationed in France in 1944.

In 1942, some twenty-four (some sources state sixty) H-39s (including at least one H-JJ) were converted to 75mm PaK 40 L/46 anti-tank gun carriers (Panzerjäger), designated as '7.5cm PaK4O(Sf) auf Geschutzwagen 39H(f)' but more commonly referred to as Marder I. A similar conversion was also completed in 1942 by converting 48 H-39s to 105mm leFH 16 L/22 and leFH 18 (18/40) L/28 (leichte Feldhaubitze - light field howitzer) carriers, designated as '10.5cm leFH18(Sf) auf Geschützwagen 39H(f)'. In both conversions armament was mounted in an open-topped superstructure. Both conversions were completed by Captain Alfred Becker's Baukommando in Paris and at Krefeld (in co-operation with Alkett in Berlin) and served with units stationed in France, including 8th Panzerartillerie Abteilung and Sturmgeschütz Abteilung 200, commanded by Major Alfred Becker. The turrets of vehicles converted to weapon carriers were used in fortifications; some tanks were even dug in as fixed bunkers.

Another interesting conversion were 11 H-35s and H-38s mounted with '428 32cm schwere Wuhrframen 40' (280/320mm rocket projector) by Panzer Abteilung 205.

Some Hotchkiss tanks were also used in armoured trains operating in the Balkans. As late as

This unusual photograph demonstrates the lengths to which the German propaganda service were prepared to go to achieve results. The lens of a camera has replaced the machine-gun of this Panzer III.

1944 some were also used as training vehicles with their turrets and hatches removed. It was also a common practice to equip units refitting and resting in France with captured tanks for the duration of their time in the field. (The 6th Panzer Division's Panzer Regiment II was equipped in this way). As of 31 May 1943 there were 355 captured tanks in German service. According to original German captured tank inventories, as of July 1943, they were distributed as follows: 15 as part of Army Group Centre, 96 in the Balkans, 149 in the West, 68 in Norway and 33 in Lapland. Panzer Abteilung 206, which operated in the Cherbourg peninsula in June of 1944, used sixteen H-38s. A number of H-38s also saw service with the 100th Panzer Ersatz und Ausbildung Abteilung (Reserve Tank Battalion), which was supporting the 96th Infantry Division in the St. Lô-Caretan area in June 1944. As of 30 December 1944, there were still 29 (H-38s) Hotchkiss tanks in German service and even a few in 1945. At least one unarmed H-39 tank was captured and pressed into service by the insurgents during the Prague uprising in May 1945.

The Char de Cavalerie Somua S-35/Char 1935 S three man medium tank armed with 47mm SA 35 L/34 gun and 7.5mm Reibel machine gun was the best French tank as of May of 1940 and around five hundred were in service with the French Army. It was the first vehicle in the world with all-cast hull and turret. This feature, however, made it unsuitable for conversion. Some Somuas were pressed into service during the campaign by the by 3rd SS (Motorised) Division, 'Totenkopf'. Altogether, during the course of campaign, the Germans captured two hundred and ninety-seven

Somua S-35s, designated as Panzerkampfwagen 35S 739(f), and employed them mainly as commander's tanks along with some machine-gun armed command tanks with rear mounted frame antennas and additional radio equipment. The Germans modified S-35s to their standards by replacing original cupola top with split hatch covers and the addition or replacement of radio equipment. The first unit to be equipped with Somua tanks, which saw combat in Finland in the summer of 1941, was Panzer Abteilung 211. In 1941 Germans handed over some thirty-two S-35s to Italy, two to Hungary in 1943 and six to Bulgaria in 1944.

As of 20 May 1942 there were five Somua S-35 tanks with Panzer Abteilung 212 stationed on Crete.

In November 1941 some sixty Somuas had their turrets removed and were used as artillery tractors, along with ammunition carriers, on the Eastern Front. The turrets were used in fortifications on the Atlantic Wall.

Panzerkampfwagen 35S 739(f) tanks were issued to captured tank Panzer Regiments of various Panzer Divisions and saw service in France, Norway, the Balkans, Finland and Russia. S-35s were also used in equipping the newly formed 23d Panzer Division (France, 1941/42) and the 24th Panzer Division, East Prussia, in late 1941.

On the eve of D-Day, on 1st June 1944, the 21st Panzer Division stationed in Normandy had twenty-three Somua S-35s in service. A number of S-35s also saw service with the 100th Panzer Ersatz und Ausbildung Abteilung (Reserve Tank Battalion), which was supporting the 96th Infantry Division in the St. Lô-Caretan area in June of 1944. According to original German captured tank inventories, as of July 1943 there were two S-35s as part of Army Group Centre, 43 in the Balkans, 67 in the West, 17 in Norway and 16 in Lapland. There were still some thirty S-35s in German service as of 30 December 1944 and few in 1945. Some of the 'German' Somuas were captured and ended up with the French resistance.

THE SUMA FLAME-THROWERS

The Germans designated the Renault Char De Bataille B-1 (Char B) four-man heavy tanks as Panzerkampfwagen B-2 740(f). As of 10 May 1941 the French Army had some three hundred and seventy Char Bs in service and the Germans captured around one hundred and sixty of them. The Chars were altered to the German standards, along with some other minor modifications, but were not issued to troops as quickly as other captured tanks.

Sometimes fear alone is enough to overcome an enemy. This was certainly the case with flame-throwing tanks. These gruesome weapons had their main tank guns replaced with a flame-thrower which could fire a jet of flame for up to fifty yards. This was not a particularly accurate, or even an effective, weapon but both sides used them in the Second World War. They were designed to be used to winkle infantry out of strong defences, pillboxes and bunkers, but their main effectiveness lay in the fear they generated.

The flame gun fired an inflammable mixture from a 100-litre tank, which was enough to fire 80 two-second bursts of flame.

In March 1941 it was decided to convert a number of Chars to flame-thrower tanks and weapon carriers. From November 1941 to June 1942 some sixty Panzerkampfwagen B-2 740(f) tanks were converted to flame-thrower tanks, designated as Flammwagen auf Panzerkampfwagen B-2(f)/Flammpanzer 132(f). Conversion consisted of removal of the hull-mounted 75mm KwK 35(f) L/17 gun and replacement with Koebe's Flammenwerfer (flame-thrower). The flame-thrower had limited traverse of its own and the tank had to be pivoted to face the target.

This installation of the first flame-thrower was inefficient and was followed by a second model. In place of the original armament platform space was made for a special Spitzkoepf (as used in the Flammpanzer II), which housed the flame-thrower spray head and allowed it to operate at 180° radius. Along with this installation an additional visor was mounted in the frontal plate. Approximately twenty-five Chars were converted by Wegmann & Company at Kassel and Daimler-Benz in Berlin. These, along with six unmodified Chars, were issued to Panzer Abteilung (F) 102, and on 23 June 1941 arrived on the front. In Russia Panzer Abteilung (F) 102 supported the 24th and 296th Infantry Divisions. It was not a successful baptism. On 27 June 1941 Panzer Abteilung (F) 102 was disbanded and further development of flame-thrower mounts took place. A final version was now introduced, which consisted of installing a ball-mounted flame-thrower in the mantlet fixed in the location of the original armament, along with an extension of the fighting compartment. Thirty-six Chars were converted in this way, and previously converted Chars were also rebuilt to this standard.

As of 31 May 1943 the 223rd Panzer Company on the Eastern Front had four Chars and twelve flame-thrower Chars, while 7th SS-Freiwilligen-Gebirgs-Division 'Prinz Eugen' in Yugoslavia had 7 regular Chars and 10 flame-thrower Chars. In addition, the 101 Panzer Brigade in France had 10 regular Chars and 24 flame-thrower Chars, and Panzer Abteilung 213 in the Channel Islands had 10

A large number of the captured French Char B tanks were converted into the flame-thrower model and saw action in Russia with the 223rd Panzer company.

General Heinz Guderian at the front commanding his troops during the massive encirclement battles of summer 1941.

flame-thrower Chars (5 on Jersey and 5 on Guernsey) and 26 Chars (12 on Jersey and 14, including 2 command tanks, on Guernsey). Panzer Abteilung 206, which operated in the Cherbourg peninsula in June 1944, used five Chars. A Number of Chars also saw service with 100th Panzer Ersatz und Ausbildung Abteilung (Reserve Tank Battalion), which was supporting the 96th Infantry Division in the St. Lô-Caretan area in June 1944.

Following the conversion of Chars to flame-thrower tanks in 1942, 16 were converted to 105mm leFH 18/39 L/28 (leichte Feldhaubitze - light field howitzer) carriers designated as '10.5cm leFH18/3(Sf) auf Geschutzwagen B-2(f)', also known as Sturmhaubitze B-2(f). This conversion was fairly simple and consisted of the removal of original turret armed with 47mm KwK 35(f) L/34 and replacement with a superstructure housing the howitzer. Along with the removal of turret, hull mounted gun was also removed and the opening covered with a bolted plate. The entire conversion was done by Rheinmetall-Borsig in Düsseldorf, and all of the resulting vehicles were issued to Sturmgeschütz Abteilung 200 stationed in France.

Some Chars were also converted to training tanks, designated as 'Panzerkampfwagen B-2(f) als Schulfahrzeug/Fahrschulwagen B2(f)'. According to original German captured tank inventories, as of July 1943 there were six B2(f) tanks as part of Army Group A (Eastern Front), 17 in the Balkans and 81 in the West. Chars were used for internal policing and security duties and remained in service as late as May 1945 in the Channel Islands. Some were recaptured by the French Resistance (e.g. FFI -Forces Francaises de I'Intérieur - French Forces of the Interior) and used after the liberation of Paris.

The FCM Char de Rupture 2C (3C) was a heavy tank shaped by the lessons of the First World War and was the world's first multi-turreted tank, operated by a crew of 11 to 12 men. Only ten were manufactured from 1918 to 1921. In May 1940 six 3Cs were still operational but never reached the front line, due to a Luftwaffe Junkers Ju87 Stuka dive bomber attack, which immobilised the train on which they were being carried and made unloading from their special railcars an impossible task. The abandoned tanks were then captured by the 8th Panzer Regiment of the 101 Panzer Division. The Germans designated 3Cs as Panzerkampfwagen 3C 74 1 (f) but none were used, and they were only evaluated in October 1940. Afterwards they were moved to the Renault Factory, where they were all probably scrapped in 1942.

Armoured Vehicle Nomenclature

The Panzer tanks (Panzerkampfwagen) extensively used by Germany in World War II were initially abbreviated to 'PzKw', but the confusion this caused with personnel carriers known by the abbreviation 'PzK' led to a change. Halfway through the war, armoured fighting vehicles consequently came to be appointed 'PzKpfw' or 'Pz.Kpfw'. A Roman numeral distinguished one vehicle type from another - and variants were identified by a capital-letter alphabetic *Ausfuhrung* number which was abbreviated to 'Ausf'. Additionally, all special purpose vehicles of the Wehrmacht received a unique SdKfz number (Sonderkraftfahzeug), which did not adjust from one version to the next. For example, all 12 versions of the PzKpfw III were known as Sd.Kfz 141. The number was only changed if an important variant was produced.

The final three German tanks of the war also received the names Tiger, Panther and Tiger II (also widely known as the King Tiger or Konigstiger). They became, for example, PzKpfw V Panther Ausf G. The designations of some tanks were converted retroactively, for example the PzKpfw VI Tiger Ausf H (SdKfz 181) was later re-designated as the PzKpfw VI Tiger I Ausf E. The Tiger II also lost its Roman-numeral type designator, becoming the PzKpfw Tiger II Ausf B (SdKfz 182). The Ausf designators were not always apportioned in alphabetical order. With the Tiger, the original Ausf letters - H and P - actually refer to the designers, Henschel and Porsche. Subvariants sometimes received an Arabic numeral after the alphabetic designator eg: PzKpfw IV Ausf F2.

Tanks with type similarities but with different guns were set apart by a reference to its main weapon, either its nominal calibre, the length of its barrel or its own type designator. A PzKpfw III with the short-barrelled 7.5 cm gun might be referred to as a PzKpfw III (75). Tigers were often distinguished from King Tigers by the identification of their main guns. The Tiger became PzKpfw VI (8.8cm KwK 36 L/56) and the King Tiger, PzKpfw VI (8.8cm KwK 43 L/71). In the assistance of further vehicle identification, unique sub-designators were used.

From 1938, prototype and experimental tanks first received a 'VK' designator standing for Volkettenkraftfahzeug, a full-tracked motor vehicle. This was followed by four numbers, the first two describing its weight in tonnes, while the second two distinguished one prototype from another. When a similar specification was allocated to two or more manufacturers, a lettered abbreviation of their name was affixed in brackets eg: VK 3001 (H) indicated a tank made by Henschel. From 1943 onwards, experimental tanks and those under development got a similar 'E' designation (for Entwicklungstyp meaning development type) followed by an estimated weight-class.

This dramatic study shows German armour advancing past the blazing wrecks of Soviet tanks destroyed during the opening phase of Barbarossa.

CAPTURED BRITISH TANKS

Alongside the French army there was the British Expeditionary Force (BEF), 400,000 men strong with some 704 tanks of various types as of 10 May 1940.

The BEF began its evacuation from Dunkirk on 16 May 1940, which eventually evacuated some 340,000 allied soldiers but left behind all of its heavy equipment. Only 13 British tanks were brought back from France. The Germans captured all of the abandoned British tanks but only pressed around 250 into service due to their condition and a shortage of ammunition and spare parts. The majority were scrapped for parts to keep a Captured Panzer Company with three platoons equipped with British tanks into 1941.

The most numerous tank used by the BEF was the Vickers-Carden-Lloyd Light (Reconnaissance) Tank Mark VIB and VIC. Lightly armoured and armed, they were fast but unreliable and were of little or no combat value. Mark VIs were used by the Germans for training purposes by units stationed in France for the abortive Operation Seelöwe (Sea Lion) - the invasion of England - while some equipped the 1st platoon of the Captured Panzer Company as of early 1940. In order to maintain the Mark VIs a number of damaged tanks were taken apart by repair workshops to provide spare parts.

The British Mark VIs became the first foreign vehicle to be converted into mobile artillery by Captain Alfred Becker. From June to December of 1940 Becker modified and converted 18 Mark VIs to self-propelled artillery. Conversion consisted of the installation of an armoured superstructure at the rear of the vehicle, which housed the main armament. Along with these conversions, four Mark VIs were converted to unarmed radio and observation tanks. This conversion was designated as Funk und Beobachtungspanzer auf Fahrgestell Mk. VI(e) - radio (an observation tank on Mark VI(e)'s chassis). Conversions were tested on the proving grounds at Beverlo in Belgium. In October 1941 the conversions were grouped in the 15th Artillery Battery of 227th Artillery Regiment of the 227th Infantry Division commanded by Becker, which was transferred to the Northern sector (Leningrad area) of the Eastern Front. In mid-1942, an additional 12 Mark VIs were converted to ammunition carriers designated as Munitionspanzer auf Fahrgestell Mk. VI(e).

The two-man Infantry Tank MU (All) Matilda I designated by the Germans as 'Infanterie Panzerkampfwagen MU 747(e)' was reliable and well armoured, but it was also poorly armed and very slow. One hundred and thirty-nine Matilda Is were produced, 97 of which equipped two tank battalions of the BEF. The design was already obsolete by 1939 standards and the Germans made no use of any of captured Matilda Is, although it is possible that some had their turrets removed and used in the fortifications of the Atlantic Wall. Two examples were certainly tested at Kummersdorf in early 1941 but found wanting in almost every respect.

Of slightly more use was the four-man infantry tank Mark II (A12), Matilda II. This was supposedly an improved version of Matilda I, although in practice its design was completely different. The Matilda II was a very well armoured vehicle armed with a two-pounder (40mm) gun. Like the Matilda I, it was a slow but reliable vehicle. The BEF was equipped with 23 Matilda IIs and the Germans captured a few during the course of the campaign, including those abandoned and knocked out at Arras. Designated by the Germans as Infanterie Panzerkampfwagen Mk.II 748(e). Two captured Matilda IIs were tested at Kummersdorf in early 1941 along with Matilda Is. A single Matilda II (turret number 111) was used by the High Seas Instructional Command at Terneuzen in Holland for training purposes during the prelude to Operation Seelöwe (Sea Lion). A Number of Matilda IIs had the turrets removed and the original guns were replaced by 50mm KwK 38 L/42 guns, which had formally equipped PzKpfw IIIs. The gun was protected by a large, wide shield; the vehicle also mounted two MG15 machine guns and anti-aircraft defence. Conversion was done by the High Seas Instructional Command workshop and was designated as '5cm KwK L/42(M) auf Infanterie Panzerkampfwagen M II(e)' or as '5cm KwK auf Matilda(e)'. Once removed, the turrets were used in the fortifications of the Atlantic Wall.

The BEF had 57 Mark IV cruiser tanks, almost all of which were captured by the Germans, who designated them as 'Kreuzer Panzerkampfwagen Mk.IV 744(e)'. The Germans issued ten Mark IVs which were in service with the 2nd and 3rd platoon of the captured Panzer Company stationed in France in early 1941. Later on modified Mark IVs were transferred to Panzer Abteilung (Flamm) 100, which saw combat in the opening stage of the Operation Barbarossa in June and July 1941. Five tanks were scrapped for spare parts in order to keep those in service operational.

ENTER THE STURMGESCHÜTZ

One machine which had slipped quietly on to the battlefield during the French campaign was the Sturmgeschütz assault gun.

Under Blitzkrieg tactics, all of the tanks of the army were concentrated into the fast moving Panzer divisions, which would thrust deep into the rear positions of an enemy force, spreading panic and confusion as they advanced from the narrow point of penetration. As we have seen, the shock of the advance required a high level of artillery support at the point of attack, and also harnessed the extra power of air interdiction. But in the 1930s, the bulk of Germany's heavy artillery forces were still horse-drawn. What this meant was that the advancing tanks and motorised infantry would rapidly outstrip the artillery support.

Even mechanised prime movers like half-tracks had their disadvantages. The time taken to move into position and deploy the guns for action under battlefield conditions meant vital time was lost. In battle, split seconds literally meant the difference between life and death.

If artillery was to play a real role in the new mobile warfare it needed to be able to operate as close to the battle zone as possible, but the closer artillery pieces got to the action, the more vulnerable the gunners were to enemy fire. What was needed was an assault gun - a mobile artillery piece which could keep pace with the mechanised infantry, afford the gunners a measure of protection, and provide support on the battlefield at short notice, where it really mattered, in the very front line. A fully armoured and fully tracked mobile gun platform therefore had great appeal from the point of view of both mobility and crew protection. It also provided a means of providing close artillery support fire right in the very front line. Orders were dispatched for prototype vehicles.

The successful prototype was produced in 1936 by the Alkett company. The final vehicle was actually constructed from two separate elements and it mounted a heavy 75mm gun on a Panzer III tank chassis. The 75mm was a heavier weapon than could normally be carried on a Panzer III, but the extra space for the gun was achieved by

The Sturmgeschutze viewed from the enemy point of view. This propaganda photograph was probably taken in Russia during 1942.

A demonstration of the building of Sturmgeschutze and Panzer IIIs which appeared in the pages of *Signal* magazine.

dispensing with the turret and setting the gun on a fixed mount with a limited traverse. The Sturmgeschutz was born.

Naturally, the Grenadiers fighting in the front lines welcomed this development with open arms. Here was an artillery piece which could fight with the infantry at the crucial point of the battlefield and keep pace with the lightning advances of the Blitzkrieg era.

Throughout the long years of the Second World War the Sturmgeschutze crews never came to regard themselves as tank men. They wore different uniforms, and considered themselves to be artillery men who happened to man mobile assault guns - but they were still gunners at heart.

From the gunner's point of view, they quickly grew to love the Sturmgeschutz. After all, they were now protected against direct infantry fire and felt themselves impervious to anything but direct artillery fire. The powerful 75mm gun meant they packed a real punch in the attack.

The Sturmgeschütz had a crew of four: the commander, driver, loader and gunner. It soon became the proud boast of the Sturmgeschütze crews that their men were all volunteers, always ready to answer the infantryman's call to 'bring up the guns.' The new assault gunners took to the role with great enthusiasm. Although the cramped interior of each Geschütze officially had room for only 44 rounds, the crews soon found that they could carry 90 rounds of ammunition by stacking extra rounds in layers on the floor of the vehicle.

This meant the guns could stay in action and continue to give their support to the infantry for longer periods. In the coming years that would be a great advantage.

Despite the early signs of promise, these first machines were produced in small numbers and only 30 Geschütze were available for the French campaign of 1940. But they acquitted themselves well in their first actions. Orders were immediately given for the production of a further 500 machines. These machines equipped the first Sturmgeschütze batteries which served in the Blitzkrieg campaigns, through the Balkans and into Russia.

Initially, the Sturmgeschütze were organised into independent battalions. Each battalion was composed of three troops, which originally had six guns each. The commander of the battalion also had his own vehicle. In later years the number of vehicles in each troop was raised to ten and the battalions were renamed as Brigades which, in theory, fielded 31 Sturmgeschütze. In practice, these ideals were hardly ever achieved and only highly favoured formations received the full compliment.

In battle these independent brigades were allocated to support infantry formations for a specific action and came under the command of these formations. As the war developed the Sturmgeschütze commanders naturally gained a wealth of battle experience through almost constant exposure to action. In practice it was frequently the infantry commanders who took the lead from the more experienced assault gun leaders.

The official regulations stressed that the Sturmgeschütze should be employed en masse. But the constant demands of a terrible war meant that they were more often employed as single battalions or even single machines.

One shortcoming of the early Sturmgeschütz models was the lack of a machine gun for close support against enemy infantry. This was rectified in 1941 with the introduction of the machine gun mounted on the Model E, of which a further 272 were produced.

WITTMANN MOVES TO THE STURMGESCHÜTZ

Among those who would see action in the assault was Michael Wittmann. Wittmann, together with several other NCOs and men, had now transferred to Juterbog, where the self-propelled assault battery was being formed. There, he and his colleagues traded in their black Panzer uniforms for grey assault gun tunics. It was to be two years before he would see Panzer black again. This was the start of Wittmann's association with armoured fighting vehicles which was to lead him to fame and infamy throughout the civilised world. There was much to learn. As we have seen, the assault guns were armed with the short-barrelled 75mm gun, which had little in common with the feeble 20mm cannon carried by the armoured cars, but Wittmann soon showed exceptional promise with

A war artist provides a vivid impression of the cooperation between the Panzer grenadiers and the Sturmgeschutze.

the new weapon. After training, the fledgling assault gun battery was sent to garrison duty in France.

THE ALLIED VIEW

The Sturmgeschütz was to become such a fixed part of the thinking of the German forces that, five years after the French campaign, the US army handbook dedicated an extended section to the German use and handling of assault guns:

Infantry-assault gun co-ordination. The assault guns are organised in assault gun battalions and are under the control of the division commander.

The Germans regard their self-propelled assault guns as decisive weapons to be employed, particularly at the point of main effort. In cooperation with infantry they facilitate the penetration and breakthrough. These weapons, the Germans believe, complement artillery fire by their ability to follow the infantry right up to an objective. Their use for small actions before an attack is forbidden so as not to betray their presence. Surprise is sought by bringing them into position by night and camouflaging their assembly area. Used primarily to neutralise enemy support weapons at short ranges over open sights, assault guns are preferably employed in concentrations; to employ them singly or in comparatively small numbers is frowned upon by the Germans.

German assault guns advance with or just behind the infantry; they never go ahead of the infantry. When an objective is reached, the assault guns do not remain with the infantry while the position is being consolidated but retire about 1000 yards to await further assignment.

In close combat the assault guns are rather helpless and therefore it is the task of the infantry to keep the enemy away from the assault guns; newly-organised assault-gun escort batteries have the same task.

A DANGEROUS DEVELOPMENT

In early 1941 there was a further significant but ominous development. Hitler sought to rapidly expand the number of Panzer Divisions from the existing ten to a new level of 20. However, there was clearly insufficient manufacturing capacity to create the new machines, or the time to recruit and train the hundreds of thousands of men who would

An artist's impression from the pages of *Signal* magazine illustrating the difficulties of moving vehicles under combat conditions. In this evocative image a Sturmegeschze of the late war variety is being used to pull another machine out of trouble under fire.

be needed. With a typical rash flourish Hitler solved the problem at a stroke by reducing the number of regiments in a Panzer Division from two to one. He then used the extra regiments to form the tank elements of ten new Panzer Divisions. Although this exercise effectively doubled the number of Divisions in a short space of time it did so by reducing the tank strength of the Divisions from the 1940 level of over three hundred machines, to the new 1941 level of around one hundred and fifty. This dramatic reduction in fighting strength was to have dire consequences later in the war when breakdowns and casualties would frequently mean that a Panzer Division which could field 80 machines was in good shape.

OPERATION MARITA

In August 1940 German divisions began transferring to the occupied areas of Poland in order to reinforce the attenuated frontier defences. For the rest of the year the build up on the eastern front continued unabated. During this period the German forces in Poland were frequently regrouped to conceal their numbers. Before the storm could be unleashed there was another matter

to be taken care of.

With the new year there arose an unexpected opportunity for the Blitzkrieg forces to test their expertise once more. Mussolini launched an ill-advised, ill-fated campaign in Greece, which left Italian forces floundering. Early in 1941 he turned to his ally Hitler for help.

Realising that their success in repelling the Italians was likely to bring German vengeance down upon them, the Greeks appealed to their British allies for aid. The reinforcements sent by Britain proved woefully inadequate. A declaration of war against Yugoslavia and Greece simultaneously was the signal that Blitzkrieg was about to be unleashed again. It burst over Yugoslavia on 6th April.

The same day Belgrade was heavily bombed and the Germans tore through the country. Zagreb, Sarajevo and Skopje fell in quick succession and just 12 days later Yugoslavia was occupied. Greece was now the front line.

After the short burst of activity which had characterised the lightning campaign through France, the long months of barracks duty hung heavy on Wittmann, who was keen to see action again. He was not to get his wish until 6 April

1941, when the Balkans Campaign began. The German forces advanced through Yugoslavia to Greece where, in addition to Greek forces, their opponents included English and commonwealth troops. Wittmann's assault gun was involved in the fierce fighting for the Klidi Pass, which fell only after heavy resistance. Next, the Liebstandarte had to fight its way through the Klisswa Pass and on to Corinth and Olympia against fierce opposition from the Greek army. The fighting in Greece ended on 30 April 1941. After pausing to rest in Thessalia in May the Leibstandarte was sent through Yugoslavia to Camp Dieditz near Wischau, where they awaited the next phase of the war - the invasion of Russia.

Two German Corps had stormed into northern Greece from Bulgaria on the 6 April, followed on the 8th by the 2nd Panzer Division. Blitzkrieg was once again proving to be unstoppable as the invading armies drove towards the south with the British retreating before them. On the 19th the British forces had been overwhelmed and evacuated to Crete.

They were hardly given time to draw breath.

On 20 May the skies over Crete were suddenly filled with the German aircraft of Operation Merkur.

A relentless bombing raid on the island was the prelude to the first major airborne assault in history. An awesome sight met the eyes of the defenders as the departing aircraft left a cascade of parachutes behind them and the 7th Fliegerdivision dropped earthwards. What followed was due to the greatest failure of German intelligence up to that point in the war. The British were ready for the paratroopers and 50 per cent of them were dead before they reached the ground.

The carnage was no help to the British, and was almost an irrelevance in the great Blitzkrieg push. Eight days later the British were being evacuated once more and Germany seemed invincible.

The succession of victories was unbroken and thus far German casualties overall had been comparatively small, so that the nation had scarcely felt itself to be at war. People were still full of wonder and admiration. Only a handful of the highest commanders were privy to the extraordinary cataclysm which was to come.

CAPTURED BRITISH ARMOUR

The fall of Greece meant that the total 300 vehicles used by the British and Commonwealth Forces were captured by the Germans in Yugoslavia and Greece during Operation Marita. The Yugoslavian 1st Tank Battalion (Batalion Bornih Kola) also yielded some 110 tanks.

Captured Yugoslavian and Greek tanks along with tanks transferred from France were assigned to infantry divisions in Serbia, Croatia and eventually Bosnia. A number were also used for railway defence in those areas and in armoured trains.

Captured from the British were some 140 tanks, including Matilda II, Cruiser (e.g. Mark II) and Light Tanks, but it is unknown how many were pressed, if any at all, into German service.

A French tank crew is taken into captivity. The prisoners are immobilised by the simple expedient of forcing them to drop their trousers to their ankles.

Estimated German Armoured Vehicle Production 1933 - 1945

Tanks	1933-1938	1939	1940	1941	1942	1943	1944	1945	Totals
Panzer I	1000	500	-	-	-	-	-	-	1500
Panzer II	800	700	200	200	100	-	-	-	2000
Panze r III	100	200	1400	1600	1800	400	-	-	5500
Panzer IV	200	200	1000	1200	2000	2000	1700	300	8600
Panzer V	-	-	-	-	-	2000	4500	300	6800
Panzer VI	-	-	-	-	-	650	630	-	1280
Panzer VI (B)	-	-	-	-	-	-	377	107	484
Total	2100	1600	1500	3200	4000	6000	7100	707	26164

Tank Destroyers	1933-1938	1939	1940	1941	1942	1943	1944	1945	Total
PzJagI	-	-	100	100	-	-	-	-	200
Stug III/IV	-	-	40	500	1000	3000	5000	700	10,240
Marder II	-	-	-	-	200	350	-	-	550
Marder III	-	-	-	-	280	400	500	-	1180
Elefant	-	-	-	-	-	88	-	-	88
Hertzer	-	-	-	-	-	-	2000	500	2500
Nashorn	-	-	-	-	-	200	300	-	500
PzJag IV	-	-	-	-	-	700	1000	300	2000
Jagd Panther	-	-	-	-	-	-	350	32	382
Jagd Tiger	-	-	-	-	-	-	50	30	80
Brummbär	-	-	-	-	-	200	100	-	300
Sturmtiger	-	-	-	-	-	-	20	-	20
Wespe	-	-	-	-	-	400	270	-	670
Hummel	-	-	-	-	-	-	560	100	660
Totals	0	0	140	600	1480	5338	10,150	1662	19,370

THE WESTERN DESERT 1941-1942

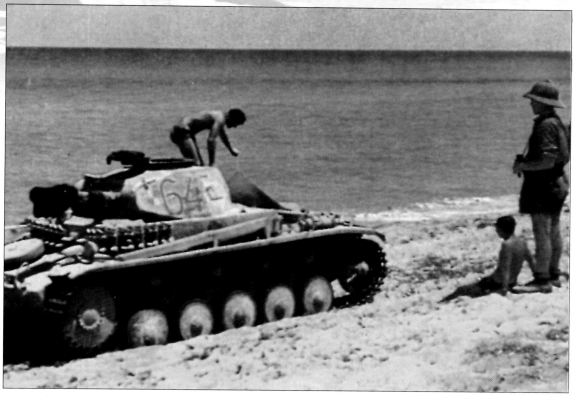

A peaceful study of a Panzer II on the shores of the Libyan coast. The crewman is in the process of spreading out an air recognition flag on the rear deck.

"It is essential that the forces fighting under my command in this theatre are properly supplied with adequate stocks of ammunition and fuel. These are the life blood of the Panzer forces."

Erwin Rommel, 1942

The fighting in the desert began with Italy's entry into the war in 1940. British forces stationed in Egypt and Sudan were confronted by much larger Italian forces on two adjoining fronts, but the British enjoyed certain advantages.

As a result of their superior training, the smaller British forces took the fight to the Italians, and appeared from nowhere with aggressive tactics, which soon won the day.

On 9 December two squadrons of Matildas under the command of General O'Connor successfully used the element of surprise and attacked a strong Italian position at Sidi Barrani without the customary opening artillery barrage. By 10.00am the fort was captured, every Italian tank was knocked out and the British had 2,000 prisoners to contend with.

'Operation Compass' followed, an astonishing 500-mile drive westwards during which ten Italian divisions were effectively destroyed, with the capture of hundreds of tanks and guns.

Casualties amongst O'Connor's men came to less than 2,000 whereas the Italians sustained losses of 100,000 dead or wounded and a further 130,000 taken prisoner. Had the Italians not escorted themselves to prison camps the logistics of dealing with so many captives would have presented major difficulties.

DIFFICULT CONDITIONS

The early battles were fought using some very humble machines. The North African desert campaign was, in many respects, the ideal battlefield for tanks. But the desert was to prove a harsh mistress offering the tantalising promise of success only to withdraw its promise just at the point where victory seemed within reach. In turn, the Italians, then the British and Germans, and finally the Americans, would each experience the thrill of conquest followed by an unexpected defeat. The first to experience the roller-coaster ride of the ebbs and flows of tank warfare in the desert were the Italians.

Italian tanks were no match for the British tanks and tactics, and in consequence the British Army enjoyed great success against the Italians. In particular, the Italian light tanks were so ineffective as to prove almost comical. But even the British medium tanks had their limitations.

In contrast to the Italian tanks, the British Matilda tank was very slow, but effective. It was the Matilda's ability to absorb punishment that earned it the nickname 'Queen of the battlefield'.

The unmistakable squat shape of the Matilda fought throughout the desert campaign. Many captured Matildas were even used by the Germans against their former owners.

While the Matilda took on the job of supporting the infantry, the armoured punch of the British tank brigade was provided by the Crusader tanks. It was their job to engage enemy tanks.

By February 1941 O'Connor was eagerly preparing to advance on Tripoli to eliminate Axis forces in Africa completely, but Churchill decided that O'Connor's battle-hardened divisions should be dispatched urgently to Greece.

The British success was so swift and comprehensive that the campaign was nearly over when Hitler at last decided to help his Italian Allies. German forces entered the campaign in February 1941 and their tactics, leadership and superior weaponry immediately changed the status quo in the desert.

The Afrika Korps typified all that was innovative in the German war machine. In its brief history, of just two years and three months, the Afrika Korps stung the allied forces into a massive war of attrition and won for itself an

The deadly '88' in action during the early stages of the North Africa campaign. These guns were to prove the most feared anti-tank weapons of the war.

honourable mention in the annals of military history.

In 1940 the Wehrmacht was singularly ill-equipped for battle beneath the relentless sun of North Africa. German military formations were created for European conditions. They did not possess even one unit specifically trained for fighting in desert conditions. By contrast the British had years of desert experience dating back to before the First World War. In fact, the British had been active in North Africa since the days of Napoleon and maintained a permanent presence in Egypt.

Desperate to keep his Axis partner in the war, in January 1941 Hitler signed Führer Directive Number 22, code-named Operation Sonnenblume, or sunflower. It authorised the transport of a small German force to Tripoli to assist the Italians in blocking further British advances.

On February 14th units of Germany's newly created Afrika Korps began to land in Tripoli. These new arrivals were already seasoned warriors and they brought with them impressive modern weaponry. They were commanded by one of Germany's most able and imaginative practitioners of tank warfare, General Erwin Rommel. Rommel was an aggressive commander who exploited any weaknesses in his enemy to the full.With a series of brilliantly executed battle plans Rommel earned the title 'The Desert Fox'. He was held in awe by his enemies.

The Matilda and the obsolete A9 Cruiser tanks now had to face German machines with better armaments, better armour and better speed and range. The British now had to contend with the Panzer II, III and IV.

The Afrika Korps was, as its name suggested, only a corps in size, but it was a relatively small corps with only two Panzer Divisions. The second 'Panzer Division' did not even arrive until May 1941. In reality the first unit was a light division, (the 5th light division).

The Desert War has often been described as the last example of a chivalrous war; nevertheless, it was a hard-fought affair.

By a series of lightning armoured reconnaissance probes, Rommel quickly established that the strength of the allied forces ranged against him had been overestimated. He was faced by the Second Army division, newly arrived from Britain, and not yet acclimatised to desert conditions. The second British armoured division consisted of one weakened armoured brigade already short of transport and with worn-out tanks. They were supported by a similarly weakened 9th Australian Division. A third British formation was held in reserve in Tobruk. These forces were under the command of General Wavell.

Wavell had been siphoning off forces for Crete and then Greece since January 1941, so when the Afrika Korps finally struck in March 1941 there was a very, very thin screen facing Rommel and his new force.

The British who had swept the Italians back were now at the end of an enormously long logistical chain; essentially, they could not support, from Egypt, the number of troops who were now in the far western desert.

The Germans had trained and developed the ideas of mobile and manoeuvrable warfare to a fine pitch during the Polish and French Campaigns which meant that the Afrika Korps was a well balanced armed force, able to traverse almost any terrain and fight almost any opponent.

As Rommel began his attacks in Cyrenaica it became abundantly clear he possessed an advantage in the quality of his weaponry. Against the British total of 22 cruiser and 25 light tanks, the 5th Panzer Regiment fielded 150 tanks - and nearly half of those were the superior Mark III and IVs. In addition, Rommel already possessed a few 88mm anti-aircraft guns, which he would use to such devastating effect as his principal anti-tank gun.

Where the British tended to use their tanks independently of their other arms, the Germans developed a very close coordination between their tanks and tank artillery and infantry. This made them a much tougher proposition in the desert battles.

Vital to Rommel's tactical success was his continued use of the bait technique, where his tanks would first attempt the allied tanks with a frontal probe. When the allied tanks then charged towards the Panzers, the German tanks would fall back behind their screen of 88mm guns which, with a greater range, could then open up with decisive killing shots on the advancing armour. This was a technique he used again and again, and it was something the British never seemed to be able to counter.

THE DESERT THEATRE

The desert in North Africa has been described as a tactician's paradise and a quartermaster's hell. For a progressive thinker like Rommel it was a paradise because of its vast, uninhabited emptiness, with no changing seasons, no partisans, no resistance groups and no urban centres to slow the movements of armoured divisions. But for the men in charge of logistical support it was a pure hell because everything - fuel, ammunition, food and weapons - had to pass along tortuously extended lines of supply which became ever more stretched as the Afrika Korps stormed eastwards.

All of the supplies for Rommel's army in terms of ammunition, petrol, food and so on had to be transported from Italy. The Italian merchant ships had to run the gauntlet, posed by the British island of Malta, with its submarines and shore-based aircraft. Although Rommel's by-line was relatively short, a matter of a mere 60 miles, it was actually a very vulnerable to British interdiction. The supplies then had to be transported over land on the one road in North Africa, the Via Balboa, built by the Italians. As Rommel's army advanced eastwards his supply line stretched; once Rommel reached El Alamein, only 60 miles from Alexandria, his supply line was 1,300 miles long, all the way from Tripoli.

One of the great problems of operating over those great distances was that the trucks themselves used fuel. It has been estimated that somewhere between ten and fifteen per cent of all the fuel that the Afrika Korps needed was actually spent in sustaining vehicles for the supply route. In those conditions, over very rough roads, vehicle breakdowns were inevitable. At any one time up to about thirty per cent of Rommel's vehicles were actually in for repair. The British helped him enormously and they seemed to abandon their tanks with careless regularity. Indeed, by the summer of 1942 virtually all of the Afrika Korps transport was composed of British trucks.

Like the Allies before them the Afrika Korps soon realised there were geographical limitations which would force them to operate within a band stretching approximately fifty miles south from the Mediterranean coast; further south than that lay the limitless sand dunes with deep desert, impassable to wheeled or tracked vehicles alike.

Within that 50-mile passable band of terrain the one road, the Via Balboa, skirted the coast, and along this tarmac artery ran Rommel's armoured units and his columns of supply lorries. Petrol was one of the most precious commodities. From the outset it was always rationed and any unauthorised use of a vehicle was heavily punished.

A WAR OF ATTRITION

Now, balanced tank forces, backed with artillery, fought each other head on in what ultimately was to became a war of attrition. The objective was to knock out the other side's tanks, deny the enemy the battlefield so he couldn't recover and repair losses. At the same time it was necessary to attack his supply routes and bases, making difficult the maintenance of his mechanised forces.

Tanks of each side took fearsome toll of each other and, contrary to popular belief, British tanks gave as good as they got. In the early months of the campaign the British in fact had the advantage in the ever-changing balance between armour and armament.

Initially the German Panzer III had only 30mm of frontal armour and the Panzer IV had even less, at 20mm; both of these machines could easily be pierced by British anti-tank weapons. In contrast the early Crusaders enjoyed 40mm whilst the redoubtable Matildas had 80mm of frontal armour. The 50mm gun of the Panzer III could not pierce the armour of the Crusader except on the side, while the Matilda could not be penetrated even at ranges as close as 500 yards.

Despite the limitations of his armour, Rommel's conduct of battle was bold and resourceful. In Panzer attacks the tanks would be used as a wedge - the 'Panzerkeil' - closely supported by other services; artillery to soften the objective, pioneers to deal with obstacles, infantry to take and hold ground, and of course the Stukas to act as supplementary artillery. Rommel led from the front and specialised in the concentration of a superior force against a single point. As the other great exponent of German tank warfare, Heinz Guderian, was fond of saying: "Kotzen, nicht kleckern". In other words "Spew, don't dribble." Rommel certainly took the message to heart.

The North Africa terrain was particularly harsh. Although one might tend to think of great swathes of sand dunes, in actual fact much of the terrain was very stony barren desert, and this took an

A Panzer III negotiates the rudimentary roads of North Africa. The fine sand and dust thrown up by the tanks had a disastrous effect on the engines and running gear.

enormous toll not just on the men, but on the vehicles too. Tank tracks were particularly susceptible to damage.

The sand blown up by the constant movement of vehicles meant that the engine air filters suffered much greater wear and tear, and the quantity of lubricants needed to keep the engines running properly and the amount of maintenance was vastly increased.

Initially, the Panzers had arrived with normal European air filters fitted to the engines. Inevitably, the sand penetrated through these filters and the cylinder walls of the engines could be scoured to a standstill within 800 or 1,000 miles.

Together, the German and Italian forces in North Africa needed at least seventy thousand tons of supplies every month. All of it had to come by sea

from ports in southern Italy, and all of it came under attack by the Royal Navy and the Royal Air Force. Minor amounts of supplies were flown in from time to time, but the unarmed Junkers 52 transport aircraft were rarely available in sufficient numbers and, in any case, they presented themselves as easy targets for any marauding RAF fighters.

The logistical difficulties faced by the Afrika Korps were enormous, and there is no question that they were usually chronically short of supplies. It is nonetheless interesting to look at the statistics for the amount of equipment which was shipped from Italy; the figures would appear to suggest that well over 90 per cent of the men, vehicles and supplies which were dispatched actually reached the Afrika Korps. Clearly there was a regular channel of supply, and it was not quite as bleak a picture as is often painted.

Rommel was eager to advance as far and as quickly as possible. He had his eyes focussed on the Suez Canal, his final objective. Frequently his supply lines were stretched to breaking point - but he was a man indifferent to such limitations. Despite the fact it was over eight hundred miles from his main supply port in Tripoli to the Egyptian frontier, Rommel viewed that as a logistical matter for the High Command to solve, whereas it was his job to fight the war on the ground.

Every German tank was fitted with wireless and had tremendous flexibility of response in a changing battle situation. The Germans were also far ahead in the techniques of anti-tank warfare. By 1941 the 37mm anti-tank gun had been replaced with the larger 50mm Pak 38. The Germans also frequently employed the famous 88mm anti-aircraft gun in the anti-tank role. This gun could even take out the sturdy Matilda at ranges of up to two thousand yards. Placed defensively, Rommel could use a screen of 88mm guns to knock out British tanks before the Panzers were even engaged. This innovative use of weapons

Rommel in Africa from the May 1941 issue of *Signal* magazine. At this time Rommel was enjoying the first fruits of success as an armoured leader and shows little sign of the enormous fatigue which characterises later pictures.

substantially reduced the advantages which came from superior numbers of British tanks.

The harsh brilliance of the desert sun imposed its own rules on the conduct of the North African campaign, with the men suffering an almost daily form of desert blindness. It was soon established that between dawn and 9am and again between 4pm and dusk a man could accurately identify friend or enemy vehicle at anything between two and five thousand yards. In the shimmering heat of full sun that accurate range dropped to 1,500 yards.

Rommel was very much a hands-on commander who always wanted to know what was happening at the sharp end. He believed that he had to have what he called a finger-tip feel for the battlefield so that he could be there in person during the crisis of a battle. This meant that Rommel was often able to react much faster to events than his British counterparts who relied upon the standard chain of command. The downside meant that Rommel left his chief of staff and headquarters often miles behind as he toured the battlefield in his personal half-track.

Rommel did have a very good radio communication system, but this was often jammed by the British, and in consequence his commanders often did not know where their Korps Commander (and later their Army Commander) actually was.

In the featureless desert the art of camouflage was another skill quickly learned by the men of the Afrika Korps. When the first Panzer Mark IIs, IIIs and IVs arrived they were painted in the Wehrmacht colours of grey green - far too highly visible in the desert. In the absence of desert colour paint those first tanks were sprayed with oil and then hot sand thrown over them until they more or less blended in with the background. The crews quickly learned to make skilful use of netting and the camel thorn bush to break up the outline of their vehicles.

As the war progressed the calibre and power of anti-tank guns increased from the relatively weak 37mm gun to the awesome power of the high velocity 88mm. The '88' was originally designed as an anti-aircraft gun, which needed to generate enormous power to fire a heavy shell 20,000 feet into the air.

When the German infantry discovered that this powerful gun could also be used to fire over a flat trajectory against tanks, a devastating new weapon was born. The massive velocity of its armour piercing shells spelt death for thousands of Russian and allied tanks during the years from 1939 to 1945.

Throughout the war the '88' was the most feared adversary for all of the tank men in the allied armies. The only drawback of this weapon was that it was very cumbersome and needed to be towed into action, but once it was deployed in concealed and camouflaged positions it was a deadly menace.

Mounted on towed trailers, the 88mm gun could be swiftly deployed and engage the enemy at 2,000 yards range - long before the allied tank guns were close enough to reply. The 88mm had one more advantage - besides the armour piercing range, it also fired high explosive shells. The Panzer Mark III and IV tanks could also fire high explosive shells which were devastating against infantry, but had little effect against the British tanks, such as the Crusader and Valentine.

Despite the fact that he personally had to cross large areas of featureless terrain, the restless energy of Rommel drove his men forward. When he was not at the helm of his command car, 'Greiff', Rommel was to be found reconnoitring the ground from the cockpit of his Feisler Storch reconnaissance aircraft, from which he was constantly urging his troops forward. Encouraged and exhorted by the gadfly energy of their commanding officer, the tank crews surged forward.

Behind Rommel's early successes in his advance eastwards was his firm belief that he could crush the allied forces and continue his advance all the way to Alexandria and the Suez canal. From there, he could set his sights on the Caucasus in the southern Soviet Union where he hoped to achieve a classic pincer movement - striking a decisive blow in Germany's war.

THE GERMAN ADVANTAGE

A major difficulty experienced by the British tanks in the desert was the lack of a dual-purpose gun, one which could fire high explosives as well as armour piercing shells. The two-pounder anti-tank guns which were standard in British tanks could not fire the effective high explosive shells which were required to deal with anti-tank guns and infantry on the battlefield.

This problem had actually been foreseen prior to the Second World War and the interim solution was

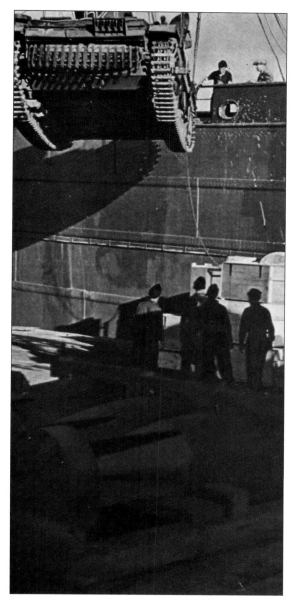

Unloading the tanks of the Afrika Korps in Tripoli during May 1941. The allied interdiction campaign, although severe, was not as all-embracing as many sources would appear to suggest. More than 90% of the armoured vehicles dispatched to Rommel actually arrived safely in Tripoli.

to provide two close-support tanks for each squadron, fitted with 3in Howitzer. Used mainly as a means of laying smoke screens, the close support tanks carried few high explosive shells on board. Generally, the Crusader was used in this role.

In the desert the battlefield was now dominated by the tanks; infantry were helpless without armoured support. The balance of power between the allied and axis forces was now measured by who could field the most tanks. Keeping these tanks in the field was another matter altogether. They required intensive servicing and repair. The harshness of the desert exacerbated this problem, and the supply line organisation assumed vital importance in bringing forward fuel, ammunition and spare parts. This over-extended supply line also dealt with the recovery of tanks from the battlefield, replacement vehicles and all of the myriad requirements for an army in the field. Attacking supply lines on land, sea or air became of crucial importance to both sides.

Not all tanks knocked out by enemy fire were actually destroyed. Often, they were brought in to be repaired; those not immediately repairable provided much needed spares for others. At the same time the enemy had to be denied the opportunity to use the battlefield losses in this way. Repaired enemy vehicles could be pressed into service against their original owners, and enemy equipment salvaged from the battlefield provided intelligence on the latest vehicles, armour, weapons and ammunition. The recovery mechanics and tank transporter drivers of both sides often plied their trade under fire. For example, at the Halfaya Pass battles the British lost 91 tanks, which included 64 Matildas. A considerable number of these losses were due to mechanical breakdowns, but a combination of time and shortage of transporters meant most ended up being left on the battlefield. In this instance the Germans were able to utilise the captured vehicles, Rommel himself acquiring a British armoured command truck, which he named 'Mammoth'.

VEHICLE RECOVERY

As Rommel's tenuous supply line grew even more difficult to maintain, it became essential to recover as many damaged or broken down vehicles as possible. While this was also a factor in British thinking, it was a less pressing issue as the Eighth Army was comparatively well served with replacements. Control of the field after the battle was vital for Rommel. It allowed the Afrika Korps to salvage allied and enemy machines alike.

Most vehicle casualties were recoverable. Obviously if a shell is blasted through the middle of a tank it usually made a wreck of the inside, but

a more common type of tank casualty would be a missing track link, damaged tracks or damaged suspensions.

INTO BATTLE

Despite the fact that in Febuary 1941 only elements of the 5th (Light) Division had arrived, Rommel wasted no time. Within ten days he launched his first assault; without waiting for his full force to be assembled he moved swiftly against the inactive forward British units, throwing them back in confusion. The British were dismayed to see shells from their two-pounder guns merely bouncing off the German armour.

The follow-up was immediate, and in early April the British were forced to evacuate Benghazi. O'Connor, hastily recalled from leave, was captured. The momentum of Rommel's brilliant offensive did not falter. Within a few months, in a spectacular change of fortunes, all of O'Connor's gains were reversed and the Afrika Korps successfully laid siege to the port stronghold of Tobruk.

During 1941 the real weakness of German tank design was still not discovered. Several false conclusions were drawn from the conquest of the Balkans and Greece. These easy victories supported the continued German belief that their tanks were the best in the world. Although the design work that was to lead to the Tiger had begun, there was little real urgency.

Up to the summer of 1941, Germany's main adversary had been Britain, and British tank design lagged behind Germany's. In the North African campaign the poor performance of the British Crusader tanks only gave fresh support to the German view that the Panzer IIIs and IVs were at least equal to anything the Allies could throw at them. The Crusader was particularly badly designed and it was plagued by a host of mechanical failures. Eventually, the British army lost faith in their own tanks altogether and in 1943, when the victorious British and American forces embarked from Africa for the invasion of Italy, all of the British tanks were left behind.

Despite the limitations of the British machines, there were signs of dangerous flaws in Germany's tank capability. In the relative backwater of the desert war, even the unspectacular British Matilda tank was considered a success against the Italian

An excellent study of a Panzer II on active service with the Afrika Korps. The 2cm gun was an improvement on the machine- gun armed Panzer I but by 1941 the Panzer II had long been eclipsed as a battle tank.

forces and frequently held its own against the Germans.

The gun on the Matilda, which was typical of most tanks of this period, was the two-pounder, a 40mm weapon, but it only fired solid shot. In other words, it was only any use firing against enemy tanks. This was fine as far as it went, but once the Germans came to the desert and started mixing tanks and anti-tank guns in the attack, a dual-purpose gun was needed, something which not only fired solid armour piercing shot to take out enemy tanks, but which could also fire high explosive shells. The advantage of this was seen when the American tanks arrived, notably the General Grant.

Once again, superior German battlefield tactics were overcoming the limitations of her armoured forces. But these successes also reinforced a leisurely attitude towards the development of new types. By 1941 the evolution of German tank design was proceeding much too slowly, and it was to have deadly consequences from which Germany would never recover. The shock was to be delivered in Russia.

In the late autumn General Auchinleck organised another offensive in the desert. For a while it enjoyed a measure of success and in December Benghazi was recaptured, but it fell again to the Germans as early in 1942. Rommel once more began to drive eastwards. Egypt itself was menaced.

After his success against the British counter-offensive, 'Operation Battleaxe', Rommel wrote to his wife, Lucy: 'I have been three days on the road going round the battlefield. The joy of my troops is tremendous.' One of his staff officers remarked: 'He is already in the process of becoming a hero'.

And he was a hero and a legend, worshipped by his men, respected by his enemies.

By this time, however, the German supply lines were uncomfortably over-extended and the number of operational tanks was depleted by such a long and arduous advance. Auchinleck decided to make a stand at El Alamein, where large salt marshes inland prevented Rommel out-flanking the British to the south. Throughout July Rommel's weakened vanguard made repeated forays against the British positions around El Alamein, but each assault was successfully beaten back. Even so, the British 8th Army remained alarmingly vulnerable.

Rommel, now created a Field Marshall following the dramatic capture of Tobruk, tried to break through the El Alamein defences and planned to use captured fuel to thrust onwards to Cairo. His first priority was to consolidate and replenish his forces. Despite receiving only limited supplies and reinforcements, by the end of August Rommel felt able to resume his offensive.

The same period saw notable changes in the British command structure. In August 1942 General Sir Bernard Montgomery took over as commander of the British Eighth Army. He was to reap the benefit of the new equipment and reinforcements pouring into the desert campaign. But Monty (as he was known to his troops) was a different breed of commander; he had taken the lessons of the First World War and the opening phase of victory in the Second World War in France to heart. He talked to his men, was seen by them, and gave them a victory at Alam el Halfa.

He realised there was one vital ridge at Alam el Halfa which Rommel must try to take. Accordingly he prepared a defence in depth. British codebreakers had deciphered the enemy signals and German convoys from Italy were regularly destroyed in the Mediterranean. Montgomery also knew when Rommel intended to strike. When it came, the battle of Alam el Halfa was brief. A deep belt of mines impeded the initial German advance and when the main offensive began the following morning the 200 German and 240 Italian tanks came under punishing bombing attacks. Rommel had achieved neither surprise nor speed and by the first week of September the Afrika Korps was back where it started.

In 1942 there was more good news for the British. The American M3 medium tank, known to the British as the 'Grant' was introduced into the

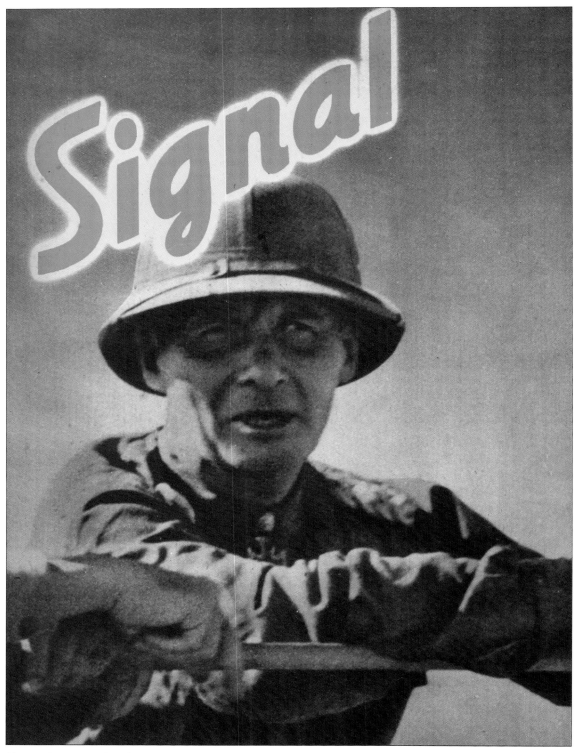

Rommel on campaign, from the font cover of *Signal* magazine, March 1942. As he is wearing the cumbersome tropical issue head gear which was largely abandoned in 1941, it is likely that this picture was taken some considerable time before publication.

campaign and first used at Gazala. The Grant mounted two tank guns to provide the solution to the need for a gun to fire high explosive and armour piercing shells. The 75mm howitzer was placed in a sponson on the right hand side of the tank - a welcome upgrading of firepower. At last the British tank forces had a good high explosive capability which could be used against German anti-tank guns and their crews. The other gun on the Grant was the anti-tank weapon, mounted in an alarmingly lofty turret perched on top of the tank, which produced a dangerously high silhouette. This height made it difficult for the Grant to adopt a hull-down position (where a tank hides its body behind cover, leaving the turret exposed, thus reducing its target area to the enemy). The two guns meant that the Grant needed a crew of six, a large number for a tank. Five hundred Grants were sent to the Middle East.

But Grant was very much an interim solution. The most important American tank to enter the North African Campaign was the M4AI medium tank, the Sherman. Shermans first appeared in action at El Alamein in November 1942. This tank would eventually become the mainstay of the allies on all battlefields. It was not a particularly heavily armoured tank but its real strength was derived from the sheer quantity manufactured. In a war of attrition the US manufacturing muscle would beat German technical superiority. The Sherman suffered the terrible attribute of bursting into flames even when hit by a non-explosive anti-tank shell. This led to it being given the nickname of the 'Ronson' because as the soldiers quipped with macabre humour, it 'lights first time'. The German nickname was equally cruel; they christened it the 'Tommycooker'! Despite its limitations, the volume of Shermans on the battlefield ultimately proved to be a deciding factor.

However, the US was not the only producer of new tanks in 1942. The British had introduced the A22, named the Churchill. This tank first appeared in March 1942 armed with the standard British two-pounder gun; the Mark III and IV variants were up-gunned to a six-pounder (57mm) gun. The Churchill, weighing in at nearly 40 tons, was powered by a 350bhp Bedford engine. Although it was a slow, ponderous tank reaching only 18 mph on a good day, its frontal armour was a massive 102mm, which gave a great deal of comfort to the five-man crew. Three Churchills took part in the

Battle of El Alamein for evaluation purposes. They passed the test and the British 21st Army Tank Brigade, which arrived in North Africa in March 1943, was fully equipped with Churchills.

The tank strength of the Eighth Army had by August 1942 reached 935 machines, with an effective strength of tanks fit for action of 762 machines. The numbers game was running against the Germans; Rommel could by now field only 200 tanks, but their qualitative situation had improved. A hundred of the tanks were now Panzer IIIs with the long-barrelled, high velocity 50mm gun, and 50 were the Panzer IVs with the even more powerful long 75mm gun.

The advantage of the desert was that it was mostly flat, with few towns or natural obstructions, but a stationary tank could be easily camouflaged. For tanks on the move, however, air cover was essential. Sand blown into the air by tank tracks could easily be detected by hostile aircraft and slow moving machines were an easy target from the air. The column of smoke from one burning tank identified the position of the unit from miles around.

For the tank crews the conditions in the desert which they had to endure were appalling. Insects were a perpetual torment. The heat inside the noisy, vibrating cabin was unbearable. The all-pervading sand caused engines to seize and turrets to jam. Sand penetrated the caterpillar tracks which then ground themselves apart. The heavy complicated machinery required continual maintenance and without their tank the crew were at the mercy of the unforgiving desert.

In battle the armour plating of the tanks protected the crew from rifle and machine gun fire and, to a varying extent, from shell fire. But even the best armoured tank was vulnerable to heavy and well-directed anti-tank fire. For many of the tank soldiers who perished in the sands, death did not come easily. A tank sustaining a direct hit might simply explode, but if it didn't the energy of the impact was converted into intense heat resulting in a dramatic increase in temperature in the interior. Burns and asphyxiation claimed many lives. Rivets commonly used in the construction of heavy tanks were an additional hazard. A hit would cause rivets to burst out, pelting the crew with red hot metal. It was said that the screams of the dying trapped inside a blazing tank were never forgotten by those who heard them.

German grenadiers inspect the knocked-out hulk of an American light tank in Tunisia in 1943.

Even when men did manage to scramble out of a blazing tank in the desert they were frequently far from proper medical facilities and during engagements water for both fit and wounded was invariably in short supply.

Ahead lay the battle of El Alamein after which the Afrika Korps would be pursued to the final battles in Tunisia.

CAPTURED BRITISH TANKS

As the Afrika Korps began to retreat they also lost the battle for another important aspect of desert tank warfare: recovery and repair. Tanks knocked out in battles by shells, mines, or breakdown could not now be rescued on the retreat.

The allies always had numerical superiority in armoured fighting vehicles but axis forces managed to capture and utilise large numbers of allied equipment. For example, the axis victory at Benghazi in late January 1942 provided them with 96 tanks, 38 guns and some one hundred and ninety vehicles, of which a fair number were utilised. The German Afrika Korps was the most notable user of all kinds of captured equipment and it was reported that sometimes the inventory consisted of more captured equipment than that of German origin. On 12 February 1942 Panzer Abteilung z.b.V Panzer Armee Afrika, a special employment unit equipped entirely with captured British and American armoured fighting vehicles, was formed.

The oldest British tank captured by the Germans in North Africa was Medium Tank Mk II, which entered service in 1925. The Medium Tank Mk II was an obsolete vehicle by any standards at the time and even the hard-pressed Germans couldn't bring themselves to use them in service.

The two man Light Tanks, Mk IIA and Mk IIB, were used during the early part of the North African campaign and a small number were captured by the DAK and pressed into temporary service. The Mk IIA and Mk IIB received the German designation Leichter Panzerkampfwagen Mk II 733(e).

The two-man Light Tank Mk V was a further development of earlier light tanks, and also saw service in the early part of the North African campaign. As with the Mk IIA and Mk IIB, the small number which were captured by the Afrika Korps were pressed into temporary service as Leichter Panzerkampfwagen Mk IV 734(e).

The DAK also utilised other British vehicles, which had been previously encountered in France. The Matilda II, designated as Infanterie Panzerkampfwagen Mk II 748(e), was one which saw extensive service on the German side in the desert war. In early August 1941 the 15th Panzer Division's 8th Panzer Regiment had one platoon entirely made up of captured tanks including seven Matilda IIs. One of the captured Matilda IIs was nicknamed 'Dreadnought' by its British crew It was captured along with six more, at Halfaya Pass in May 1941. In late August 1941 seven Matilda IIs were transferred from the 8th Panzer Regiment to the 33rd Panzer Pionere (engineer) Battalion and, as of November 1941, there were still five Matilda IIs in service. In June 1941 the 21st Panzer Division's Panzer Regiment also had one platoon equipped with captured tanks, including Matilda IIs, but in August 1941 only one was still in service. In July additional Matilda IIs were captured near Bardia. The best known photo of a captured Matilda II from the 21st Panzer Division's Panzer Regiment was taken when Allied soldiers (possibly New Zealanders) recaptured it. Matilda IIs were easily repaired by German workshops. Unserviceable vehicles were scrapped for spare parts, and in some cases spare parts were even shipped from France where large numbers of Matilda II tanks, captured in May 1940, were still available. Some Matilda IIs turrets were mounted in the Halfaya Pass on concrete emplacements as fortifications.

The Cruiser Tank Mk VI (AI 5)Crusader, was the development of an unsuccessful Mk V Covenanter. It inherited Mk V's poor armour protection and unreliability but still saw extensive service in North Africa from 1941. The Crusader was produced in five variants: Mk VI Crusader I armed with a two-pounder, Mk-VI Crusader 1 CS armed with a 3inch Howitzer, Mk VI Crusader II armed with a two-pounder, Mk VI Crusader II CS armed with a three inch Howitzer, and the Mk VI Crusader III armed with a six-pounder. The first examples were captured as early as June 1941, and the Crusader received the German designation of Kreuzer Panzerkampfwagen Mk VI 746(e). A number of Crusaders were captured in good condition - due to the high incidence of mechanical breakdowns their crews often abandoned them. German repair shops were able to fix a number of them by using other Crusaders as sources for spare parts. In some cases parts were again shipped from France, where Crusader tanks captured in May 1940 were still available. Captured models of the Crusader type were pressed into either short-term service or long-term service, for example in the previously mentioned Panzer Abteilung z.b.V Panzer Armee.

The DAK had a platoon of Crusaders in service from February to December of 1942. Besides the vehicles in service with this unit, additional tanks were in service with a variety of units, including the 21st Panzer Division's 5th Panzer Regiment

and the 90th Light African Division's 605th Panzerjäger Abteilung. A Number of Crusader tanks were captured after the Sollum Battle of June 1941. When, on 13 May 1943 DAK surrendered, the few Crusaders which were still in service were recaptured. In general, the Germans liked Crusaders for their speed and manoeuvrability.

The British Infantry Tank Mk III Valentine was produced in eleven main variants designated Mk I to Mk XI. Allied forces in North Africa utilised the first five variants all armed with two-pounder (40mm) guns. The Valentine Mk I and Mk II were operated by a three-man crew, while the Mk III to Mk XI were operated by a four-man crew. The Germans designated Valentine as 'Infanterie Panzerkampfwagen Mk III 749(e)'. The Valentine was also used as a base for the Bishop self-propelled gun, armed with a 25-pounder (87.6mm) field gun, which also saw service in North Africa. In 1941/42 the Germans captured a number of Valentines, mainly Mk IIs, which were then pressed into service with (Beute) Panzer Abteilung z.b.V Panzer Armee Afrika, which had as many as 12 of them at any one time. Additionally, at least five Valentines were in service with the 90th Light African Division's 605th Panzerjäger Abteilung. A single Valentine was also shipped back to Kummersdorf for testing purposes. Probably the best known picture of a captured Valentine is that of Mk V in service with 10th Panzer Division's 7th Panzer Regiment in Tunisia in early 1943. Unserviceable tanks were either scrapped for parts or were dug in as defensive positions. When the DAK surrendered, a few Valentines, which were still in service, were recaptured by their former owners.

The four-man American M3 Light Tank armed with 37mm gun was known to the British unofficially as the 'Honey' and to the Americans as the 'Stuart'. The Honey saw service with the British before the arrival of American troops in North Africa, and then with Americans. Only a small number of Honey and Stuart light tanks were captured and pressed into service by DAK. They were designated as Panzerkampfwagen M3 740(a). On 22 and 23 November 1941 the 15th Panzer Division captured 35 Stuarts, most of which were badly damaged, near Gabr Saleh in Libya. A few were made serviceable and were maintained using spare parts from damaged vehicles. Twelve Stuart tanks captured in June

Inside the tank works tracks are tested for use with the Panzer III.

1942 were also pressed into service by the Panzer Company of Rommel's Kampfstaffel and remained in service as late as March 1943 in Tunisia. The M3 was followed by an improved version M5 Light Tank, also used in North Africa. Only a few M5 tanks were captured by DAK and temporarily used as Panzerkampfwagen M3 740(a).

The six-man American M3 Medium Tank was an interim solution before the introduction of M4 Sherman Medium Tank. It was produced in two versions designated as the 'Grant' and the 'Lee'. The Grant was a version produced with a British-designed turret and saw service with the British before the arrival of American troops in North Africa. The Lee was a standard version produced for the American Army. Both versions were armed with a turret-mounted 37mm gun and a hull-mounted 75mm gun. A Small number of M3 medium tanks were captured by DAK and pressed into temporary service as Panzerkampfwagen M3 747(a).

DIEPPE 1942

On 19 August 1942 allied forces made up mainly of Canadians performed an unsuccessful raid on the French port of Dieppe, code-named Operation Jubilee. The raid was unsuccessful, with a high casualty rate because of the incorrect assessment of the German strength in the area including the presence of the 10th Panzer Division. The landing forces included some 30 Churchill tanks and some seven scout cars. Only 15 of the Churchills managed to leave the beaches before being stopped by roadblocks. It was, however, the first time that armoured fighting vehicles had taken part in an amphibious landing.

The five-man Infantry Tank Mk IV Churchill (A22) was largely based on experiences of the Western Front from 1914 to 1918, although the first was produced in May 1941. It was a slow and well-armoured tank with a design that resembled First World War tank mounted with a turret. The Churchill became the most important and successful of British tanks and was produced in ten main versions, along with a variety of special purpose tanks. Three main models of Churchills were used during the Dieppe raid. The Mk I was armed with a turret-mounted two-pounder (40mm) gun and a hull-mounted three inch (76.2mm) Howitzer. The Mk II had a machine gun instead of the Howitzer and the Mk III was armed with a turret-mounted six-pounder (57mm) gun. The Germans captured and salvaged 23 Churchill infantry tanks, most damaged after heavy fighting. The most numerous was Mk III, of which ten were acquired, along with five Mk II and six Mk I tanks, although only a few were in a state to be repaired. Vehicles beyond repair were scrapped for spare parts and then used for target practice or other training exercises. A single example of every model was transferred to the Army Weapons Office for evaluation and testing purposes. A small number of Churchills, mainly Mk III were taken into German service, including one Mk III nicknamed 'Blondie', previously commanded by Corporal Jordan. Churchills equipped the Captured Panzer Company, which in late 1942 became Panzer Regiment 100. In late 1943 there were still two Mk III tanks in service with Panzer Regiment 100 and they were eventually transferred to Panzer Abteilung 205 in early 1944. It was very hard to maintain Churchills in running condition since there were only spare parts available from scrapped tanks along with a limited supply of ammunition. One of the Mk III tanks was personally inspected by Albert Speer, the Minister for Armaments and Munitions. The Churchill received the German designation of Infanterie Panzerkampfwagen Mk IV(e).

BARBAROSSA

A propaganda image which has become one of the most famous of World War II is this study of a Panzer III from the 18th Panzer Division crossing the River Bug in June 1941.

"Seven weeks of the most important and historic events are behind us. Stalin's main armies are shattered, his powerful Panzer forces are almost completely destroyed. The door to Moscow has been forced open, the Reds will will not succeed in closing it again."

Generaloberst Hoth, August 1941

The launch of Operation Barbarossa, the invasion of the Soviet Union, on 22 June 1941, was Hitler's most desperate gamble of the Second World War. It was a gamble Hitler felt compelled to take, if his ambition of the complete subjugation of Europe was to become a reality. Four-fifths of Germany's total armies, three million men, were committed to the most appalling conflict in the history of warfare.

In 1941 the conquest of Russia would not only have provided Germany with the agricultural and industrial supplies to ensure Hitler's mastery of Europe, it would have simultaneously rid him of the only military power capable of challenging his domination. The deaths of tens of millions of Russians was not simply an economic necessity, their destruction would pave the way for the 'Grossraum', a concept already under development by Heinrich Himmler as the culmination of Hitler's call for 'Lebensraum'. The Grossraum was envisaged as a gigantic Germanic state stretching from the Atlantic Ocean in the west to the mountains of the Urals, in the east.

Standing between Hitler and the realisation of

this vision were the armies of the Union of Soviet Socialist Republics, a fighting force whose condition of unpreparedness was a testament to the paranoia of its political leadership and the excesses of a state which vied with Germany in the extent of its totalitarian oppression. Hitler's first Barbarossa directive ominously stated that the USSR might be invaded even before the war with Great Britain was over.

Though Stalin accepted that war was now inevitable, he believed Russia had until the spring of 1942 to prepare herself. His fanatical rejection of counter-information was so fierce that vital intelligence concerning German preparations was kept from him by subordinates fearful of the violence of his reaction.

As the German build-up toward Operation Barbarossa continued, Stalin's attempts to pacify Hitler grew more desperate. He had already stated in an interview with PRAVDA in November 1939 that it was not Germany who had attacked Britain and France, but Britain and France who had attacked Germany. Stalin now forbade any criticism of Germany to be printed in the newspapers. He increased Russian supplies to Germany and withdrew recognition of the Norwegian and Belgian governments in exile. When Hitler successfully invaded Greece and Yugoslavia, Stalin expelled the Yugoslavian ambassador to Moscow and refused a request to recognise the Greek government in exile.

Stalin felt he was continuing to buy time by these unrequited concessions, but the breathing space he obtained was totally devoid of any worthwhile attempt to remedy his military disadvantages. By May 1940 170 Soviet divisions were stationed in newly occupied Polish territories, with the result that over half the army were occupying positions with fortifications and rearward communications which were incomplete. Indeed, by June, with a German attack imminent, Western Special Military District was a complete shambles.

Many formations were between six and seven thousand men short of wartime establishment. Numbers of experienced personnel had been hived off to build new tank and aviation units. Only one of six mechanised Corps had received their full complement of equipment. Three of the four motorised divisions had no tanks and four out of every five vehicles in the tank fleets were

obsolete. Four of the Corps had only one quarter of their designated motor vehicles, and in another Corps one in three motor vehicles needed repairs. Therefore, although the opposing forces had amassed vast amounts of weaponry along their common borders, the Soviet Red Army and the German Wehrmacht were anything but equal adversaries.

The awesome German armies, which the 170 under-strength divisions of the Russian troops faced, were divided into three large groups. These consisted of 148 fully manned and equipped divisions of which 19 were Panzer and 15 Panzer Grenadier divisions. The Army Group South was commanded by Field Marshall Gerd von Runstedt and was charged with seizing Kiev and taking control of the Ukraine as far as the river Dnieper. Field Marshall von Bock's Army Group Centre was to strike towards Smolensk. Army Group North under Field Marshall von Lieb was to attack through the Baltic States and seize Leningrad.

The three German army groups were supplemented by 500,000 Finnish troops advancing from their homeland in 14 divisions and 150,000 Romanians attacking along the Black Sea towards Odessa. These forces, together with the Luftwaffe, which had devoted 80 per cent of its operational strength - 2,770 aircraft - to the build up of Barbarossa, fielded over three thousand three hundred and fifty tanks, over seven thousand artillery pieces, 60,000 motor vehicles and 625,000 horses.

There was, however, one vital flaw in the German organisation, previously mentioned - the questionable decision to reduce the tank strength of each of the divisions from a two-regiment brigade to a single regiment. At a stroke the tank strength of the division was reduced from 340 to 170 tanks. The initial compensation for the dilution of strength in the Panzer Divisions came in the form of the deployment of more Divisions. The resulting Panzer Divisions within each of the separate army groups were bought together to form miniature Panzer armies. By concentrating a number of Panzer divisions together the Germans were able to achieve a massive local superiority of numbers at the point of decision. In the early part of the campaign the far-sighted use of armoured formations went a great deal towards offsetting the dilution of the tank strengths of the Divisions.

The Russian army still clung to its peacetime

structure. Should war occur, each military district would be transformed into army groupings similar in structure to the German forces opposing them. The Soviet Northern front was to repel advances through the Balkans and defend Leningrad from Finnish attack. The North-West, West and South-West fronts would engage the three main German army groups, and the Southern front would deal with any advance towards Odessa.

Behind these lines, the contrast between the warring nations could not have been greater. While Germany boasted one of the finest industrial infrastructures in the world, Russia had still not completed her industrial revolution. By 1941 a generation of upheaval had left its mark economically and psychologically. Revolution and civil war had been followed by the destruction of the peasantry and their enforced collectivisation. Whole segments of the population had been uprooted and transported to work the new industries set up in the mineral rich regions of Siberia, the Urals and Kazakstan.

At 4am on the 22 June 1941 the maelstrom that was Barbarossa finally erupted. The German armies of the Blitzkrieg sliced through the

Russian forces on every front. Faced by the results of his intransigent refusal to act, Stalin became frozen with indecision. While his army headquarters desperately tried to piece together the most rudimentary picture of what was happening, he ordered an immediate counter-offensive on all fronts. As the first reports of the devastation his own command had helped to create filtered through, he was shattered.

"All that Lenin created we have lost forever," he declared. He finally retreated to his dacha, not to emerge until 3 July.

At the front, the concerted rapier thrusts of the German Panzer divisions were skewering through the chaotic Russian defences. The Panzer groups created deadly breaches in the Soviet line, slicing the Red Army forces into isolated segments. The supporting German divisions then moved forward in encircling advances which surrounded these pockets of defenders. The ferocity and effectiveness of the Panzer attacks were so great that some of the pockets were gigantic. Groups of up to fifteen Russian divisions were surrounded and mercilessly bludgeoned into surrender.

The encirclement of Minsk by the right flank of

The effects of the long campaign have begun to show on these Panzer IIIs halted in a Russian village just before the onset of winter 1941.

The men of the Panzertruppen were as ill-prepared as the rest of the German army for the onset of the Russian winter. These men are wearing 1941 pattern greatcoats which proved to be hopelessly inadequate for the conditions. In the case of the vehicles the situation was even worse; neither lubricants nor machinery had been designed to withstand the conditions they were about to face.

Army Group North and the left flank of Army Group Centre yielded 300,000 prisoners, 2,500 tanks and 1,400 artillery pieces. Thirty-two of the 43 Russian divisions were destroyed within a week and the road to Moscow penetrated to a depth of 300km.

The remainder of Army Group North led by Panzer Group IV, under Hoepner, scythed into the Baltic States, capturing Riga, the Latvian capital. Only in the south were the German forces limited to shallow advances toward Lvov and Rovno.

On the ground chaos reigned. The Luftwaffe were pulverising the road and rail links behind the Russian lines. Many Russian officers were not even using code in their desperate radio requests for instructions from their headquarters. Struggling masses of uncoordinated troops were being slaughtered by the German troops as they attempted to obey Stalin's orders to counter-attack. Others were being machine-gunned by their own military police for fleeing from positions which were worse than hopeless.

By 3 July the battle for the frontier was over. The German armies had advanced along a line from the river Dvina in the north to the Dnieper in the south. General Halder, Chief of German General Staff, declared that the war against the Soviet

Union had taken only 14 days to win. But German intelligence had totally underestimated the reserves which Russia could command. By 1 July 5,300,000 men had been mobilised and Stalin had emerged from his isolation to broadcast a message of patriotism and resistance to the nation. For once, the Russian people were told the truth. The pre-war complacency which Stalin had done so much to foster had rapidly to be undone. Stalin now took direct control of the Red Army. But the general mobilisation of Russian troops failed to curtail the German advance.

Four reserve armies of 37 divisions were despatched to bolster West Front in the general area of Smolensk. The Germans countered with yet another encirclement and the Panzer groups of Generals Hoth and Guderian smashed through the Soviet line and manoeuvred 300,000 Russian troops into an indefensible pocket. Another 150,000 prisoners, 2,000 tanks and 2,000 artillery pieces fell into German hands.

Goebbels announced that: "The eastern continent lies like a limp virgin in the mighty arms of the German Mars".

Army Group South finally broke through the Russian South-West Front and another pocket yielded a further toll of 100,000 prisoners.

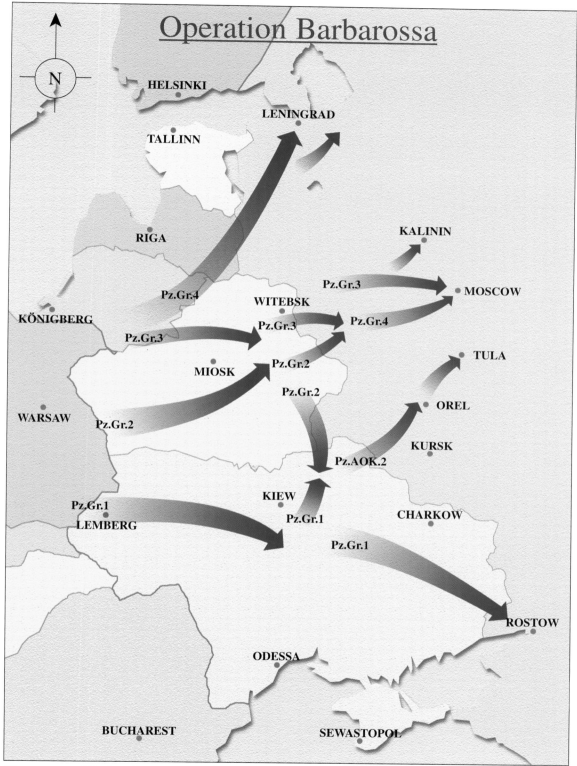

Operation Barbarossa

N

HELSINKI

LENINGRAD

TALLINN

RIGA

KALININ

Pz.Gr.4

WITEBSK

Pz.Gr.3

MOSCOW

KÖNIGBERG

Pz.Gr.3

Pz.Gr.3

Pz.Gr.4

MIOSK

Pz.Gr.2

TULA

Pz.Gr.2

WARSAW

Pz.Gr.2

OREL

Pz.Gr.2

Pz.AOK.2

KURSK

KIEW

Pz.Gr.1

LEMBERG

Pz.Gr.1

CHARKOW

Pz.Gr.1

ROSTOW

ODESSA

BUCHAREST

SEWASTOPOL

The progress of the four Panzer groups during the initial phases of Operation Barbarossa and Operation Typhoon from May to December 1941.

WITTMANN JOINS THE FRAY

Although the war in Russia began with Operation Barbarossa towards the end of June, the Leibstandarte wasn't initially committed, so the war in the Soviet Union for Michael Wittmann actually began a month later, in July 1941. It was like a second baptism of fire for Wittmann, who faced an attack by 18 Russian tanks on his Sturmgeschütze Battery's first day in action.

He had encountered nothing like this in Poland and Greece, but Wittmann was a natural fighter and he succeeded in knocking out six enemy tanks in succession. The rest fled the field in disarray. This was Wittmann's first striking success, and the incident provided the first signs of his supreme talent as commander of an armoured fighting vehicle.

On 12 July 1941, in recognition of his great feat on his first day in action in Russia, Wittmann was decorated with the Iron cross - Second Class.

But there was little time for celebration, as the advance continued.

The short 75mm gun of the German Assault gun in the early war years was an inferior weapon to the long 76mm gun of the Russian T-34 tanks, but despite this disadvantage Wittmann proved himself a master of armoured warfare.

Combat in Russia placed terrific demands on the assault gun crews. Frequently, Wittmann and his

Men of the 11th Panzer Division advance cautiously through the streets of a Russian village in December 1941.

crew were on their own, separated from the rest of the assault gun battery. In this hostile environment, he showed himself to be a successful lone fighter with initiative. Nevertheless, he remained popular with his comrades. Wittmann's gunner at that time, Otto Schalte, described him as a modest man; "Michael was a quiet, gifted, friendly NCO with firm goals in front of him."

With 2,000 miles of front to fight over, the German armoured forces were spread incredibly thinly. It was lucky for Wittmann that he was such a good lone warrior, as the assault guns were rarely employed en masse, as the standing orders required, so his skills were forged in the hard battles of the summer of 1941. Unit commanders were always happy to have an assault gun assigned to their sector, particularly one commanded by him.

The German advance along the Black Sea began in the first weeks of August 1941. Wittmann fought near Sasselje and Nowyj Bug from the 10-17 August and on the 19th at Kherson. In the course of the fighting for the port city of Kherson, a bizarre incident took place as the assault guns commanded by Wittmann and Beck engaged first an enemy gunboat, then a submarine. The gunboat was sunk, but the effects of the fire directed at the submarine are not recorded.

Wittmann had destroyed ten enemy tanks by this point in his career.

But his luck was about to change for the worse, as a direct hit on his vehicle, though it failed to penetrate the armour, nonetheless left Wittmann wounded in the face and back by shell fragments. However, Wittmann's tally continued to rise to 25 enemy tanks and 32 anti-tank guns destroyed. Yet combat losses were not just on the Russian side. Those on his own also rose steadily.

In February 1942 the depleted assault gun battery was brought up to battalion strength through new additions from Germany, and the transfer of a battery from the SS Wiking Division.

As a result of this expansion, Wittmann was made an SS officer candidate in early 1942. He left the battalion in June in order to attend the Candidate Training Course at the SS-Junkerschule in Bad Tolz. Wittmann learned tactical lessons which he combined with his practical battlefield experience. The 28-year-old Wittmann now served as Platoon Commander in the 2nd Company of the SS Panzer Replacement Battalion.

A mixed force of Panzer IIs and IIIs halt for the night in a Russian village at the time of Operation Typhoon in December 1941.

TOWN AND STREET FIGHTING

For the tank men the opening weeks of the offensive had gone like clockwork. However, all of the lessons from the Polish campaign had obviously not been fully assimilated and the German forces once again found themselves drawn into fighting for towns and cities, with resulting high casualties in men and machines.

In attacking a town or village, the German tactics were to employ flanking and encircling tactics. They attempted to cut off water, electricity, gas, and other utilities. While carrying out the flanking manoeuvre, they tried to pin down the defenders with heavy artillery fire and aerial bombardment. When it was necessary to make a direct assault, the German tactics were to concentrate all available heavy weapons, including artillery and air units, on one target. They favoured as targets for their massed fire the forward edges of the community, especially detached groups of buildings and isolated houses. During the artillery fire concentration the infantry would assemble and attack their objective immediately upon termination of artillery barrage. Tanks and assault guns accompanied the infantry, and with their fire immobilised any new enemy forces which appeared. They also supported the infantry in

sweeping away barricades, blasting passages through walls, and crushing wire obstacles. Guns and mortars were used against concealed positions, with anti-tank guns to cover side streets against possible flanking operations. Machine guns engaged snipers on roofs.

The immediate objective of the German thrust into a built-up area was to divide the area occupied by the enemy. These areas were then isolated into as many smaller areas as possible, in order to deny freedom of movement.

Russian armoured warfare was inhibited by Stalin's disenchantment with tank divisions, which had led him in the '30s to utilise his armour only in the support of infantry formations. After witnessing German successes on the western front, Stalin changed his mind, but a reorganisation on that scale meant that the reshuffle of Russian armour was not completed before the launch of Barbarossa. Even though Russian tanks outnumbered German two to one at the front and six to one overall, tactical ineffectiveness, obsolete models and widespread disrepair tipped the advantage overwhelmingly in favour of Germany during the first stages of the conflict.

But ground forces were only part of a Blitzkrieg operation, which saw German advances of up to fifty miles per day. The fast-moving Panzer Groups were again supported by Junkers Ju87 two-seater bombers, which were protected by Messerschmit 109 fighters. The Ju87, more familiarly known as the Stuka, was one of the most versatile machines of all time. Used as a night bomber, torpedo launcher, trainer, long range reconnaissance aircraft and for a host of other specialist tasks, it was at its most fearsome as a dive-bomber. Screeching out of the sky like some furious bird of prey, its airbrakes allowed it to slow to a speed which enabled its bomb load to be delivered with almost pinpoint accuracy.

THE ADVANCE CONTINUES

After a month of victorious progress, the German High Command were disconcerted by the rapidity of their own advance. Their armies were now fighting on a front 1,000 miles wide. The Stukas could no longer deliver the concerted hammer blows which had punched the holes in the Russian lines which the Panzers had so mercilessly exploited. Even though the Soviet airforce had by now lost approximately five thousand aircraft, the supply of replacements seemed endless. The factories in the east, which were churning out more effective fighter models, were out of Luftwaffe bombing range. The German air assault began to run low on fighters.

The Luftwaffe also had serious supply problems. The distance from home base and the destruction of the transport infrastructure meant that aircraft replacement parts had to be flown to forward airfields. The lengthening supply lines were also affecting the German ground forces. Tank commanders, hundreds of miles from their Polish depots, nevertheless pressed for the final thrust toward Moscow. They argued that only the continuation of the offensive would prevent the Russians from organising a fresh line of resistance. While many of Hitler's generals disagreed that such an attack should be launched immediately, they were almost unanimous in recommending that Moscow should become the primary objective of the next phase of the war.

Hitler, on the other hand, was worried about the possibility of the gaps between the Panzer divisions and the main armies being exploited by Russian reinforcements. He also feared that the hundreds of thousands of Soviet troops left behind the German lines in the wake of the advance might

co-ordinate their actions into an effective guerrilla movement.

Hitler had never been fully convinced of the importance of Moscow and continued to regard it as a secondary objective. The debate stretched out until mid-August. A vital month of summer weather was wasted. The Russians had the breathing space to throw reserve divisions into the gaps in their defences. Though barely trained, poorly equipped, some in the battered remnants of their civilian clothing, their stubborn ferocity meant that they were still a force to be reckoned with.

Eventually, the generals were silenced and two major objectives were prioritised: the capture of Moscow and the fall of the Ukraine.

A giant pincer movement, involving Guderian's Panzer Group II in a movement from the North and Panzer Group I under von Kleist who were to sweep up from the south, began to close its jaws on a huge pocket of Russian forces to the rear of Kiev. Field Marshall Zhukov, the Soviet Chief of Staff, pleaded with Stalin for a strategic withdrawal of the troops defending the city. He was dismissed from his post. Marshall Timoshenko, the newly appointed South-West commander, arrived just in

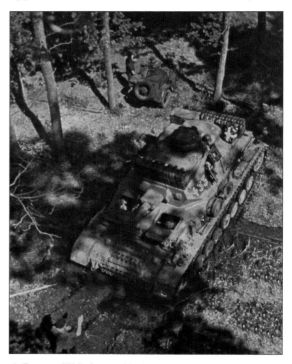

A Panzer IV being guided into a concealed position in a Russian forest.

time to see the Soviet divisions trapped. The 600,000 prisoners taken by the Germans remain the highest number ever captured in a single engagement.

The battle for the Ukraine now centred on the Crimean Peninsula where the right flank of Army Group South pressed the Soviet 51st army back towards Sebastapol. While half of the German Group Centre were engaged in subduing the Ukraine, Marshall Zhukov was transferred to the reserve forces behind West Front, and seized the opportunity to attack the German 4th army. Occupying a salient near Smolensk, the Germans were now themselves vulnerable to encirclement. The 4th army were thrown back 12km but, without sufficient tanks and aircraft, Zhukov failed to tighten the noose he had made. However, in terms of morale, Zhukov's counter thrust was highly significant. His action was the first substantial Soviet counter-attack of the war.

Hitler's response was to regroup Army Group Centre and prepare the most critical operation of the campaign. Operation Typhoon, the drive toward Moscow, was finally under way. Seventy divisions, spearheaded by the 1,500 tanks of Panzer Groups 2 and 3, would race toward the Russian capital before the rains of autumn or the snows of winter could halt their progress.

On 30 September General Heinz Guderian's 2nd Panzer Group almost inevitably broke through the Soviet line and had encircled the defending Bryansk Front by 6 October. Simultaneously, the Western Front, commanded by Marshall Timoshenko, fell into a similar trap. The pockets of Vyazma and Bryansk containing nine armies of 71 divisions were almost completely destroyed. Another 660,000 troops faced the grim brutality that the German army meted out to prisoners of war and the road to Moscow lay open.

In the Baltic States von Lieb's Army Group North had captured the city of Novgorod by 16 August, a vital target in the approach to Leningrad. The beleaguered defenders had fought to the death following the German discovery of the city's defensive plans on the corpse of a Soviet officer. General Hoepner's 4th Panzer Group resumed its drive toward Leningrad, but without supporting infantry its progress was limited.

Leningrad was a vital centre of the wartime production industry, and reserves and equipment were poured into the defence of the city. The

An early version of the Stug III moving up in support of the infantry through a blazing Soviet landscape.

citizens themselves formed into militia, divisions of which were flung against the Germans more in despair than hope. Following a basic training period averaging 16 hours, the first militia divisions were sent to the front, six days after being formed; the second, two days, and the third, the same day it was established.

Despite such gargantuan efforts, the first shells began to pour down on Leningrad early in September. With the arrival of the 18th Army to reinforce the Panzers on the 8th, the German stranglehold on the city tightened further. The capture of Schlusselburg to the east signalled the end of rail transport.

When Marshall Zhukov arrived to take over the defence of the city on 10 September, he found the defenders in an advanced state of disorganisation and the inhabitants close to panic. Undaunted, he briskly set about bolstering its defences. A shortage of anti-tank guns was dealt with by converting anti-aircraft artillery to the task of attempting to halt the Panzers. Six brigades of naval infantry and students were formed and reinforcements drafted in from the Karelian Isthmus. Zhukov began to take the fight to the Germans, through raids and counter-attacks, but by now the German troops had pierced the inner circle of defences and were rampaging through the suburbs.

After a furious exchange of advances and retreats, at the end of the month the defenders were still hanging on to their city by their fingernails. It seemed inevitable that Leningrad would capitulate.

But as Zhukov awaited a renewed assault, the 4th Panzer Group suddenly departed. They had been ordered south to join the battle for Moscow and the remaining German forces began to build siege lines. Leningrad would not now be taken by force, it would be starved into submission.

The German invaders now controlled all of western Russia on a line from Leningrad in the north to Rostov on the Black Sea, and the Red Army was still retreating before them. The countryside they left behind was a wasteland. The first few months of the war had robbed the nation of nearly fifty per cent of her grain-producing lands.

But the fighting spirit of the Russians was far from crushed. It had been inflamed by accounts of the slaughter of prisoners of war, and the murder and torture committed by the German invaders. Even the constant series of military reverses failed to dampen the ardour of defenders whose motherland had been ravaged.

THE T-34 MENACE

When Hitler ordered the conquest of Russia in the summer of 1941, confidence among the Panzer force was at an all time high. The desert war was progressing well and the German tactics of mixing tank and anti-tank forces together concealed the deficiencies in tank design, in some cases from the Germans themselves.

Despite the understandable cockiness of the German High Command, a few lessons from earlier campaigns had been absorbed, and the make-up of the tank force which shook Stalin to the core had a much higher proportion of the heavier Mark III and IV tanks, instead of the lightweight Panzer Is and IIs. This trend illustrated the steadily increasing reliance on heavier armour, which was to continue throughout the war. It was just as well, because the Wehrmacht was about to meet with a very nasty surprise.

After a few weeks of the campaign, during which the German armour had faced only obsolete Russian tanks such as the lumbering T-28 and the outdated BT-7, the German forces suddenly encountered two of the new Russian tanks which were to change the course of the war.

The first was the Heavy KV-I, a 46-ton monster, with superior heavy armour and a vicious 76mm gun capable of destroying any German tank from most ranges on the battlefield. In 1941 this was a deadly adversary indeed.

The Soviet KV-1 was a fine example of a tank

Photographic proof that even the legendary T-34 was not always equal to the Russian terrain. These three machines were bogged-down in marshy ground and abandoned by their crews. The wooden planks used to try and free the top machine are still visible.

made for specific conditions. It had broad tracks for dealing with mud and snow, and a diesel engine for operating in the coldest possible weather. It was a superb design and absolutely dominated the battlefield.

The other unpleasant surprise for the Germans was, of course, the arrival of the T-34, a medium tank far better armed and equipped than the German Mark IV. It was also better equipped to deal with the extreme Russian weather conditions. Its wide tracks made it equally at home in dry conditions or in the mud and snow. In addition, the sloping armour presented an angled front to German fire, designed to cause shells to glance off the armour.

The T-34 was to become the real nemesis of the German army. It was built for mass assembly, and the crude welding lines can be clearly seen on surviving examples. It was no beauty, but it was tough, and it possessed a rare in-built ability to be upgraded as the situation changed.

When the T-34 first appeared in service it was fitted with a 76mm gun and had a two-man crew in the turret. By 1944, the Soviets had not only up-gunned the tank to an 88mm weapon, they had also increased the turret size to enable it to take three men, which made for a far more efficient tank on the battlefield.

Although the Germans would devise better tanks, they could never hope to compete in terms of the sheer number of T-34s.

The T-34 was the most prolific tank of the Second World War and when we consider that the Soviets achieved that and moved their tank producing facilities right across the country under German pressure, it really is a remarkable achievement. The workmanship was crude enough to make the average British or American factory worker weep, but that was not the main concern for the Russians. They were out to produce as many reliable, tough fighting tanks as possible, and in the T-34 they achieved it.

Time and time again veterans of the Russian front will praise the T-34. Sixty years later, Russian Front veteran Gerhard Majewski recalled the effectiveness of the machines he fought against.

"The T-34 at its time was by far and away the best tank the world had ever seen. It was actually second to none. The shape is followed even to this day - the outline of the tank. It was the mother so to speak of all modern tanks. It was just right in

every respect, the guns, the armour, the speed, the lot."

The T-34 was by no means the best tank to emerge from the Second World War, but it was more than adequate for the task and the huge numbers manufactured would ultimately tip the balance of the whole war.

THE KV-I IN ACTION

It was now, almost too late, that the German High Command began to urgently request new tanks with superior armour and more effective guns, to combat the KV-1 and T-34. This report, from a unit of Panzer Group IV facing the KV-I for the first time, gives a clear indication of just how unprepared the German forces were when faced with the new breed of Russian armour:

"The Russian armoured force played only a subordinate role at the beginning of the war. In the advance of 1941, our troops encountered only small units which supported the infantry in the same manner as our own self-propelled assault guns. The Russian tanks operated in a very clumsy manner and were quickly eliminated by our anti-tank weapons. The Russians carried out counter-attacks with large tank forces, either alone or in combined operations with other arms, only at individual, important sectors.

On 23 June 1942 our 4th Panzer Group, after a thrust from East Prussia, had reached the Dubysa and had formed several bridgeheads. The defeated enemy infantry units scattered into the extensive forests and high grain fields, where they constituted a threat to our supply lines. As early as 25 June the Russians launched a surprise counter-attack on the southern bridgehead in the direction of Raseiniai with their hastily brought-up XIV Tank Corps. They overpowered the 6th Motorcycle Battalion which was committed in the bridgehead, took the bridge, and pushed on in the direction of the city. Our 114th Armoured Infantry Regiment, reinforced by two artillery battalions and 100 tanks, was immediately put into action and stopped the main body of enemy forces. Then there suddenly appeared, for the first time, a battalion of heavy enemy tanks of a previously unknown type. The tanks overran the armoured infantry regiment and broke through into the artillery position. The projectiles of all defence weapons (except the 88mm flak) bounced off the thick enemy armour.

The one hundred German tanks were unable to check the 20 Russian Dreadnoughts, and suffered losses. Several Czech-built tanks of the type 35(t), which had bogged down in the grain fields because of mechanical trouble, were flattened by the enemy monsters. The same fate befell a 150mm medium howitzer battery which kept on firing until the last minute. Despite the fact that it scored numerous direct hits from as close a range as 200 yards, its heavy shells were unable to put even a single tank out of action. The situation became critical. Only the 88mm flak finally knocked out a few of the Russian KV-1s and forced the others to withdraw into the woods.

One of the KV-1s even managed to reach the only supply route of our task force located in the northern bridgehead, and blocked it for several days. The first unsuspecting trucks to arrive with supplies were immediately shot afire by the tank.

There were practically no means of eliminating the monster. It was impossible to bypass it because of the swampy surrounding terrain. Neither supplies nor ammunition could be brought up. The severely wounded could not be removed to the hospital for the necessary operations, so they died. The attempt to put the tank out of action with the 50mm anti-tank gun battery, which had just been introduced at that time, at a range of 500 yards, ended with heavy losses to crews and equipment of the battery. The tank remained undamaged in spite of the fact that, as was later determined, it got fourteen direct hits. These merely produced blue spots on its armour. When a camouflaged 88mm flak gun was brought up, the tank calmly permitted it to be put into position at a distance of 700 yards, and then smashed it and its crew before it was even ready to fire. The attempt of engineers to blow it up at night likewise proved abortive. To be sure, the engineers managed to get to the tank after midnight, and laid the prescribed demolition charge under the caterpillar tracks. The charge went off according to plan, but was insufficient for the oversized tracks. Pieces were broken off the tracks, but the tank remained mobile and continued to molest the rear of the front and to block all supplies. At first it received supplies at night from scattered Russian groups and civilians, but we later prevented this procedure by blocking off the surrounding area. However, even this isolation did not induce it to give up its favourable position. It finally became the victim of a ruse. Fifty tanks were ordered to feign an attack from three sides and to fire on it so as to draw all of its attention in those directions. Under the protection of this feint it was possible to set up and camouflage another 88mm flak gun to the rear of the tank, so that this time it actually was able to fire. Of the 12 direct hits scored by this medium gun, three pierced the tank and destroyed it."

To combat the KV-I and the T-34 a new heavy tank was needed urgently, but, in the form of the Tiger, it wouldn't be available for at least a year.

To further compound matters, mistaken assessments based on experience in France, had led to even the heaviest German tank, the Mark IV, still being equipped with short barrelled 75mm guns which were developed for the infantry support role. While Germany scrambled to produce the new heavy tanks, the Mark IVs were urgently re-equipped with long barrelled 75mm guns which gave them the high velocity which was required to deal with the T-34. Extra welded steel skirts were also added as defence against the new Russian hollow charged weapons.

Measures like these helped to keep up the momentum of the German advance in 1942 but, all the while, the Panzer Divisions were increasingly hard pressed by the growing numbers of T-34s and KVIs. Guderian himself, in November 1941, ran into a T-34 ambush and he witnessed his force being completely destroyed. It was then that the Germans began to realise they were up against something which they had not counted on.

In the German Reich it was felt that the deadly 88mm anti-tank gun was the ideal weapon for the task of destroying the hordes of T-34s. But the '88' was originally designed as an anti-aircraft gun. It was very large and not designed to be carried in the turret of a tank. What the Germans now needed was a tank big enough to house such a gun and well armoured enough to withstand the punishment which it would receive on the battlefield. It would take time to develop such a machine and, in 1941, one stop-gap measure was to increase the production of assault guns in the form of the Sturmgeschütze, which utilised the Panzer III chassis and now also carried a high velocity 75mm gun.

There were two big advantages to the Sturmgeschütze. Firstly they were quicker and cheaper to produce, and secondly, they could actually fit a far larger gun than could normally be fitted into the turret of the Panzer III. The disadvantage, of course, was that the Sturmgeschütze would never be as effective in open battle as the Russian tanks. It had no turret to swing round, and to fire in a different direction meant moving the whole vehicle round.

In 1941 the puny 50mm gun was still the standard anti-tank armament for German Panzer III tanks. The experience of tank ace Herman Bix was typical of the desperate straits many German tank commanders now found themselves in. Bix saw a dozen of his shells bounce off a KV-I even at the closest ranges. Eventually he managed to silence the steel monster as it swung its turret to take aim against him by the expedient of a well aimed shot deliberately fired through the barrel of his opponents main gun.

Men like Bix were part of a new breed of German tank commanders who achieved incredible victories against superior forces. But these superior forces were now also armed with better equipment and a deadly race would now develop between the Russian capacity to manufacture more tanks and the Germans' ability to engineer better tanks.

Although the German engineers would prove themselves winners, they were let down by their manufacturing capacity. The German war effort was being run inefficiently and by 1942 Germany was being targeted by wave after wave of allied bombers which were reducing her war industries to rubble, while Stalin had wisely moved his factories back into the interior of Russia, out of harm's way. The workers from one tank factory actually walked along railway lines under German gunfire to get in the trains to be moved out. It was the largest industrial migration in the history of the world; well over one thousand nine hundred plants were moved eastwards.

GERMAN COMMAND TANKS

To compensate for the low quality of their guns, the Germans further extended their technological lead by refining the special command tanks which had the main guns removed to make room for additional radio equipment.

These command tanks (Befehlspanzer) were factory conversions of ordinary gun tanks which were used by relatively senior tank commanders at

This artist's impression conveys something of the shock which the German tank forces experienced under attack by the KV-1 for the first time. The superior power and armour of the KV-1 is well represented in this dramatic but accurate propaganda drawing for *Signal* magazine.

squadron, company, battalion or regiment level to observe and to coordinate the actions of their subordinates on the battlefield. Command tanks generally mounted extra wireless sets, for these purposes, and in order to incorporate these extra wireless sets and sometimes extra wireless operators, something usually had to be removed from the tank. Generally speaking this was either ammunition, which is extremely bulky, or the main armament of the tank itself. Obviously removing either, and particularly the main gun, considerably disadvantaged a command tank on the battlefield.

The cohesion which came from a smooth flow of commands was one of the obvious reasons that the inferior German tanks of 1941 and 1942 were able to overcome the superior T-34s and KV-Is, but these command tanks soon drew special attention and attempts were made to disguise them with dummy guns - a length of wood or pipe, fashioned to represent the main gun.

Even when a dummy gun was used, however, the extra wireless antennae needed were another way with which the enemy could identify enemy command tanks and knock them out. This disconcerting factor was not mitigated by the rigid German practice of numbering their tanks in sequence, starting with the commander's vehicle, which frequently carried the number 001, displayed prominently on the turret - a sure invitation!

During 1942, the Red Army's armada of T-34s was growing ominously. New Russian tank armies were coming into being, and in the wake of the terrible defeat at Stalingrad the German soldiers prayed for an answer. It was now a race between German engineering and Soviet manufacturing.

CAPTURED RUSSIAN TANKS

As the war progressed, a large number of captured Soviet T-60s were pressed into service by the Germans but rarely as combat tanks. The majority were used as light and medium artillery tractors with or without turrets designated as Gepanzerter Artillerie Schlepper T-60(r).

The T-70 light tank was designed as a replacement for the T-60; although it was an improved version, it was also operated by just a two-man crew, but its armament consisted of a turret-mounted 45mm gun and a 7.62mm machine gun. According to original German captured tank inventories, as of July 1943 there was only one T-70(r) as part of Army Group South and three tanks as part of Army Group Centre.

The Germans found the BT series tanks to be technically unreliable, but they were able to maintain a number of them by using other tanks for spare parts. Some BT series tanks were still in service in 1944. As of 15 October 1941, there were officially ten BT series tanks in service with German units: the 1st Panzer Division had two BTs, the 8th Panzer Division had three BT-7s and the 19th Panzer Division had five BTs. A number of BT tanks were also known to be in service with the 3rd SS (Motorised) Division, 'Totenkopf' and 4th SS Polizei Panzer Grenadier Division. BT series tanks were used a combat tanks until 1942, when they were relegated to second line duties, including policing and security, in the Ukraine and Byelorussia. They were still in service in 1944.

The T-28 Medium Tank was a six-man lightly armoured tank inspired by the British Vickers-Armstrong A6 Medium Tank. It was produced in four versions. There is no evidence of them being used by the Germans, but possibly a number were used as fixed fortifications, while the rest were scrapped.

Along with other tanks, the Soviet Army had two main heavy tanks in service as at 22 June 1941. These included some forty T-35 and approximately five hundred of the KV series heavy tanks.

The T-35 Heavy Tank was a 10-11 man multi-turreted tank inspired, to some extent, by the British Vickers A1E1 Independent Tank. It was produced in two versions and was armed with a single 76.2mm L/24 gun, two 37mm (model 1933) or two 45mm (model 1937) guns and six 7.62mm DT machine guns installed in five turrets. A number of these lumbering machines were captured intact by the Germans, either abandoned by their crews, or broken down through lack of fuel. The T-35A (model 1933) was an early production model designated by the Germans as Panzerkampfwagen T-35A 751(r), while T-35C (model 1937) was a late production model with conical turrets and was designated by the Germans as Panzerkampfwagen T-35C 752(r). It is also possible that in the confusion designation of Panzerkampfwagen T-35C 752(r) was also given to the SMK heavy tank (named after Sergius Mironovitch Kirov), which was a prototype of a T-35 replacement, eventually abandoned. T-35 tanks were of great of interest to the Germans, who inspected them carefully and took numerous pictures, although there is no evidence of them being used in combat. Possibly a few were used as fixed fortifications, while the majority were scrapped. It is also reported that the few that were kept in reserve were used by the Germans in the defence of Königsberg, Berlin and Kummersdorf in 1945.

In addition to the KV-I there were also KV-2 close support tanks armed with turret-mounted 152mm howitzer. The main armament was installed in a large slab-sided high turret and the vehicle was operated by a six-man crew. Two versions were produced: KV-2A model in 1940 and improved KV-2B model in 1941. The Germans designated captured KV-2 tanks as Sturmpanzer KV-2 754(r). Only a few were pressed into service because of their limited combat value and the need for constant maintenance. The most publicised captured KV-2 tank was taken near Dubno by the 2nd Battalion of the Regiment 'General Göring' on 29 June 1941. It was painted with this message '2./Regiment General-Göring donated to our Führer! Dubno 29.6.41'. This machine became the subject of numerous propaganda photographs and newsreels. In addition to the Dubno machine it is also known that 8th Panzer Division used a single KV-2 in the winter of 1942. Along with a single

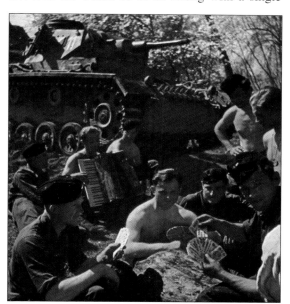

Tank crews relax in the shelter of a Panzer III during a brief lull in the fighting during the summer of 1941.

KV-I, another KV-2 was also shown during special exhibitions in Germany. This particular KV-2 was found in the Krupp factory in Essen in 1945, where it was used for target practice. A number of KV-2 tanks were extensively tested at Kummersdorf, while seven were ordered to be maintained in perfect condition for unknown reasons. Badly damaged tanks were used for spare parts and eventually scrapped. In 1942 a single KV-2 and a T-34/76 were used to form 66th Panzer Company for the planned Invasion of Malta, code-named Herkules. Overall, the Germans only pressed the KV-2 into limited and temporary service. According to original German captured tank inventories of July 1943, there was only one KV-2(r) as part of Army Group Centre.

THE STURMGESCHÜTZ IN RUSSIA

The Sturmgeschütz made a valuable contribution to the success of Operation Barbarossa, but, despite the initial successes, by late 1941 it was apparent that the German armoured force as a whole was seriously under-gunned. The armoured forces of the Wehrmacht were in danger of being swamped by the new Russian T-34 tanks.

We have seen that the short 75mm gun of the Sturmgeschütz was really designed to fire low velocity, high explosive shells in support of infantry formations, and although it used the relatively small chassis of the Panzer III, the fact that it had no turret allowed the Stug to be up-gunned to incorporate the deadly long-barrelled 75mm gun, which could not be fitted to a Panzer III.

With this gun, the Sturmgeschütz was now a match for the T-34, and much more than an infantry support weapon. It was now apparent that, with its low silhouette, the Stug was a much harder target to hit than the Russian T-34. The sloped armour also helped to deflect shots away from the vehicle, and the scales gradually began to tip back in Germany's favour during the fierce tank battles of 1942.

This much-needed upgrade was first incorporated into the Sturmgeschütz Model F in 1942. The long barrelled L/43 gun gave the armour piercing shells fired by the Geschütze a much higher muzzle velocity and therefore a far greater tank killing capability than the 50mm gun of the Panzer III. It was now obvious that the Panzer III had evolved as far as it could and the model was phased out. From 1943 the Panzer III chassis was used exclusively for the manufacture of Sturmgeschütze, production of which continued right up to the last days of the war.

The pressure of battle on the Eastern Front ensured that, almost by accident, the German forces had evolved a very successful example of a new breed of fighting vehicle - the Panzerjäger or Tank Hunters. It was in this role that most Sturmgeschütze were to be employed for the rest of the war, and 20,000 enemy tank kills were claimed by assault gun crews up to the early months of 1944.

The Sturmgeschütze manual stressed time and time again the need for the gun to be stationary when firing. In this way the highest level of accuracy was achieved. When the commanders heeded this request, the results were devastating.

In a mobile battle, where every second counts, the lack of a turret was a very real disadvantage, but Sturmgeschütze crews learned to adopt defensive tactics designed to lure Russian tanks into carefully constructed killing grounds.

The new tactics certainly worked, and in early 1943 there was another increase in gun power with the introduction of the long 48calibre gun, which gave extra velocity.

It was this new gun which equipped the definitive Sturmgeschütze, the Model G, of which 7720 were eventually manufactured. The sheer number produced is a reflection of just how effective and popular it was in battle.

By comparison to the 11,500 Sturmgeschütze manufactured, only 4,500 Panzer IIIs, 6,800 Panzer IVs and 6,000 Panthers were manufactured in the same period.

While the turreted tanks took on the role of the battlefield rovers, designed to forge ahead of the infantry in wide ranging strategic advances, it was the Sturmgeschütze which accompanied the Grenadiers during the dogged fighting on the ground. As the war dragged on, they became the infantry's rock in defence and his armoured fist in attack.

By 1943 the Sturmgeschütz was an indispensable part of both the Panzer Division and the ordinary infantry division. The infantry soon came to know that as long as the Geschütze were in the line, things were in control.

Extraordinary results were achieved by skilled

A Panzer III of the 11th Panzer Division rumbles past a blazing farm in the opening days of the Russian campaign.

crews in Russia, who sometimes accounted for dozens of Russian machines in a single action. In those actions, a major issue for the Sturmgeschütze commanders was the limited fuel and ammunition capacity of their cramped vehicles which produced a constant need to leave the battlefield. As the war progressed, the soldiers in the front line increasingly took strength from the presence of the Geschütze, so the tactical manual for their employment went to great lengths to stress the importance of the Sturmgeschütz commander keeping his infantry commanders informed that his guns were leaving the line only to re-arm and re-fuel.

It was a standard rule of Sturmgeschütz tactical doctrine that, if possible, not all machines would be withdrawn from the line at the same time, but that they should leave the field in relays, otherwise there was a real danger that the morale of the infantry might collapse if they saw their beloved Geschütze withdrawing from the field.

Despite its undoubted success as a tank killer, there was still an infantry support role for the Sturmgeschütz. The low trajectory 7.5mm gun was an excellent anti-tank gun, but to reach infantry hiding behind obstacles or other terrain features, a high trajectory howitzer was still required. A further 1,100 Sturmgeschüetze were therefore manufactured with the 10.5cm Howitzer which packed a deadly, high explosive punch which could be used in support of the infantry, either in attack or (more usually) desperate defence. The theory was that for every two troops of 75mm armoured Geschütze to deal with enemy tanks, there would be one troop of howitzer-armoured Geschütze to deal with the infantry. Problems with supplies of vehicles meant that this situation was very rarely achieved in practice.

The tactics set down for cooperation between the two types of assault guns was that the guns armed with 7.5cm guns would target any enemy armour, while the howitzer-armoured vehicles would concentrate on the infantry who accompanied the tanks. In this way, countless Russian attacks came to grief on the bulwark provided by the Sturmgeschütze battalions.

By 1943 the obvious success of the Sturmgeschütz in the field led the allies to target the Alkett factory responsible for the production of Stug IIIs for priority bombing. The resultant saturation bombing severely damaged the production factories.

During the period of rebuilding production was switched from Alkett to the Krupp's tank works, but Krupp made Panzer IVs not Panzer IIIs.

During 1943 the 1500 Sturmgeschütze manufactured by Krupp used the Panzer IV tank chassis, combined with the highly successful L/48 gun. These machines, known as Sturmgeschütze IVs, were no less successful than the old Stug IIIs.

By the end of the war over thirty thousand enemy tanks had been destroyed by the Geschütze crews, a ratio of approximately three enemy vehicles to every Stug deployed. It was a mark of the achievement of the guns and the crews that Russian orders forbade their tank commanders from entering into anti-tank duels with the Geschütze head to head, ordering them instead to manoeuvre to find the weaker side and rear armour.

One famous variant of the Stug IV was a real heavyweight, the forerunner of the SturmTiger. This was the mighty Brumbär (the grizzly bear, or grumbler), which carried a powerful 15cm Howitzer. The Brumbär had sloping frontal armour 100mm thick and was designed to rumble up to infantry fortifications before firing its massive shell at point blank range.

The Brumbär was originally developed to cope with the close-quarter street fighting at Stalingrad but delays in production meant that they did not see active service until the battle of Kursk in 1943.

After Kursk, Germany was largely fighting a defensive war, but on the few occasions when the Brumbär saw action they acquitted themselves well, and over three hundred were produced by the end of the war.

The eventual production of Sturmgeschütze totalled some 11,500 vehicles, more than any other mark of German fighting vehicle. There were sound reasons for this, as not only was the Sturmgeschütz successful on the battlefield, it was also far less expensive, quicker and easier to manufacture than fully turreted tanks built on the same chassis - a vital consideration for Germany's hard pressed manufacturing industry. German armies on all fronts were desperate for armoured fighting vehicles to stem the flood of Russian and allied armour, so production resources were increasingly switched to the production of Sturmgeschütze, which were well suited to fighting a defensive war.

THE WESTERN DESERT 1942-1943

A Tiger on its way to the front is the subject of intense interest from the locals during the final battles for Tunisia.

"A tank battle of extreme violence developed with heavy casualties on both sides. Their ammunition supply was inexhaustible. Our situation on the other hand was now desperate. During the course of the day we shot off 450 tonnes of ammunition and received only 190 tonnes. Even that was delivered by destroyers to Tobruk, 300 miles away."
Lieutenant-General Fritz Bayerlein, on El Alamein

In the weeks that followed the battle of Alam el Halfa a steady supply of reinforcements, munitions and supplies poured into the British camp. The Sherman M3 Medium tank known to the British as 'The Grant' greatly strengthened British firepower with its 75mm gun. Montgomery was preparing to attack the German's position at El Alamein but had resolved that the men under his command would never be needlessly sacrificed. The offensive would begin on the night of 23 October 1942.

As the initial 1000 gun artillery barrage began, the British and Commonwealth forces outnumbered the Germans and Italians almost two-to-one in men and tanks, and had vastly superior air power. Montgomery could rapidly make good any losses, with the Royal Navy dominating the Mediterranean; Rommel could not. More critically, the Afrika Korps possessed only one-tenth of the fuel which they required for full operational mobility, and operations would soon be restricted. There had also been widespread outbreaks of disease amongst the German forces and Rommel himself had fallen ill. On the first day of the battle of El Alamein Rommel was convalescing in Austria.

Montgomery's initial plan was for a major thrust to the north screened by a feint to the south. The first two days were spent probing passages through the deep minefields in what Montgomery called the 'crumbling process' - the wearing down of the enemy's entrenched defences. The German anti-tank positions proved too resilient and the hope for breakthrough into the open desert to the German rear did not succeed.

The adaptable Montgomery decided on a change of tactics and on 28 October he struck north towards the coast. Rommel rapidly and successfully countered. In these fierce tank battles the Germans were destroying four machines for every one lost. Montgomery again changed tactics and a third attack began on November 2nd. It met with fierce resistance and at the end of the day 200 tanks on both sides were out of action, but a corridor had been forced through the German defences. The two armoured divisions comprising the main striking arm of the Afrika Korps had now dwindled to 2,000 men and some thirty-five tanks.

On 3 November Rommel was forced to organise a general withdrawal. Montgomery had won the battle for El Alamein.

It was now that Montgomery's instinctive caution worked against him. The follow-up was slow and hesitant. With a combination of skill and luck Rommel's small forces eluded the vastly superior British and Commonwealth forces. However, Operation Torch was just round the corner and on 8 November British and American Forces began to land in north-west Africa. Rommel launched his last counter-attack on 16 March in an attempt to hold the Mareth line in Libya, but it was easily beaten off. Shortly thereafter he was recalled to Germany. Hitler was disappointed in his Field Marshall but he wanted him well out of the way before the ignominy of final capitulation.

TIGERS IN THE DESERT

The Western Allies first encountered the legendary Tiger tank in Tunisia in December 1942. Rommel's desert war had been going from bad to worse for the hard pressed men of the Afrika Korps, and they urgently needed a morale booster.

They got it in the form of the new Panzer VI - the Tiger. Its appearance came as an unpleasant surprise and was a shock to the Allies. The Tiger boasted a squat purposeful shape, and its deadly high velocity gun attained such notoriety that soon the mere appearance of the Tiger on the battlefield was enough to cause panic in the allied forces. The psychological power of the Tiger legend was so powerful that the sighting of any German tank force was enough to set the rumour running that Tigers were on the way.

With the very limited numbers which actually reached Tunisia, the Tiger menace was in some respects as much psychological as physical; nonetheless, that was no consolation for the allied tank crews who actually met the Tiger. Tank crews of the Allied Forces were disadvantaged by the superior range, killing power and armour of the Tigers. Allied tank men watched in horror as their own shells simply bounced off its thick armour plate.

In response to the Allied landings under Operation Torch in November 1942, the German high command had at last sent reinforcements to the hard pressed German forces in Tunisia. At an earlier meeting, Hitler had personally promised Rommel that he would have the new Tiger tank as soon as it was available and, sure enough, it was among the reinforcements to arrive in Tunisia, but as with all of Hitler's pledges, there were certain omissions.

The actual Tiger strength which appeared was just two companies of Schwere Panzer Abteilung 501, with 18 tigers each, and one company of the Schwere Panzer Abteilung 504 with eight machines. These units later merged to form one Abteilung.

The miracle machines were in such short supply that it led to a certain amount of unseemly squabbling among the German commanders. Field Marshall Rommel recorded that, before the start of his thrust towards Tebessa, he had asked General Von Arnim to send him the 19 Tiger Tanks that were with the Fifth Panzer Army. Von Arnim demurred on the grounds that all Tigers were undergoing repair. Rommel later pointed out with some pique that this statement was patently untrue.

Against all expectations a British Army unit, 48 Royal Tank Regiment, actually captured one of the precious Tigers at Medjez El Bab on 21 April 1943. The Tigers, in company with supporting Panzer III and IV tanks, had already taken out the leading machines in a formation of Churchill tanks, when a shot from one of the remaining Churchill's six-pounder guns hit the bottom of the Tigers' gun mantlet. The shell was deflected into the turret ring, which jammed the gun turret. Another shell then hit a turret lifting bracket and wounded the Tiger's commander. The German crew then abandoned the Tiger, allowing the British to capture an intact tank.

Shipped back to Britain, the tank was stripped down and provided much intelligence on German tank technology. That same Tiger tank, number 131 of 504 Schwere Panzer Abteilung, now rests at Bovington Tank museum, England.

Having been forced out of Libya and with German forces now in and around Mareth, Rommel intended to concentrate the mass of his motorised force and attack the British/American Forces in Western Tunisia with the aim of forcing withdrawal. This operation, code named 'Spring Wind', saw the capture of the Faid and Kasserine Passes through the hills as crucial. Rommel stated that he feared no effective attack from Montgomery during this phase, until the British had mustered powerful air and artillery forces.

The 21st Panzer Division, up to strength again and now under the command of 5th Panzer Army Afrika, was to attack Faid pass. The pass was required as a start point for the thrust to Sidi Banzed and Sbeitla. The attack was a success, resulting in the capture of over one thousand six hundred American prisoners and 150 tanks, including 86 US medium tanks. All of these machines were part of the US First Division.

With the movement of the Germans in the area the Allies put all forces they could muster into northern Tunisia. Fighting came down to control of the passes. The weather made the going bad for vehicles but at the same time kept the Allied Air Force at home. Air attacks would have been disastrous within the confines of the narrow passes.

Rommel thought the Allies weaker at Kasserine than at Sbiba, therefore he placed the weight of his attack there on 20 February 1943. Panzer Grenadier Regiment 'Menton' attacked, but was halted by well-placed American artillery and mortar fire from the surrounding hills. The 10th Panzer Division's Motor Cycle Battalion was thrown in to the fray. 'Nebelwerfers' were also deployed for the first time in Africa and proved very effective. By 5pm the Germans controlled the Kasserine Pass.

A US Armoured Group situated in a side pass was to have aided the Kasserine defenders. Rommel pushed the 8th Panzer Regiment across the Hatab River and caught this US Force by surprise.

A constant flow of JU52 transport aircraft was required to ferry in fuel, seen being collected together in the foreground.

A Panzer IV rolls past the wreckage of a knocked-out British light tank in the Western desert campaign in 1943.

Opening fire at point-blank range the Germans devastated the Americans. The 8th Panzer Division also captured 20 US tanks and 30 armoured troop carriers, most of which were towing 75mm anti-tank guns.

Rommel kept the 10th Panzer Division and the Afrika Korps column around the Kasserine area in case of a counter attack. However, during the night they moved northwards along the Kasserine-Thalu road and westwards to Tebessa. But the enemy had gone.

Driving through the debris of the aftermath of the battles Rommel was impressed with the Americans who the Germans had described as 'fantastically well equipped'. He went on to say: 'We (the Germans) had a lot to learn organisationally. One particularly striking feature was the standardisation of their vehicles and spare parts.' British experience had been put to good use in American equipment.

Although the Tigers had played a major part in the battle it would be true to say that, had the allied planes put in an appearance, things would have been very different. Also, of course, for the American troops it was their first meeting with the Panzers.

UPGRADING THE GERMAN ARMOUR

During 1942 the German response to the superior numbers of allied tanks lay in the development of more new tanks and up-gunning existing models. The Tiger and Panther were on their way, but in the meantime the Panzer IV was now the mainstay of the German Tank Divisions and it was still found to be capable of further development.

Only a few modifications were required to upgrade the tank to accept the highly effective long-barrelled L/43 gun, although the gun itself had to be fitted with a muzzle brake in order to prevent the gun recoil from taking off the breechblock. (The muzzle brake on a gun is fitted on the barrelled end to allow gases to vent from behind the shell before it leaves the muzzle, thus reducing the recoil force). Many of the early Panzer IVs were actually fitted with the new long L/43 gun in the field.

The last variants of the Panzer IV to appear in Africa were fitted with a more powerful gun, the L/48, which fired a shell at even higher velocity.

The Panzer IIIs in the desert theatre were also modified. The increased use of the Panzer IV in the anti-tank role left a need for infantry support tanks. The British called these upgraded tanks the 'Specials'. As the Panzer IV was being fitted with the long-barrelled 75mm the Panzer III was now fitted with the short-barrelled infantry support gun which had originally equipped the Panzer IV. In effect the two tanks had swapped roles in mid-campaign.

After the fall of Tripoli on 23 January 1943 the Afrika Korps fell back before the advancing

British Eighth Army. The Germans left in their wake mines, booby traps and demolitions. These caused problems for the British troops unable to deploy off the main axis route due to salt marshes and soft sand.

The Germans next stand was at the Tadjera hills, which sat on the approach to the Mareth Line. A brilliant move by 22nd Army Tank Brigade put the British in a position to bring effective fire upon the Germans. This resulted in the German forces abandoning the Tadjera position, allowing British observation of the Mareth Line.

The Mareth Line lay 80 miles inside the frontier of Tunisia between the sea and the Matmata hills. The Mareth Line has been 'over-rated as a defensive line. The original defences were a line of antiquated blockhouses built by the French, of little use in modern warfare, except as shelter from artillery fire. The French had also believed that either a salt marsh or steep wadis would stop attackers, and that it could not be outflanked.

Rommel's inspection of the area led him to believe that well-trained soldiers could surmount these difficulties. The British advance proved him correct.

Rommel had wished to concentrate on the Akarit line, which could not be outflanked, but his superiors thought otherwise. On 15 February 1943 the rearguard of the 15th Panzer Division took up these positions in the Mareth Line. The long retreat from El Alamein was over.

This was Rommel's command position from which he commanded his last action in the desert war; the writing was on the wall for the Afrika Korps.

Rommel, now a disillusioned and physically sick man, was ordered to leave his beloved Africa Korps on 9 March 1943. He flew back to Europe, deep in despair about the approach of the inevitable end. Hitler this time refused to allow him to return to Africa where his men, now under the command of General von Armin, soldiered on. The axis forces retreated all the way into Tunisia and to Enfidaville, some twenty-five miles south of the Cape Bon peninsula and between the mountains and the sea. Here the 90th Light Division dug in around the hills while the 21st Panzer Division prepared to meet a head on thrust from the massed allied forces.

During the first days of May an incredibly ferocious artillery and air bombardment ripped into the German positions. At the heart of the defence of Tunis the 15th Panzer made a desperate last attempt to combat the overwhelming allied forces.

Inspecting one of a group of knocked-out British Matildas. These machines were taken and used by the Afrika Korps in surprisingly large numbers.

A Bersaglieri despatch rider from the Italian Ariete division arriving with a message at an Sd Kfz 263 eight-wheeled radio car.

The guns fired until there was no more ammunition. The tanks, when their petrol was gone, carried on firing from where they stopped until they, too, ran out of ammunition. The official report of Army Group Africa preserved to this day, records simply: 'The bulk of 15th Panzer Division must be deemed to have been destroyed'.

In early May, slowly, reluctantly, the white flags of surrender began to appear from the men whom Hitler had ordered to fight to the last. The allies marched triumphantly into Tunis. Rommel's Afrika Korps had existed for two years and three months. Out-gunned, out-supplied, out-numbered, but rarely out-manoeuvred, the Afrika Korps marched proudly into the pages of German military history.

CAPTURED ALLIED TANKS

The four-man American M4 Sherman medium tank armed with the 75mm gun was to become the main and most numerous American produced tank of the war. The DAK first encountered British-operated Shermans in October 1942, and then American operated Shermans in Tunisia. A small number of Shermans were captured by the Afrika Korps and designated as Panzerkampfwagen M4 748(a). One particular machine was nicknamed 'War Daddy' from the 3rd Battalion of the 5th American Armoured Division, captured by Corporal Thull of the 501st Schwere Panzer Abteilung, a heavy tank unit equipped with Tiger tanks. It was taken on 22 February 1943, near Sbeitla in Tunisia, and shortly after was sent over to the Army Weapons Office in Germany for evaluation and tests. Later on, in mid- 1943, 'War Daddy' took part in the tests with early model Panther Ausf D to 'prove' the Panther's superiority, which were staged for propaganda purposes. In the resulting newsreel the enthusiastic commentator shrieked with delight as the American-made machine failed to live up to the performance of the Panther. 'General Sherman fell back. His German opponent, our new heavy tank, succeeds where the Yankee failed'. Although the entire comparison was made to boost the German morale, it is well worth searching out a copy of the film for the tank enthusiast.

Panzerkampfwagen VI Sd.Kfz. 182

Nicknamed the 'furniture van' by the Germans because of its bulkiness and 57 ton weight, the Panzer VI went into production in 1942 following further demands from Hitler that the Army needed heavier tanks. Henschel and Porsche both submitted prototypes, but Henschel was chosen as the manufacturer as his design appeared to break down less than Porsche's design. The 'Tiger Model E', as it was first called, initially saw military action at Leningrad in August 1942.

The Model E, designated Tiger I, equipped the special heavy tank units of the Wehrmacht and the Waffen SS and saw service until the end of the war. However, like the Panther, the Tiger entered service too early and was faced with technical difficulties resulting in continual breakdowns. The Tiger I had the powerful 88mm gun and thick frontal armour making it virtually indestructible. In late 1942 British troops in Tunisia met the Tiger I and soon discovered that two of the main problems with the Tiger were its thin rear armour plate and an engine which demanded constant maintenance.

Two types of Tiger I were produced - the Ausf H and the Ausf E(HI) - both were soon replaced by the introduction of the Tiger II, designed in 1943.

From July 1942, only 1,355 were manufactured by Henschel and Wegmann with production continuing as late as August of 1944. Tiger production reached its highest point in April 1944, when 105 were produced. The main reasons for the low numbers were the Tiger's difficult production and its cost.

Out of the entire number produced some 500 saw service with SS heavy tank units. A very small number of Tigers were sold to Hungary in 1944. On June 7th 1943 the Japanese ambassador in Germany, General Oshima, was shown a Tiger from sPzAbt 502. A single Tiger was then sold to Japan in 1943, but was never delivered due to the war situation and was loaned by Japan to the German Army (sSSPzAbt 101). Henschel charged Japan 645.000 Reichsmarks for the fully equipped Tiger (with ammunition and radio equipment), while the regular price for the same Tiger was only 300.000 Reichsmarks. Some sources state that Spain was interested in acquiring a number of Tigers but the transaction was never finalized.

Armour (mm/angle) Ausf H/E
Front Turret: 100/8
Front Upper Hull: 100/10
Front Lower Hull: 100/24
Side Turret: 80/0
Side Upper Hull: 80/0
Side Lower Hull: 80/8
Rear Turret: 80/0
Rear Hull: 80/8
Turret Top / Bottom: 25/81-90
Upper Hull Top / Bottom: 25/90
Lower Hull Top / Bottom: 25/90
Gun Mantlet: 100-110/0

Model:	Ausf H/E
Weight: (tonnes)	56.9
Crew:	5
Engine:	Ausf H = Maybach HL210 P 45, V-12, 650 bhp Ausf E = Maybach HL230 P 45, V-12, 700 bhp
Speed: (road)	38 km/h
Range: (road)	90 km
(crosscountry)	60 km
Fuel Capacity:	534 litres
Length:	8.24 m
Width:	3.73 m
Height:	2.88 m
Armament:	L/56 & 2 x 7.92mm MG

The Department of Weaponry of the Red Army made these interesting observations in late 1944;

"It is suggested to the Red Army to use such German tanks as StuG III and Pz IV due to their reliability and availability of spare parts. The new German Panther and Tiger can be used until they are broken down without trying to repair them. They have bad engines, transmission and suspension."

Tigers were equipped with two kinds of tracks, 520mm narrow tracks (used for transportation) and 720mm battle (wider) tracks. Also special railroad flatbed cars were produced in order to transport and unload Tigers more quickly. From mid-1943, Tigers were very commonly coated with Zimmerite anti-magnetic paste. Late production Tigers differed slightly from early models and shared many common parts with the Panzer V Panther in order to simplify their production. There was also an experimental mounting of the 88mm KwK 43 L/71 gun on the Tiger E but it was delayed and abandoned in favour of the development of Tiger II, which eventually replaced the Tiger I. The massive Panzerkampfwagen VI Tiger will remain forever a symbol of formidable German Panzer formations of World War II.

The crew of a Tiger make essential checks before moving into action during the winter of 1942/1943.

122

A brand new Tiger fresh from the factory. This picture gives a great impression of the uncompromising flat armour.

CONVERSIONS

- Befehlswagen Tiger I Ausf. E (Sd. Kfz. 267/268) command tank

- Sturmpanzer (Sturmmorser) Sturmtiger Ausf E - heavy mortar carrier

- Bergewagen Bergetiger - heavy recovery vehicle

- Tiger (P) - Porsche design (5 produced)

- Schwerst-Flammpanzer auf Tiger I - long range flamethrower tank (planned)

- Sturmpanzer Bar - 305mm L/16 gun carrier (planned)

- Sturmpanzer Tiger I - 170mm Kanone 44 gun carrier

- Sturmpanzer Tiger I - 210mm Moerser 18/43 mortar carrier (project)

- Sturmpanzer Tiger I - Skoda's 305mm Granatwerfer heavy mortar carrier (project)

- Tiger I - 240mm Kanone 4 transport vehicle (project)

- Panzerkampfwagen VI Tiger II Ausf B

HIGH NOON AT KURSK

A rare colour shot of the Tiger from the pages of *Signal* magazine.

"As we passed the unfamiliar column of Panzers, it was soon obvious that there had been a serious problem with one machine in particular that was reduced to a burnt out wreck with no sign of any enemy activity. We later learnt that this was the Panther - Guderian's problem child!"

SS Panzer Grenadier Hofstetter , on Kursk.

Under peacetime conditions, normally, a new fighting vehicle would be designed, built and tested over a period of something like five years. Between 1941 and 1945 some very successful designs were produced in as many months. They had to be. The war in the East was a demanding and remorseless taskmaster which consumed every new offering as soon as it was ready for action. The price of failure was unthinkable.

From 1943 onwards German engineers were driven by the desperate demands of a voracious front line which threatened to consume their very homeland if they did not supply exactly the right technology.

Despite the vile excesses of the regime under which they toiled, German factories produced an outstanding variety of armoured fighting vehicles in an incredibly short period of time. It has often been said that the German armaments industry placed the best possible weapons in the worst possible hands; that is certainly true of the armoured fighting vehicles.

Obviously, there were many failures, but against heavy odds, there were also a large number of successful vehicle types which shaped the face of armoured warfare for years to come.

SELF-PROPELLED ARTILLERY

One successful new breed, created in response to the demands of the Russian front, were the self-propelled artillery vehicles which were rushed into production from the war-ravaged German factories to shore up the defensive battles of that terrible conflict. Mobile artillery on fully-tracked chassis had been proposed as early as 1936 by Heinz Guderian, who for a long time harboured a grudge over its rejection. Now with the Panzer Divisions deployed in the role of a mobile fire brigade which could be rushed from place to place on the crumbling front, mobile artillery was to supply the needs of a military situation which was declining on an almost daily basis.

By 1942 the use of tracked vehicles to support the objectives of the Wehrmacht had grown exponentially. The army of 1942 was much more mobile, Panzer Grenadiers moving swiftly around the battlefield in armoured half tracks which had gone from 60 in service in Poland to 6,000 in service in Russia. But even mobile infantry still required equally mobile artillery support to achieve many of their objectives.

The Sturmgeschutz assault gun had originally been designed to provide this support, but by 1942 battlefield necessities meant that they were often hijacked into the role of tank destroyers. This left a gap which could not be filled by conventional medium or heavy artillery, these heavier guns often lagging behind the motorised troops across the huge distances which had to be covered in Russia.

In Europe, during the campaigns of 1939-1941, where roads were good, it was found that conventional artillery could be moved and deployed reasonably easily. But in Russia the dirt roads turned to rivers of mud with the arrival of spring and autumn rains, and they were frequently covered in deep snow during the winter months.

It was now belatedly recognised that Guderian had been correct, and the best possible solution was the deployment of large calibre self-propelled guns on fully tracked carriages. These vehicles could stick reasonably close to the fast-moving Panzer divisions, and provide them with the same heavy artillery support which would normally require horse-drawn or motorised transport.

Ultimately, thousands of self-propelled guns in a bewildering variety of variations would be employed.

Although it was the insistent demands of the Russian front which provided the real catalyst for the development of self propelled guns, there were a number of earlier precedents. Limited numbers of self-propelled guns called Schwere Infanterie Geschutz, or SIG for short, had been successfully deployed in the 1940 campaign in France.

Initially, these vehicles used the ridiculously light Panzer I chassis to carry the heavy 15cm infantry gun. The troops advanced using the gun to blast infantry from buildings and strong points and, despite the obvious limitations of these first self-propelled guns, the high command was now aware that there was an increased role for them.

The Germans have long been famous for the quality of their engineering work. They are also justifiably renowned for their meticulousness. A demonstration of this can be seen in the thorough manner in which every tank chassis manufactured during the Second World War was methodically exploited, with uniform thoroughness and regularity, to produce a wide array of specialist vehicles to cater for every need on the battlefield.

Each of the tank chassis produced by German manufacturers or by her Czechoslovakian satellite suppliers, was systematically altered to produce, not just the main battle tanks themselves, but, in almost every case, a tank destroyer variant, and a self-propelled artillery variant. There were also command tanks, anti-aircraft tanks, armoured ammunition carriers, armoured recovery vehicles and even flame-throwing tanks.

In the case of self-propelled artillery, this systematic approach to the design possibilities of each model was first seen in the Panzer I, Germany's first and smallest tank. It had proved to be hopelessly inadequate under combat conditions. The armour was too thin and the two-machine-gun armament was ineffective, but the chassis itself was a good one and German engineers immediately set to work to produce specialist variants for other battlefield tasks.

It was the successful adaptation of the Panzer I

chassis which allowed the Sig 33 to carry a heavy 15cm gun, to give a heavy self-propelled artillery piece which could be moved right up to the front line.

However, there was one major drawback in that the arrangement of such a big gun on such a small chassis: it was so top-heavy that the gun was very liable to tilt over. This undignified trait led to the search for a better alternative. Naturally, the first step was to examine the larger chassis of the other German light tank in service, the Panzer II.

Like the Panzer I, the Panzer II battle tank was found to be woefully inadequate under combat conditions, and, like the Panzer I, an extended Panzer II chassis was successfully developed as a 15cm self-propelled gun carriage in an attempt to extend the life of the design.

In this respect, the Panzer II worked only a little better than the Panzer I. Although it gave a slightly lower profile, and hence better stability and a greater measure of protection to the crew, it was only manufactured in tiny quantities. Only 12 were made and all appear to have been despatched to Africa to equip the Afrika Korps.

In practice, neither the Panzer I or the Panzer II chassis could really deal with the requirement of the heavy 15cm gun which they were being adapted to carry. The lateral solution to the problem was found by reducing the weight of the gun. This produced the Wespe (or Wasp) which combined the lighter 10.5cm gun on a Panzer II chassis. The Wespe was an excellent design, light enough to keep up with the troops, but heavy enough to produce an effective barrage. 682 of

these machines were produced from 1942 to 1944. They were welcomed with open arms by the hard-pressed men in the front lines. One thing which did not find favour was the name; it did not suggest power and presence, and was dropped on the personal orders of Hitler in 1944. However, they continued to be known as Wasps to the troops, who did value their considerable sting in battle.

With the introduction of the Wespe, the possibilities for the Panzer II chassis appeared to have been exhausted. The Russian front required heavier guns, so German engineers moved on to examine the possibilities inherent in the Panzer III, which was Germany's main battle tank in the early years of the war. This proved to be a much more fertile hunting ground.

The main variant produced using the Panzer III chassis was, of course, the famous Sturmgeschütz.

To supplement the assault guns it was now obvious that the Wehrmacht needed a purpose-designed vehicle capable of heavier artillery support.

The solution was to adapt the Panzer IV chassis to produce the Hummel or 'Bumble Bee'. The Hummel carried a heavy 15cm gun for mobile artillery bombardment. This vehicle overcame all of the drawbacks of the previous self-propelled guns: it carried a much heavier punch, could be very rapidly deployed and, of course, it could be easily moved to avoid counter-barrages by enemy guns. 666 machines eventually entered service - there was a huge demand from the front line units and there were never enough to go round.

The Hummel and the Wespe were to prove highly

This photograph is part of a sequence which originally appeared in *Signal* magazine in February 1943 showing the construction of an assembly line to make Marder tank destroyers. The haste with which the plant had to be designed and built mirrors the speed with which the Marder had to be completed and thrown into action, despite its less than satisfactory design.

successful under battlefield conditions. Both could give mobile artillery support to the hard-pressed Panzer divisions then quickly move location.

In total, some 1,300 of these two types of self-propelled guns were made from 1942 to 1945, during which time they provided essential artillery support to the great advances of 1942 and covering fire for the desperate Wehrmacht divisions during their headlong retreat back into Germany during 1944.

The only major drawback of these self-propelled guns was the lack of storage space for stocks of ammunition. In the case of the Hummel, there was only enough room for 18 rounds. Constant re-supplying was therefore required during any significant bombardments.

However, by 1944 ammunition supplies were strictly limited in the German forces and, unlike the glory days of 1941, even these limited stocks had to be shepherded very carefully indeed.

In line with the German factories, the tank-producing Skoda works in Czechoslovakia also produced self-propelled artillery using the chassis from the Czech manufactured tanks. The Czech-made Panzer 38(t) equipped many German units during the early years of the war, and when the tanks were withdrawn from front line service in 1942 it made sense to convert the highly serviceable chassis into a self-propelled artillery role.

The resultant machine which combined a 10.5cm Howitzer with the 38(t) chassis was known to the Germans as the 'Grille', or Cricket. In post-war years a number of authorities have suggested it was also known to the troops as 'the Bison', although the sources for this are uncertain. No action reports refer to these vehicles by any other name than Crickets. They were never as popular as The Wespe or The Hummel; nevertheless, 282 machines were manufactured and they saw action mainly in Russia. A few were also used in the campaign in the west after the Allied landings.

Unlike the Panzer I, II and III, the Panzer IV remained in service throughout the war, so there was never likely to be a surplus of redundant vehicles for conversion. In any case, the successful introduction of the Wespe and Hummel solved the technical problems of mobile heavy artillery support. In consequence, further attempts to use the Panzer IV chassis for self-propelled artillery were limited to a few experiments which produced

a machine nicknamed the Grasshopper. This is a very rare machine indeed, of which only a few were produced. Some sources put the figure as low as two machines, others say 14 were made. With the warped logic which led to its creation, that's no great surprise.

In order to allow for the turret to give the protection the crew needed, the gun size had to be reduced to 10.5cm, when what was actually demanded were heavier calibre guns, but the Panzer IV produced one of the most successful designs in the form of the Panzerjäger IV, a superb tank hunter.

By this stage of the war time was beginning to run against the Germans, and the Panzer V and VI chassis did not produce as many conversions as previous vehicles.

THE PRELUDE TO KURSK

In the wake of the German disaster at Stalingrad in February 1943, the Red Army continued its lightning advance. Finally the 1st SS Panzer Corps, who were part of Army Group South, managed to halt the Soviet thrust around Kharkov in March 1943. To the North, the hard-pushed Army Group Centre had also managed to stall the Russian advance around the region of Orel. Together these two German Army Groups were just about managing to hold the Russian attacks. However, between their positions was a huge Russian bulge. The width of the salient was about one hundred miles wide and eighty miles deep, centred around the town of Kursk. Hitler ordered that this salient was to be cut off and the Soviet forces inside destroyed.

The plan itself was simple; it called for the inspirational handling of armoured forces. With their proven record of success the men of the German tank corps felt they were equal to the task. The 9th Army would attack from Orel in the north, the 4th Panzer Army would attack from Belgorod in the south. These two great advances would meet in the middle and trap the Russians inside a huge pocket. They could then concentrate on the destruction of these trapped forces. The architect of this great scheme was Field Marshall Von Manstein, who was an experienced veteran with a good understanding of armour in battle.

The Russian forces facing the Zitadelle offensive were aware that their forces were vulnerable here.

Both sides could see that this area could represent the decisive battle of the campaign so far. Germany was keen to regain the initiative in Russia after the Stalingrad debacle, and the recent success at Kharkov had provided an important but small taste of what could be achieved. Nonetheless, Hitler did have misgivings about this offensive and he even confessed to Guderian that the thought of it 'made his stomach turn over'. To the troops, however, he stressed the importance of this forthcoming battle. He boasted that the coming victory at Kursk will be a 'beacon for the whole world'. It was a measure of his anxiety that the out-of-favour General Heinz Guderian was recalled to oversee the preparation of the new armoured forces for the battle. This led to the creation of a specialist Tank Ordnance headquarters.

EQUIPMENT AND AMMUNITION ORGANISATION

Previously the same organisation had served the Panzer forces as well as the other formations of the Wehrmacht. The agencies responsible for most of the storage, issue, and repair of equipment and for the storage, issue, and salvaging of ammunition belonged to a separate branch of the Army, the Ordnance Branch (Feldzeugwesen). This branch was headed by the Chief Army Ordnance Officer (Feldzeugmeister), who worked through his staff, the Ordnance Inspectorate (Feldzeuginspektion) in the General Army Office (Allgemeines Heeresamt). From the Ordnance Inspectorate the chain of command led through three regional commands, called Ordnance Groups (Feldzeuggruppen), with

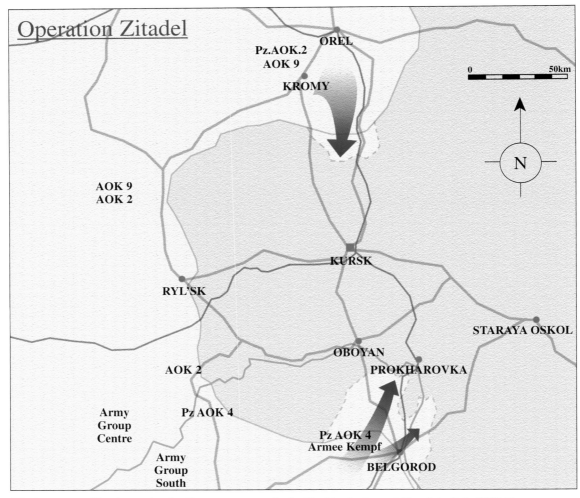

The last great offensive action by German armour in the East took place at Kursk in July 1943. Progress was limited on both sectors but particularly in the North.

The difficult logistics of moving tanks by trailer meant that the Panzers were frequently driven long distances on these trailers resulting in a high level of breakdowns.

headquarters in Berlin, Kassel, and Munich, to the Ordnance Headquarters (Feldzeugkommandos) which were at the level of the corps areas but not affiliated with the latter. There was one Ordnance Headquarters in each corps area, where it controlled a varying number of equipment and ammunition depots. The Ordnance Headquarters was the lowest controlling agency for the storage and issue of equipment and ammunition, below this level they were handled by two separate types of depots. The Ordnance Headquarters was designated by the number of the corps area. Ordanance Headquarters and the depots it controlled were not, however, part of the corps area organisation.

In addition to the Ordnance Headquarters designated by the corps area numbers, there existed an Ordnance Headquarters, which was in charge of a great number of subterranean ammunition depots in central Germany. In 1943 the special Tank Ordnance Headquarters, (Panzer-Feldzeugkommando), was created. This was done in order to centralise the supply of all types of armoured fighting vehicles and their spare parts throughout the German forces.

FUELS AND LUBRICANTS

The question of fuel supply may seem rather unspectacular but it was the life blood of the Panzer Divisions. The system was complex. Fuel from home fuel depots or from Field Army mobile reserves was directed to the railheads. Sometimes the fuel was kept loaded in tanker trains (Eisenbahntankstellen) near the railhead

and transferred from these directly to fuel columns, but preferably it was laid down in 20 and 200-litre containers in Army Fuel Dumps (Armeebetriebesstofflager) forward of the railhead. From these dumps the fuel was taken on to Division Fuel Distributing Points (Divsionsbetriebsstoffausgabestellen) or, in the case of armoured divisions, to Division Fuel Dumps (Divisionsbetriebsstofflager). Fuel was then forwarded from the division area to lower echelon supply points and to fuel points that were set aside for the use of single vehicles (Tankstellen fur Einzelkraftfahrzeuge). The latter could also be supplied from the army fuel stores.

Perhaps even more important than the Field Army Motor Transport Parks were the Field Army Tank Parks or Bases (Stutzpunkte). These were established on the basis of one per army group. Their importance was increased by the fact that armies did not ordinarily maintain fixed installations for the repair of tanks, although armies had semi-permanent tank workshops. The tank bases were reception or control centres from which tanks could be dispatched to workshops in the near vicinity for repairs, or returned to home depots and factories for rear echelon maintenance.

SUPPLY REQUIREMENTS

The determination of the overall requirements necessary to maintain a German field division presented a number of difficulties. This is best shown by a review of the German supply expenditures in Russia in 1941. Armoured divisions averaged some 30 tons daily when inactive and about 700 tons a day when engaged in heavy fighting; infantry divisions required 80 tons a day when inactive and 1,100 tons during a day of heavy fighting. When engaged in defensive, mopping-up, or minor offensive activities, the divisions required supplies in amounts somewhere between the two extremes. By far the most important variable in this campaign was the amount of ammunition expended. Requirements of fuel and equipment also varied considerably particularly among the armoured divisions, while rations and clothing consumption remained relatively static. Expenditures depended upon the nature of the action involved, the types of units engaged, the zone of action, the season of the year, the amount of material available for consumption, and the facility with which supply movements could be made.

PANZER MAINTENANCE

Minor repairs to armoured vehicles (including tanks, self-propelled weapons and other armoured vehicles) were made by unit mechanics and by mobile tank-workshop units. If the repairs could not be completed in the division area within three days, the vehicles were sent to semi-permanent army tank workshops or to Field Army Tank Parks or Bases. When armoured vehicles were so badly damaged that they could not be repaired in the field, they were cannibalised or forwarded to tank equipment depots or factories in the home area. In the latter case the vehicles were no longer under Field Army control and were not returned to the units to which they were originally assigned.

Armoured vehicles were of course repaired on the spot if possible. Otherwise they were moved rearward under their own power. Tank transporters were used only when long movements were contemplated or when vehicles could not move under their own power.

For the coming offensive at Kursk, Hitler knew that he was approaching his last opportunity to win a decisive victory in the East. For that reason he ordered the deployment of some of the latest designs in German tanks, even though some of them had not been properly tested.

One such variant was the Rhinoceros or Nashorn;

it carried the 88cm Pak 43, the latest 88mm anti-tank gun, mounted on the hybrid chassis of the Pz. Kpfw. III and IV. The vehicle's silhouette was very high and the armour protection given to the crew by the thin-skinned superstructure was very poor. The gun, however, was able to engage tanks at very long range and was loved by its crews.

HERR SENEBERG

A veteran of the Kursk battle was Herr Seneberg. He was a gun-loader on a Nashorn self-propelled tank-hunter, and sixty years later recalled his experiences in the build-up to Kursk:

"The veterans who marched on Stalingrad said to us, "Hopefully we'll get better tanks now." They had marched on Stalingrad and they were still partially equipped with tanks that had the 50mm - the 'door knocker' we called it. We were inferior to the Russians as far as tanks were concerned. They had the legendary T-34, a completely different type of tank weapon.

Once we had been withdrawn, we were told that we would be getting new tank-destroyers with the 88mm - a long-barrelled gun - and that's what happened. We were given new 'tanks' but, as we were anti-tank gunners, we had a long-barrelled 88mm gun on an open carriage. The body of the tank was from a Mark III with our gun on top. Yes, we had armour, but the tank was open on the upper part. A normal tank could swing the turret - we couldn't. We had an action radius of only 45 degrees and the rest was up to the driver who had to direct the tank to the left or right. With this new anti-tank gun we were more than a match for the Russians - we destroyed over thirty T-34's.

After we had been trained on the new guns we were sent to the area of Orel, Kursk - the Kursk Bend we called it - where a final attempt was to be made by the German army to go on the offensive. To the south of us, in Prokhorovka, was the greatest mass of our tanks ever collected in battle.

Then it started. We wanted to attack but the Russians intended to do the same thing, and one offensive met the other. The Russians were stronger in material and had a greater number of men. When we advanced on this offensive there came a dreadful barrage. And what was it like for me? The worst thing I ever experienced. My father, who had been injured in the First World War at Verdun, told me what that was like. I think this must have been the same. The ground looked as if it had been ploughed up. The barrage ended after three hours and then the fighting began.

At first our tanks were called 'Nashorner' or 'Rhinoceroses', but so that the Russians would get fooled, the name was later changed to 'Hornisse' or 'Hornets'. After our offensive collapsed we were fighting near Orel. The Russians were superior and we had to retreat further and further. We were then given assistance from a tank called the 'Ferdinand'. The biggest tank shell could hit it - it was practically invulnerable. There were still some left after the Kursk battle. The name came ostensibly from Ferdinand Porsche - that's why it was called the Ferdinand. The earth was practically shaking when the Ferdinand was three kilometres away. I know people say they are no good, but I saw them destroy a number of enemy tanks. However, autumn weather set in and the ground went soggy - the Ferdinand was not prepared for that. The Ferdinands which were left after the big battle got damaged motors and they all broke down.

Eventually we got a direct hit, it must have penetrated the armour at the front where the driver

A study of a column of Sturmgeschütze armed with the long-barrelled 75mm gun moving into action.

sat with the radio operator. I sat up at the top as I was a gun-loader, and I fed the shells into the barrel. I remember the tank shook, the tracks burst off and we had to jump out at the back. There were four of us left - the Commander, me and the two others. They trampled on top of me and I fell over and saw them running to the left across a cornfield towards the wood. Then I heard them screaming terribly because they had been caught in the machine-gun fire. I had good luck - I ran off to the right and got away."

ENTER THE PANTHER

One vehicle with more than its fair share of teething problems was the new Panzer Mk V, better known as the Panther. With the emergence of the Russian T-34 in the autumn of 1941 the Germans quickly realised that they would have to come up with an effective antidote. The plans for a heavier tank were revisited and work began in earnest. The resultant design produced a 45-ton tank, which was still classed as a 'medium' tank by the Germans.

The Panther had the same sloping armour, wide tracks and a similar 75mm gun. Developed with breakneck speed, and rushed into production, the Panther made its debut at the Battle of Kursk, before it was really proven. Engine and transmission problems abounded. Engine fires were commonplace, dozens broke down and some vehicles went into their first action pouring fire from the exhaust pipes. Not surprisingly, the Panther was a disappointment at Kursk, but once it had overcome its initial teething problems, it would prove itself the best 'medium' of the war.

The Panther was a far better vehicle than the T-34 but it was never to be available in the quantities which the war in the East demanded. Although 6,000 would be built, that was never enough, as the numbers destroyed always kept pace with supply.

The advent of the Panther and the Tiger represented almost the end of the evolutionary trail in the Second World War. German tank sizes had steadily increased, from the 6-ton Panzer I to the 22-ton Panzer III and now onto the 62-ton Tiger. It would reach a peak with the 70-ton Tiger B, or King Tiger. The weight and superior armour certainly made the difference but the quality had been achieved at the expense of quantity and it was quantity which Germany needed.

Panzerkampfwagen V Sd.Kfz.171

By the end of the first year of the war it was clear that the Panzer IIs and IIIs were not suitable for combat with stronger British, French and Russian tanks. In 1941, Hitler decided that a prototype for a 'heavy' tank should be designed to provide the German Army with heavier fighting vehicles. The result was the Panzer V Panther and possibly the most well known and outstanding German tank of World War II.

From the two prototypes designed by MAN and Daimler-Benz, the MAN design was the one which went into production. Initially, Hitler preferred the Daimler-Benz design but it was rejected by the "Panther Committee" on account of identification problems with the vehicle. By the end of 1942 a pre-production series of 20 tanks were produced under the name Null-Serie. They were designated as PzKpfw V Panther Ausf A; lightly armoured (60mm frontal armour), deployed a 75mm KwK 42 L/70 gun and were powered by a Maybach HL2 10 P45 engine. Technically, these early versions were very different from later prototypes in the series.

Also, by December 1942, a newly moderated version of the Panther, designated the Ausf D, was ready and had entered production. A month later the first Panzer Ausf D with improved armoured protection and re-versioned gun left the factory. The first 250 Panther Ausf Ds were also referred to as the Ausf D I. These machines made their combat debut during Operation Citadel in July 1943, but due to technical problems many Panthers broke down in action and

from the original 250 only 43 were in still service the following year.

Production of a further 600 Ausf D - designated Ausf D2 - had a more powerful HL230 P30 engine which then became standard for future models. In August 1943, the next model was the Ausf A instead of the expected Ausf E and between the four manufacturers of MAN, Daimler-Benz, MNH and DEMAG, 1,788 models were constructed.

Further modifications saw the next model, the Panther Ausf G, become the most numerous model with 3,740 being produced between March 1944 and April 1945, by MAN, Daimler-Benz and MNH. The hull was redesigned with thicker sides, the hatches for the hull gunner and driver were hinged making them easier to open, and the ammunition storage increased from 79 to 82 rounds.

Armour (mm/angle) Ausf G
Front Turret: 110/11
Front Upper Hull: 80/55
Front Lower Hull: 60/55
Side Turret: 45/25
Side Upper Hull: 50/30
Side Lower Hull: 40/0
Rear Turret: 45/25
Rear Lower Hull: 40/30
Turret Top / Bottom: 16/84 / 16/90
Upper Hull Top / Bottom: 40/90 / 16/90
Lower Hull Top / Bottom: 30/90 / 16/90
Gun Mantlet: 100/round

Model:	Ausf D	Ausf A	Ausf G
Weight: (tonnes)	44	45.5	44.8
Crew:	5	5	5
Engine:	Maybach HL230 P30 V-12 700 bhp	Maybach HL230 P30 V-12 700 bhp	Maybach HL230 P30 V-12 700 bhp
Speed: (road)	46 km/h	46 km/h	46 km/h
Range: (road)	160 km	160 km	160 km
(crosscountry)	100 km	100 km	100 km
Fuel Capacity:	730 litres	730 litres	730 litres
Length:	6.87 m	6.87 m	6.87 m
Width:	3.27 m	3.27 m	3.27 m
Height:	2.95 m	3.1 m	2.95 m
Armament:	L/70 & 2 x 7.92mm MG	L/70 & 3 x 7.92mm MG	L/70 & 3 x 7.92mm MG

In 1936, AEG were ordered to start the development of infrared night-vision devices, and in 1939 the first successful prototype unit was ready for use with 37mm Pak 35136 L/45 anti-tank gun. In autumn of 1942, a unit for use with 75mm PaK 40 L/46 anti-tank gun was constructed and was also mounted on Marder II (Sd.Kfz.131).

In June 1943 tests started with infrared night-vision (Nacht Jager) devices and telescopic rangefinders mounted on a Panther. Two different arrangements were created and used on Panther tanks.

Solution A - Sperber (Sparrow Hawk) was made up of one 30cm infrared searchlight (with range of 600m) and image converter operated by the commander - FG 1250. From late 1944 to March of 1945, some Panzerkampfwagen V Panther Ausf G's (and other variants) mounted with FG 1250 were successfully tested. From March to April of 1945, approximately 50 Panther Ausf G's (and other variants) mounted with FG 1250 saw combat service on the Eastern and Western Fronts. Panthers with IR operated with SdKfz.251/20 Uhu (Owl) half-track with a 60cm infra-red searchlight and Sd.Kfz.251/21 Falke (Falcon). This solution could easily be mounted on any type of armoured fighting vehicle.

Solution B - The second and more complicated arrangement was the "Biwa" (Bildwandler), which provided the driver, gunner and commander with one 30cm infrared searchlight (with a range of 600m) and image converter. Various variants of Panthers were converted and mounted with "Biwa". It was reported that tests were successful, but there were very few combat reports from the Eastern or Western Fronts.

In May 1944, the newly designd Ausf F was to be manufactured exclusively with steel-rimmed road-wheels and increased armour protection. The prototype Ausf G was completed in January 1945 and although it is possible that a few were completed and used in combat before the war ended, it is more commonly thought that only certain key components were ever assembled by Daimler-Benz.

The Panther endured an inauspicious birth at Kursk but it was to become one of the best medium tanks of the war.

The well sloped frontal armour of the Panther and the wide tracks were two features first seen in the T-34. At one stage it was suggested that the German army simply copied the T-34, but Hitler's pride overruled any further discussion.

CONVERSIONS

- Befehlswagen Ausf D/A/G (Sd.Kfz.267) - command tank

- Befehlswagen Ausf D/A/G (Sd.Kfz.268) - ground to air liason tank

- Beobachtungspanzer Panther Ausf D - observation tank

- Bergepanther (Sd.Kfz.179) - recovery vehicle

- Munisionspanzer Panther - ammunition carrier

- Panzerjager jagdpanther (Sd.Kfz. 173)

- Flakpanzer V Coelian - 2 x 37mm/55mm Flak gun - planned

- Flakpanzer V / Grille 10 - (lengthened chasis) - prototype

- Grille 10 - 100mm K gun carrier (planned)

- Grille 10 - 105mm leFH 43/35 (planned)

- Minenraumpanzer Panther - mine clearing tank (prototype stage)

- Ramschaufelpanzer Panther - dozer tank

- Munition Schlepper Panther (2 produced)

- Munition Schlepper/Waffentrager Panther (shortened chasis planned)

- Grille 12 - 128mm K 43/44 gun carrier by Krupp (planned)

- Skorpion - 128mm K 43 gun carrier by Rhienmetal (planned)

- Grille 15 - 150mm sFH 43/44 howitzer carrier (planned)

- 88mm Flakwagen Panther

- Sturmpanther - 150mm StuH 43/1 gun carrier

- Panther with 105mm rocket launcher

- Panther II (prototype stage)

THE TIGER IN RUSSIA

The Tiger first saw action near Leningrad in August 1942. The results were poor due to inadequate infantry protection and poor deployment. The Russians were able to knock the tanks out by aiming at the tracks. The Germans quickly learned their lesson and future use of the Tiger I was carefully managed. The first large employment of the tank was at Kursk, when approximately one hundred were used. Almost half of these were issued to the elite formations of the Waffen-SS and the Grossdeutchland Division. The Tiger I quickly earned a fearsome reputation among its enemies. This tank only saw action for two years, but its reputation still endures today.

Unlike the Panther, the Tiger was designed on familiar German lines, but all the dimensions were increased. The main armament was the 8.8cm Kw.K 36, which was essentially the 8.8cm Flak 36 adapted for turret mounting. The mounting of such a heavy gun raised considerable problems of rigidity, and consequently the hull was constructed of large plates entirely welded together. The superstructure was made up in one unit, and welded to the hull. The turret wall was made from a single large piece of armour, 82mm thick, bent into a horseshoe shape. To give further protection all the armour plates were interlocked, in addition to being welded. The armour of the Tiger, at the time of its appearance, was the thickest ever to be fitted on any German tank; the front vertical plate was 102mm thick and the hull sides 62mm.

The suspension, which employed interleaved, Christie-type bogie wheels with a very wide track, was reasonably simple and was an effective solution to the problems of such a large and heavy vehicle.

The Tiger engine required very skilled driving and maintenance to get the best performance, and in the hands of insufficiently trained crews mechanical troubles were apt to appear. This characteristic was the tank's principal disadvantage.

THE TIGER IN ACTION

The five-man crew was the standard for all German medium and heavy tanks. The crew of a Tiger consisted firstly of the commander, who was in charge of the vehicle and selected targets. He also fired the turret machine gun. Next came the gunner, who sat next to the commander and targeted his enemies through his gun sights. In many respects, he was the most vital member of the crew. In battle, every shot had to count. The flight of a shell is affected by many factors, including wind direction, rain, snow and other atmospheric conditions. The gunner had to gauge the range to the target, allow for any climatic factors and compensate for the speed of any moving targets, which were more difficult to hit. One miss could allow an enemy tank to get in the first vital shot, which spelt death in the tense tank duels of the Second World War.

The main 88mm armament of the Tiger was aimed and fired as a result of a team effort. It was the job of all members of the Tiger crew to use their vision devices to identify potential targets and to report them to the commander. The Tiger commander would then prioritise the target and would give orders to engage it. The gunner would traverse the Tiger's turret using a hydraulic system controlled by a foot pedal, aim the gun using a binocular telescope sight and then fire the gun using an electrical ignition system.

The loader was responsible for selecting the correct type of ammunition from the ammunition bins, which were included in the Tiger's structure, and using an automatic or semi-automatic loading system to load the gun.

After each engagement he also had the laborious job of emptying the shell cases and restocking the tank with the cumbersome rounds for the main gun.

Inside the hull, towards the front of the vehicle, sat the driver. On his right was the radio operator, who fulfilled the vital communications function, and also manned the hull machine gun.

The usual practice was for the crew of a tank to paint a white ring around the gun barrel for every enemy tank destroyed. Some crews were so successful that a thick white ring had to be painted, representing ten kills. The most successful commanders proudly carried an array of kill rings like so many strutting peacocks.

WITTMAN AND THE TIGER

During his time away from action, Michael Wittmann was promoted to SS-Untersturmführer. On Christmas Day 1942 he received his transfer to

A Tiger rolls past a group of grenadiers during the build-up to the battle of Kursk. Although the Tigers acquitted themselves well in the battle, poor battlefield reconnaissance resulted in large numbers being lost to minefields which had not been adequately cleared.

Fallingbostel for the formation of the new heavy tank company. Wittmann once again changed his grey assault gun uniform for a black Panzer uniform.

There were rumours of a new miracle weapon which filled Michael Wittmann and his colleagues with anticipation. For once, these rumours were true. The Germans were to be equipped with the mighty Tiger tanks, but there was also disappointment for Wittmann. Each Tiger company had a few of the old Panzer IIIs for scouting and support. As he had experience in armoured cars and had trained using these machines, Wittmann was assigned to a Panzer III.

Wittmann was anxious for a Tiger of his own, but he had a long wait. Finally, in March 1943, he achieved his aim and stood, for the first time, in the turret of a Tiger, as its commander.

Wittmann could afford no time to reflect on his new status. The strategic situation on the Russian front was desperate, and the Tigers were pitched straight into action. Massive tank duels, the bitter one-to-one combats, and tank battles against anti-tank guns were the daily work of Michael Wittmann.

His first great moment of triumph came in the titanic battle of Kursk.

THE ELEFANT

The Tiger may have proved itself to be a good design, but the first tank destroyer which was based on it was a misguided failure; this was the 'Elefant'.

The gun was mounted on the Tiger (P) chassis, a discarded prototype version of the Tiger made by Porsche. It incorporated twin gasoline generating units with direct electric drive. Although protected by heavy armour, this vehicle was unsuccessful, not least because it was ponderous and difficult to manoeuvre.

Like the Panther, this vehicle was rushed through the production stage so that it could be ready for the Kursk offensive. One major design flaw was the lack of a machine gun to back up the main gun, which was to have serious consequences for crews during battle. The suspension was also under immense strain due to the weight of the vehicle and resulted in the vehicle getting easily bogged down.

THE ATTACK ORDERS

Positioned on the opposite side of the turret from the gunner was the loader. He did the heavy manual work of loading the gun.

Although the orders for the preparation of the assault were issued in April, the actual attack did not take place until three months later in July. The delays were for a number of reasons. Hitler wanted no room for failure, so the plans were revised again and again to ensure no detail had been left out. In addition, the Führer had an almost child-like faith in the power of new weapons. He believed that the new generation of Panzers would win the war and he wanted the new Panthers and Elefants to be used in the battle. Despite the fact that the field trials of these new Panzers were not complete, they were committed to the battle anyway. This decision would prove costly during the ensuing clashes. The delays caused further, unforeseen problems. The Russians had been made aware of the German plans through the help of the 'Lucy' spy ring that had been passing decoded Ultra messages from Bletchley Park in England. They could also observe the massive German preparations for the battle and they began to make plans.

Initially Stalin had ordered a Soviet offensive to be launched to thwart the German plans. His Generals, however, had persuaded him to adopt a defensive stance instead. The idea was to draw the German armoured forces into a well-prepared trap and destroy them with anti-tank defences. When they were on the point of destruction, a heavy armoured counter-attack would be launched to finish them off. The Russians knew that the Germans would be concentrating large amounts of

Tiger tanks roll along a muddy road in the southern sector of the front during the first rains of autumn 1943. By now the Tiger had become established as a symbol of German tank power on the Eastern Front. Although only 1700 of these machines were ever manufactured, they were to forge a legend out of all proportion to their relatively small numbers.

armour in the area, so particular attention was paid to anti-tank defences. Anti-tank guns and anti-tank mines were laid out in pre-prepared areas that would blunt the German armour as they tried to punch through. The Russian defences overall consisted of extensive lines of trenches, minefields and pre-prepared killing grounds. These were arranged one behind the other and presented a formidable obstacle. The number of mines laid was as high as 5,000 per mile in some areas.

ANTI-TANK MEASURES

By 1943 a tank was no place to be. Infantry had, by now, developed extra killing power in the form of magnetic mines, Bazookas and the Panzerfausts. These deadly weapons could all blast through the armour of a tank. Early in the war the Russians found that the simple expedient of a bottle filled with petrol, lighted and thrown onto the engine decks, could disable even the largest tanks. Their tank hunting teams soon became very adept at wielding this simple improvised device.

The ever-present danger for tanks was less spectacular than the anti-tank guns and tank hunting teams, but equally deadly. Anti-tank mines could be placed in great numbers to protect a defensive position. These mines would support the weight of a man without detonating, so infantry

teams often passed by unsuspecting, but as soon as the weight of a tank was sensed it would explode with tremendous force.

Although tanks were sometimes destroyed by mines, the most frequent result was that they lost a track. This resulted in crews having to leave their vehicle to attempt to repair these massive iron tracks in the heat of battle.

The job of testing for mines and clearing a path through them was the job of the Pioneer sections. Occasionally, this vital task was given insufficient time and care. At Kursk, General Heinz Guderian, the inspector of armour in the German army at the time of the crucial battle, was left livid with rage. His new Tiger tanks had rolled into action through uncleared minefields, with the result that many of his most effective machines, the spearhead of the army, were rendered immobile by a threat which could easily have been anticipated and cleared.

THE PRELUDE TO KURSK

During the three-month delay before the battle, the Russians had pushed vast amounts of men and material into the area. They also enlisted the help of an 'army' consisting of hundreds of thousands of civilian helpers from the surrounding areas to construct the defensive trenches needed. When completed, these trenches would stretch for over six thousand miles. A vast number of civilians also helped construct a new rail line that would be used when the counter-attack was launched.

Over twenty thousand artillery pieces were moved into the area by the Soviets, together with over three thousand tanks, two thousand planes and over one million men. The Russians had General Vatutin's Voronezh Front and General Rokossovsky's Central Front in the salient. In reserve would be General Konev's Steppe Front. The brilliant tactician Marshall Zhukov was in overall command. One mistake that the Russians made was in the assessment of where the main German attack would fall. They believed that it would come from the north and they arranged their forces accordingly. This resulted in a very tough defensive wall that would meet Model's forces head on. However, the Germans had assembled their main attacking forces in the south as part of Hoth's 4th Panzer Army. This would cause the Russians some real headaches in the days ahead.

The opening stages of the battle began just before 5am on the morning of the 5 July 1943. Through their highly developed intelligence sources, the Russians knew when the Germans were going to launch their attack. In a well-planned move, Zhukov ordered the Soviets to launch a pre-emptive artillery barrage. This strike had the desired result of catching the Germans out in the open during the forming up stage. The ensuing panic and destruction offered a taste of what was to come. To add to the carnage, the Germans now launched their artillery strike. The resulting noise and destruction presented a devastating and awe-inspiring sight. Although lasting less than one hour in total, this opening phase reached new heights of ferocity. The Russian artillery bombardment delayed the start of the German attack, which did get under way about two hours late, with the infantry leading the way.

With the 9th Army in the north, Field Marshall Model had four Panzer Divisions to call on, the 2nd, 9th, 18th and 20th Panzer Divisions, plus three heavy tank battalions. The heavy tank battalions consisted of the 505th heavy tank battalion equipped with 30 Tigers and the 653rd and 654th heavy tank battalions equipped with a total of 90 of the new Ferdinand heavy tank destroyer. The emphasis of the German attack lay in the south with General Hoth's 4th Panzer Army and Army Detachment Kempf. There were a total

of nine infantry Divisions in this area, together with the Grossdeutchland Panzer Grenadier Division and the SS Panzer Divisions Leibstandarte Adolf Hitler, Das Reich and Totenkopf. The four SS Divisions each had an attached Kompanie of 15 Tigers, the Leibstandarte and Das Reich Divisions were also equipped with the new Panthers. The crack Grossdeutchland Division was also equipped with a Tiger Kompanie and a number of Panthers. To back this already powerful armoured force up the 503rd heavy tank battalion was also allocated to this section with a further 45 Tigers. This made for a very impressive line-up and represented the best that Germany had to offer at that time, both in men and machines. One important feature that the Germans lacked was a suitable reserve force. The Russians had a very sizeable reserve to call upon, but the Germans had been badly mauled by two years of fighting in Russia.

It was not just on the ground that new German weapons were being tested. One important new development made its arrival from the air during the Kursk offensive. Hans-Ulrich Rudel, the famous Stuka pilot, was responsible for battle testing a new addition to the Stuka that would prove itself a menace for the Red Army tank men. A pair of 37mm Flak cannon were fitted to the underside of the aircraft. It was found that this weapon was very accurate and very effective at destroying enemy tanks from the air. To make this new weapon work, however, the pilot had to go into a shallow dive and get within close range of his target, a task that presented its own dangers, but it worked, and the number of Russian tanks that fell to this new weapon grew steadily throughout the Kursk offensive.

THE OFFENSIVE BEGINS

As the offensive began to gather momentum, the 9th Army began their advance along the main Orel to Kursk railway line. They quickly ran into the first defensive line and the number of casualties began to rise. Within the first two days the 9th Army's attack was halted near Olkhovatka. They had advanced only 12 miles from their start point, but the concentration of the Russian forces in this sector had proved fatal for Model's forces. The revitalised Russian airforce also helped to defeat the advance.

To compound the problems, in the North the new German tanks that had been expected to yield excellent results had performed miserably in battle. The Elefants started well, and had advanced only a few miles into enemy territory. Initially, the thick frontal armour proved a good defence against enemy attempts to disable them but, lacking a machine gun, they could not completely neutralise enemy infantry positions without supporting efforts. Accurate, sustained fire from the Soviet positions prevented the German infantry from following behind the tanks. The Ferdinands ran into difficulties when they became separated from their infantry support. The disastrous failure to fit an on-board machine gun prevented them from defending themselves against the enemy infantry. The Russians were able to get up close and disable or capture these new machines.

A different series of problems were visited on the Panther-equipped companies. Many of these tanks broke down on their way to the start point. Another worrying problem for the Panther crews was the fact that many of them actually caught fire, due to a badly designed exhaust system that accumulated unburned fuel. This first model of the Panther earned the nickname of 'Guderian's problem child'. Around two hundred of these new tanks were sent to the Kursk area, and most broke down. The Tigers too experienced problems, especially with the retrieval of vehicles which were damaged by the extensive Russian minefields, which had been insufficiently cleared.

TANK RECOVERY

With the huge weight of the later war tanks, such as the Tiger, immobilised tanks could often only be moved by the power of another Tiger. The heaviest tractor in the German army was the 18-ton Famo, but it took three of these harnessed together to move one broken down Tiger, and in the midst of the battlefield the tractors were highly vulnerable to anti-tank rounds, high explosive shells and the hand held weapons of the infantry.

The Tiger tanks, which each weighed about sixty tons, were prone to a range of mechanical and electrical failures. In addition, they were extremely expensive valuable assets that could not afford to be wasted. Because of this, recovering Tiger tanks was particularly important. There were a range of options available to the SS and the army tank

battalions which operated Tigers. Most obviously, they could use their own gun tanks to tow other tanks out of trouble. The problem with this is that it tended to cause electrical, engine or transmission malfunctions in the Tigers doing the towing. Alternatively, unarmoured half tracks could be used, but unfortunately several of these needed to be used to tow a single Tiger, and because they were unarmoured they were vulnerable. Quite clearly what one required was an armoured recovery vehicle that could tow a Tiger on its own and which was capable of operating in intense combat conditions.

Once again, the solution to the problem was to develop a specialist recovery vehicle, known as a Bergenpanzer. These machines dispensed with the turret and replaced it with a box-like wooden structure. They were designed to run quickly up to disabled tanks and tow them away from enemy reach. Every tank carried heavy towing cables ready to be hitched up to a recovery vehicle or a friendly tank. Most sensible commanders went into action with their cables already hooked up, just in case.

The Tiger tanks may have looked incredibly robust, but in many respects they were surprisingly vulnerable. They required high maintenance, and also shed their caterpillar tracks with infuriating regularity, especially in thick mud, when crossing obstacles, or as a result of anti-tank fire and minefields. Veteran Jerry Majeuski recalled the problems with the Tigers:

"Tank tracks, as you might guess, are the most important part on a tank and they frequently had to be changed. For instance, if one link just breaks, one pin, and you haven't got a track any more. From enemy action tracks are often hit by enemy shells and damaged and have to be changed. It is a very hard job and takes a lot of effort to do it. The whole crew is involved. I have never done it myself under enemy action but I shudder to think what it would take."

In the south, Hoth's forces got off to a better start than Model's. The Tigers were placed at the head of the advance with the Panthers providing flank cover; the weaker Panzer IIIs and IVs came in behind in what was known as a 'Panzer-Kiel', or armoured-wedge. The Russians had spread out their forces in the south. This helped the 4th Panzer Army to make relatively good progress. By the end of day one, the 4th Panzer Army had advanced 15 miles to the town of Prokhorovka. The advance slowed considerably after this as the Russians poured in waves of reserves to meet the threat. As the advance slowed, the emphasis of the attack was shifted northwards. The SS Divisions had reached, and forced a crossing of, the Psel River by 11 July, bringing them close to the town of Prokhorovka. They prepared to advance further as Army Detachment Kempf moved parallel to their left flank, about twelve miles from their positions.

On the day that the great battle began, Wittmann destroyed eight tanks, and in the following tank battles he emerged as an unmatched tank ace. He overran batteries, picked out even the most cleverly-camouflaged anti-tank gun nests, and constantly out-fought enemy tanks. He was cautious when he had to be, aggressive when it paid off, his keen hunter instincts, combined with a huge slice of luck, allowing him to emerge unscathed through five furious days of the biggest tank battles in history. Over and over again enemy tanks went up like blazing torches before him, and when Michael Wittmann washed his sweaty, powder-smeared face on the evening of the fifth day of battle, he knew that he had left behind him 30 wrecked T-34s, and had destroyed 28 Soviet anti-tank guns and two batteries of artillery.

By the 11 July Hoth's forces were only 12 miles from the town of Oboyan. This was where the Russians had centred their defences for the whole of the southern part of the Kursk salient and the Germans knew that this area was a Russian strongpoint. Army Detachment Kempf was fighting to the south-east, towards Rzhavets. Hoth planned to turn to the east, away from Oboyan, and

An artist's impression from *Signal* magazine pays tribute to the services of the mobile workshops which kept the Panzers in the field. Without these back-up services tank formations soon ground to a halt.

destroy the enemy to the south. He could then link with Kempf's forces and force a new path towards Kursk. The town that lay in Hoth's way was Prokhorovka. Success at Prokhorovka was essential to the continuation of the German advance.

Up to 12 July 1943, Prokhorovka was an unknown village. By the end of that day it would earn its place in the history of the Second World War. The Russians, who could see the threat posed by the SS-led armoured advance, poured strong armoured reserves into this area. Among these reserves was the 5th Guards Tank Army who were placed north-east of Prokhorovka alongside 5th Guards Army. The 5th Guards Tank Army could boast a strength of 850 various tanks including T34s and KV-1s. At this stage the Russians estimated that the German armoured advance consisted of 700 vehicles. The truth, however, was very different. Hoth's SS force had been severely weakened by the advance through the extensive enemy defences. By 11 July the II SS Panzer Korps could only muster 300 battle ready machines and a further 230 German armoured vehicles were fighting to their left with the rest of Hoth's forces. One major failure on the part of the Germans was that they failed to detect the formidable enemy force that lay in wait for them. Hoth felt confident that the enemy had been severely weakened and that the German attack would open up the east flank and push the enemy back towards Oboyan. All of this assembled armour was situated in an area of less than three square miles.

The start of the great armoured clash was preceded by air attacks launched by both sides. The Russians also delivered an artillery attack towards the German lines. This was quickly followed by the start of the Russian tank advance. Almost at the same time the Germans moved from their start points towards the Russian lines. The two sides met head-on and a state of extreme confusion soon developed. Any hope of control over these formations was lost as both sides locked horns in a struggle for survival. At such short range the German Tigers and Panthers could not rely upon their far superior, long-range guns. The T-34s and other Russian machines found that they could destroy the German monsters as easily as they could be destroyed themselves. Also, in acts of suicide, Russian tanks were seen driving straight

The Pz. Kpfw VI - The Tiger was the long awaited solution to the qualitative advantages enjoyed by Soviet armour in the Russian campaign. There were never enough manufactured to overcome the massive advantages in numbers that the Soviet forces enjoyed.

into the Tigers and ramming them, the resultant explosion assuring the complete destruction of both machines. In addition the planes and artillery from both sides could not play any part in deciding the outcome, as the danger of destroying friendly forces was too great.

The entire battle had lasted for 12 hours. In this short space of time the finest Divisions in Hitler's Army had been fought to a standstill. They had suffered heavy infantry casualties and could not break through the Russian lines. At the end of this time both sides settled back and assumed defensive positions. They both counted their losses and decided what to do next. The battle at Prokhorovka had resulted in losses for the Germans, but contrary to popular belief, these losses amounted to no more than one hundred and fifty machines in total. The Germans managed to keep their battle-ready tank numbers at a fairly even number around this period; the majority of their losses had taken place in the first few days of the Kursk offensive. After Prokhorovka, the Germans simply lacked the strength and forces necessary to continue the advance. By this stage they were completely exhausted. The Russian tank losses during Prokhorovka stood at around four hundred tanks and this spelt a temporary setback in this area for

them. In the overall plan they knew that they had yet to deliver the main attack elsewhere. Throughout the night of 12 July the Russians and Germans recovered what vehicles they could from Prokhorovka and returned them to the repair shops in an attempt to make their losses good. The engineers destroyed whatever could not be recovered. Smaller scale fighting did continue in this area for the next few days, but the fact was that both the Russians and Germans were exhausted. Hitler called off the Zitadelle offensive on 13 July.

For a number of reasons 12 July 1943 proved a decisive day. Two days earlier on 10 July the allies invaded the island of Sicily. This had been achieved with complete surprise and the invading force consisted of over three thousand ships, a force that the thinly-stretched resources of Germany could never hope to match. By the 12th the allies had landed over one hundred and fifty thousand men and over five hundred tanks on the island. Germany did not have the forces available to defeat this new threat. Hitler was now faced with the one thing he had tried desperately to avoid: a two-front war. There was worse to come.

As the clash of tanks was taking place at Prokhorovka, the Russians were preparing for the counter-attack in other areas. They had amassed a formidable attacking force in the north of the salient. Even as the German offensive continued, they began their probing attacks on 12 July, near Orel. The Germans began to fall back under the weight of this attack. They were weakened beyond repair and on top of this Hitler withdrew the elite 1st SS Panzer Division and sent them south towards the new threat in Italy. At the start of August, the Russian offensive began in full. It quickly gained ground and less than a week after the start of the attack, the Russians had retaken most of the lost areas. By the end of August they even managed Kharkov. This was the fourth and last time this Russian city would change hands. In some areas the going was tough for the Russians. The Germans had dug in well and got the chance to exact a measure of revenge for the losses they had endured. Von Manstein himself directed these defensive battles but the end was now in sight.

Germany had thrown the very best of its armoured forces into this battle in an attempt to win the decisive victory it needed. Hitler had placed all of his hopes in the Waffen-SS formations that had won him victory at Kharkov in March. He ensured that they were given preference in receiving the new Panthers and Tigers, but not even these new heavy tanks could win the day. At the end of this struggle these units, together with the rest of the forces involved, had suffered heavy losses in men and machines. This was to be the last offensive operation mounted by the Germans in the east. What it spelt for the Germans was the start of the end of the Russian campaign. The armies of Adolf Hitler faced a one-way move back towards their homeland. Local successes did take place, but they were not enough to alter the final outcome.

For the Russians, it allowed them to seize the decisive advantage over the Germans. The carefully planned counter-attack tore large gaps in the German front line. They had at last proved that the mighty German Army was beatable. With regards to tanks, sheer numerical superiority overwhelmed the technical superiority of the Panthers and Tigers. This victory did provide a beacon for the whole world; the victory however, lay not with the forces of Hitler, but with the forces of Stalin.

Despite these reverses, Michael Wittmann continued his success in late autumn. Near Brusilov he ran into a Soviet tank assembly area, taking the enemy by surprise, and in that single action, blasted ten tanks from the mass of Soviet armour. Three more fell prey to his Tiger later that afternoon. Wittmann marked every tank eliminated, but he rated the anti-tank guns he destroyed twice as high. He hated these concealed nests, which he called 'the hiding places of death'. By this stage of the war, Wittmann professed that enemy tanks had ceased to be a strain on his nerves, and only the anti-tank guns still made him uncomfortable.

The Nazi propaganda department were naturally keen to capitalise on Wittmann's success and a war writer was sent to join him in his tank. He filed this report:

'In an attack against a large town guarded strongly by tanks and anti-tank guns, we cleared the way rather quickly by destroying several tanks and anti-tank guns and soon reached the town. Our targets were all to the right of our direction of travel, from our twelve to approximately three o'clock positions. Suddenly to our left, behind a haystack, we sighted a Joseph Stalin I with its gun trained on us. Wittmann: "Turn left, target 100 metres, go!". And that was it'.

This action resulted in the destruction of 15 enemy tanks in a single day. Wittmann frequently manoeuvred the Tiger based on his experience in assault guns. From a static position, he would swing the whole vehicle round, rather than waste time moving the turret. Moving the Tiger in this way was accomplished by one track turning forward and the other in reverse. This called for extreme caution with the Tiger however, because of the great danger of shedding one of the huge tracks while turning in place, which could cause soil to accumulate under the idler wheels and the tracks to snap.

Unlike most tank crews, Wittmann's gunner, 'Bobby' Woll, often fired without a target designation from his commander, for, as Wittmann frequently put it, there was no time for a conversation, and Bobby Woll often acquired the target in the few split seconds which meant the difference between life and death.

On 15 January 1944 armoured groups of Leibstandarte and Das Reich divisions were ordered to drive further north-west in the direction of Ljubar. This armoured advance was stopped, principally by heavy fire from anti-tank guns and mortars. Those two days of intense fighting saw Wittmann destroy six enemy tanks, 20 anti-tank guns, 60 guns, 32 trucks and countless other vehicles. On 16 January 1944 both Wittmann and Bobby Woll received the Knight's Cross. Woll was the first soldier holding rank as low as gunner to be awarded such a high decoration. There were now two wearers of the Knight's Cross in Wittmann's Tiger.

As a member of Wittmann's crew, Woll's success surpassed that of every other gunner in the winter battles of 1943 and 1944.

By January, he had destroyed 80 tanks and 107 anti-tank guns. Bobby Woll played an important part in the success of Michael Wittmann. With his quick reactions and good eye, he was a master behind the mighty 'eighty-eight' gun. Confident of Woll's ability, Wittmann was not intimidated and would often take on superior numbers of enemy tanks. The two made a fine team and Woll knew Wittmann's ways to the letter. While a crew's driver, radio operator and loader often changed, the commander and gunner stayed together whenever possible.

Making up the rest of Wittmann's crew in January 1944 were Werner Irrgang (radio operator), Eugen Schmidt (driver) and Sepp Robner (loader).

Balthasar Woll, Michael Wittmann's Tiger gunner, used a rather idiosyncratic method; he pre-set his sights to 800m which was the kind of average length or distance at which a Tiger would engage a target. He would then correct the targets that were closer or further away using his great experience and essentially intuition in order to fire the gun either higher or lower than the point which was directed by the sight, a very quick and efficient way of firing the gun.

The Tigers were feared by the Soviets and the heavy German tanks often drew heavy anti-tank fire in their attacks. They were used as weapons to smash gaps in enemy positions for the grenadiers to move up in support. In countless attacks they breached anti-tank fronts and destroyed enemy artillery positions. With their high rate of fire, they could out-fight any tank on the battlefield. Although few in number, the Tigers performed outstanding feats in the offensive and defensive roles. Constantly under a hail of fire from anti-tank rifles, anti-tank guns and rocket launchers, the Tigers did not get off unscathed. However, thanks to their strong frontal armour they were difficult to knock out. Often shells fired by enemy tanks and anti-tank guns simply bounced off. Nevertheless, the Tiger was not invulnerable, and losses always

kept pace with the slow trickle of new machines arriving at the front from the hard-pressed German factories.

The incredible achievements of Wittmann on the battlefield did not go unnoticed. He was fast becoming a national hero. On 2 February 1944 he was summoned to Hitler's headquarters. Michael Wittmann received the Knight's Cross with Oak Leaves from the hand of Adolf Hitler. In the course of his conversation with Wittmann, Hitler noticed that he was missing a front tooth. He subsequently sent him to his dentist to have the tooth replaced.

CAPTURED SOVIET TANKS T-34/76

When captured - as a large number were - the T-34/76 was designated by the Germans as Panzerkampfwagen T-34 747(r). The Germans were always more than happy to employ as many captured examples as they could and many served with various units. The first examples of captured T-34/76 were in service with 1st, 8th and 11th Panzer Divisions during the summer of 1941, although the crews considered it a dangerous undertaking to utilise captured T-34/76 tanks as many anti-tank gunners fired on sight of the feared T-34 silhouette rather than waiting to see the exact markings. In order to prevent such mistakes the crews of captured T-34s painted large crosses and swastikas on the turret. It was also very common to paint a cross or swastika on top of the turret in order to prevent the Luftwaffe from attacking. Another way to overcome this problem was to use captured T-34/76s in an infantry support role, where recognition problems were less common. The T-34/76D (model 1943) tanks with round twin turret hatches were often nicknamed 'Mickey Mouse' by the Germans because of their comic appearance when both hatches were open.

From late 1941 onwards captured T-34/76 tanks were transported to a workshop in Riga for repairs and modifications, while in 1943 Mercedes-Benz in Marienfelde and Wumag in Goerlitz (now Zgorzelec) were also repairing and modifying T-34s. Captured T-34/76 tanks were modified to German standards by the installation of a commander's cupola and radio equipment. Other non-standard field modifications were also made by the their new crews. Spare parts were never a significant problem and some three hundred

Captured Russian T-34 tanks were sent into action with German markings. This could prove to be a hazardous introduction as frequently German anti-tank teams opened fire at the first sighting of this familiar silhouette without looking to identify the makings.

captured vehicles were maintained on a long term basis. T-34/76s tanks were also used as artillery tractors and ammunition carriers, and badly damaged tanks were either dug in as pillboxes or used for testing and training purposes.

Known users of captured T-34/76 tanks were numerous although there were probably countless occasions on which these machines were used but not recorded. As early as 15 October 1941 the 1st Panzer Division had six T-34/76 tanks. T-34/76 tanks were also in service with the 2nd Panzer Division, 9th Panzer Division, 10th Panzer Division, 20th Panzer Division and the 23rd Panzer Division. A number of T-34/76 tanks were still in service in 1945, for example with the 23rd Panzer Division in Slovakia and East Prussia. In the summer of 1943 a few captured T-34/76 tanks were even operated by Italian crews. According to original German captured tank inventories, as of July 1943 there were 28 T-34(r) serving as part of Army Group South and 22 as part of Army Group Centre. In September of 1943, a R0NA (Russian Army of Liberation) unit commanded by Mieczyslaw Kaminski operated some twenty-four captured T-34/76 tanks against Soviet partisans in Byelorussia. Even elite units such as

Panzergrenadier Division 'Grossdeutschland' used some captured examples as late as 1945. The Waffen-SS units too did not hesitate to use captured T-34/76 tanks and both the 2nd SS Panzer Division 'Das Reich' and the 3rd SS Panzer Division 'Totenkopf' are known to have pressed significant numbers into service. T-34/76 tanks used by 'Das Reich' are of particular interest. When in March 1943, the 1st SS Panzer Corps recaptured Kharkov, 50 models of the T-34/76 tank were captured. All of these had been undergoing repair in a local tractor factory that was overrun and re-designated as the SS Panzerwerk (SS Tank Workshop). Shortly afterwards they were repaired and modified to German standards, repainted and given German markings. Modifications included the installation of commander's cupola (from damaged Panzerkampfwagen III and IV tanks), and the addition of Schurzen (armour skirts). Other equipment such as Notek light, storage boxes, tools, radio equipment and new radio antenna was also added. Twenty-five of these machines entered service with the newly created 3rd SS Panzer Battalion of the 2nd SS Panzer Regiment 'Das Reich'. SS Hauptscharfuhrer Emil Seibold from the 3rd SS Panzer Battalion scored 69 kills during his career, including a number using his Panzerkampfwagen T-34 747(r)in July and August of 1943, during the Battle of Kursk Salient. Seibold received the Knight's Cross during the last decoration ceremony on 6 May 1945. The 3rd SS Panzer Division 'Totenkopf' also pressed a number of captured T-34s into service and there were at least twenty-two T-34/76 tanks in service with this SS Panzer Division during the Battle of Kursk Salient, which means that 'Totenkopf' probably fielded more T-34s than Tigers!

On 30 December 1944 some 29 Panzerkampfwagen T-34 747(r) were in service with 100th Gebirgsjager Regiment. In 1942, a single T-34/76 and KV-2 were used to form 661 Panzer Company for the planned invasion of Malta. Two T-34/76 tanks were certainly captured by Schwere Panzer Abteilung 502 on the Leningrad Front in November 1943 and were pressed into service. There were also some T-34/76 tanks in service with Hermann Goring Fallschirm-Panzer Division which took part in the suppression of the Warsaw Uprising in 1944. In the summer of 1944 the Germans sold three captured T-34/76 tanks to Finland.

LATE WAR CAPTURED TANKS

Late in 1943 an improved model of the T-34 operated by a five-man crew and armed with an 85mm gun and machine gun was introduced. It was designated as T-34/85 and by the end of the war 29,430 of these tanks were produced. Only a few were captured and even fewer actually made it into German service. On 6 September 1944 the 5th SS Panzer Division 'Viking', during heavy fighting on the Vistula front near Warsaw (north of Serock), captured two T-34/85 tanks and used them in action. The 252nd Infantry Division, during their combat in East Prussia, also used a captured T-34/85 in battle.

SELF-PROPELLED ARTILLERY

Once again the US handbook on the German Army of 1945 provides a good insight into how German armour was viewed by the allies. The correct use of self-propelled artillery from 1943 onwards excited considerable interest from the allies, and this contemporary record clearly illustrates the allied concern over these machines,

which first began to make a real impact around the time of the battle of Kursk:

'*DEVELOPMENT. German self-propelled artillery has now developed to a point where there is scarcely any artillery piece up to and including 150mm calibre which has not appeared on at least one self-propelled chassis. Some of these have been experimental, but others have been standardised and have appeared in large numbers.*

PRODUCTION METHODS. Self-propelled artillery has been produced in three different ways. First, there are the gun-chassis combinations which have been designed and engineered carefully to fill a particular role. These were produced in quantity by major armament factories in Germany and exist in large numbers. The 75mm and 105mm assault guns are examples of this type. Second, there are the standard guns fitted on standard tank chassis. Conversion has been carried out in accordance with well-engineered designs at considerable expense of time and skill. Among these are the 10.5cm le. F. H. 1812 on the Gw. II (Wespe) and the 15cm s. F. 11. 1811 on the Gw. III/IV (Hummel). Third, there is a large class of self-propelled guns produced by field conversion, carried out in unit or base workshops, and requiring little skill, time, or material. An example of this is the 15cm s. I. G. 33 mounted on the chassis of the Pz. Kpfw. I

TACTICAL USES. German self-propelled artillery may be divided into four types from a tactical point of view, but the line of demarcation often is not clear, as many self-propelled artillery pieces have dual missions. These types are: close-support artillery, including assault guns; field and medium artillery; tank destroyers; and anti-aircraft artillery.

Close-support and assault guns. The development of close-support and assault guns was begun about 1940. Assault guns are designed for the close support of infantry, and normally consist of a gun of limited traverse on an armoured self-propelled chassis carrying heavy frontal armour. They are inclined to be slower and less manoeuvrable than tanks but are suited particularly well for attacks on enemy infantry heavy weapons and main points of resistance.

Field and medium self-propelled artillery. Field and medium self-propelled artillery was introduced first about the middle of 1942. Both types of howitzers (10.5 cm. le F. H. 18 and 15 cm s. F. H. 18) in the division artillery now may be found on self-propelled chassis.

Self-propelled anti-tank guns. The first self-propelled anti-tank gun was the 4.7 cm Pak. (t) mounted on the then (1941) obsolescent chassis of the Pz. Kpfw. I b. Anti-tank guns now form the numerically largest class of self-propelled artillery weapons.

Self-propelled anti-aircraft artillery. Self-propelled anti-aircraft artillery actually was developed before any attempt was made to apply this principle to other types of weapons, but so far no serious effort has been made to mount anti-aircraft guns larger than 37-mm on motor-driven carriages.

GUN AND CHASSIS MODIFICATIONS. Guns, with the exception of assault guns, are mounted normally on their self-propelled carriages without any major alteration. Assault guns usually are fitted with electric firing devices and modified recoil systems. The chassis, however, particularly in cases where they are those of existing tanks, have undergone considerable modification. Not only have the superstructures been altered, but in some cases the engine has been moved from the rear to a central position to enable the gun crew to stand on the floor of the hull to serve the gun.'

ALLIED TANK LOSSES

It has been estimated that from May 1944 until the end of the war, on any given day, on average, only 600 tanks were available for action in the entire German army. The allies could call on some twenty thousand.

With this tremendous disparity in numbers, the German tank divisions would had to have destroyed ten Russian tanks for every one of their own lost.

In fact, by the end of the war it is estimated that five Russian tanks were destroyed for every German tank. But it was never enough to affect the huge numerical superiority enjoyed by the allies. Even on the Western Front, four allied tanks were being destroyed for every German machine lost.

For the Western allies, the solution was very much the same as the Russians. It was to abandon the search for tactical advances, take a simple workable design and manufacture it in vast quantities. The allied option was the Sherman. It had numerous flaws, chief among them its very high profile, which made an easy target, but it was available in huge numbers. So many Shermans were manufactured that they were even shipped to the East to help the Russian war effort. The Russian response was politely muted as the Sherman never matched the standards of the T-34. Even when it was upgraded to include a high velocity 85mm weapon, the tank was really no match for the new breed of German armour such as the Tiger. As further proof of the Sherman's weakness, it is interesting to note that only a small proportion of Tiger tanks were actually destroyed by allied tanks. The vast majority either fell victim to allied fighter bombers or had to be abandoned and destroyed by their crews when they experienced mechanical difficulties, or, more frequently, ran out of fuel.

From 1944 the allied bombing campaigns were really beginning to bite and the shortage of fuel and spare parts was killing the Panzer formations as effectively as the allied armies were.

Two Panzer IVs and a Marder tank-destroyer are shown in action during the intense battles which led to the recapture of Kharkov.

ACTION IN ITALY AND NORMANDY

Large numbers of self propelled guns finally began to arrive at the front during 1943.

> "In the West we suffered from a severe shortage of heavy weapons and particularly in tanks. Repeated crises in the East had constantly drawn away our tank strength. In June 1944 we were still using some French tanks which we had captured in 1940."
>
> *Lieutenant-General Bodo Zimmerman, on Normandy*

On 25 July 1943 Benito Mussolini was arrested and Marshal Pietro Badoglio became his successor. On 8 September 1943 the Italian Government announced the armistice and Italy dropped out of its alliance with Germany. On 9 September 1943 the Germans quickly occupied Italy, the Italian armed forces were disarmed and equipment confiscated in Operation Achse (Axis). Following the operation Italy declared war on Germany on 13 September. On 15 September Mussolini's New Fascist State, the Salo Republic (or Italian Social Republic -

Republica Sociale Italiana - RSI) was set up in Northern Italy and loyal forces continued fighting alongside the Germans until the end of the war. During Operation Axis the Germans captured large number of Italian armoured fighting vehicles, the majority of which they were familiar with from North Africa. The Germans also occupied many of the Northern Italian plants where the Italian tanks were produced. In addition a large number of other vehicles was also captured. Some captured armoured fighting vehicles were handed over to the armed forces of the Italian Social Republic.

After the completely successful withdrawal from Sicily in 1943, the main focus of the German campaign in Italy lay in dogged defence and it was for this reason that armour was mainly deployed.

Outside of the powerful counter-attacks which were launched against the allied landings at Salerno and Anzio the German tanks were chiefly used as mobile strong points. They were often dug into the ruins of buildings or carefully placed to cover one of the innumerable mountain passes which dotted the Italian countryside.

The US military handbook of 1945 provides a good insight into the German ability to put the lessons from the years of mobile war into the fight against superior numbers of allied machines:

"ANTI-MECHANIZED DEFENCE. In constructing a defensive position the Germans stress construction of obstacles and anti-tank defences. If possible they select tank-proof terrain, and natural tank obstacles, such as steep slopes, are improved. Very steep forward slopes are made at least eight yards deep, while uphill slopes are made 2 to 3 yards high. Originally the Germans constructed anti-tank ditches well forward of the main line of resistance, but experience taught them that such ditches offered favourable jumping-off positions for hostile infantry and also revealed the location of the main line of resistance. At the present time, therefore, anti-tank ditches normally are dug in the area between the main line of resistance and the artillery positions. They are built in an uninterrupted line to avoid leaving passages that can be exploited by the enemy. All crossings essential to assure the maneuvrability of friendly troops are built so that they can be blown up on the shortest notice.

The Germans are aware that obstacles of any kind are effective only when covered by fire from various weapons. Consequently, there usually are trenches behind the anti-tank ditches from which machine-gun and anti-tank-gun fire can cover the entire length of the tank obstacle.

The Germans learned that dense minefields in front of their positions were an inadequate tank obstacle, because the enemy usually neutralised them by massed artillery fire or by concentrated air bombardment before launching a large-scale attack. Now German minefields normally are laid within the main battle position, and only single mines are dispersed in pattern at wide intervals in front of the main line of resistance. Particular stress is placed on the mining of roads. Routes of withdrawal which have to be left open are prepared for mining, and, if time does not permit placing of actual mines, dummy mines are installed.

The Germans employ many kinds of tank obstacles. They recently have used static flame throwers dug into the ground. Usually sited in pairs and in conjunction with other tank obstacles, they are fired by well concealed personnel as soon as hostile tanks come within range.

German anti-tank guns are disposed in depth, with some well forward. They often are dug in and carefully concealed to prevent the enemy from discovering the location and strength of the anti-tank defences prior to attack. In emplacing anti-tank guns, the Germans prefer positions in enfilade or on reverse slopes. They normally employ two to three anti-tank guns in each position, protecting them from infantry attacks with light machine guns. Ranges at which the Germans open fire upon hostile tanks vary according to the caliber of the gun and its position. Although single anti-tank guns sometimes engage enemy tanks at ranges up to 1,000 yards, main anti-tank defenses usually hold their fire until the range is reduced to about 150 to 300 yards. The employment of close-combat anti-tank teams supplements the anti-tank defense. When the hostile tank attack is repulsed, the anti-tank guns move to alternate positions.

The Germans emphasize that the use of smoke can be of great assistance in defeating enemy tank attacks. Smoke shells are fired into the attacking formation about one-third the distance back from the leading echelon. Thus the Germans avoid blinding their own anti-tank gunners, and leading hostile tanks not only are left without adequate support but are silhouetted against the smoke. The Germans also rely on the smoke being sucked into the tanks and forcing the crews to dismount."

THE DEFENCE OF ROME AGAINST THE GERMANS

The German forces fighting in Italy should have been augmented by Italian armour but, as we have seen, most of the Italian machines were of very little fighting value. The Carro Armato (Pesante) P26/40 four-man medium tank was the most modern tank in the Italian Army's arsenal, but only five pre-series vehicles were completed before

German occupation. A single P26/40 was shown to Hitler on 20 October 1943 at Arys (in East Prussia) along with wooden mock-ups of Panzerkampfwagen VI Tiger II Ausf. B (King Tiger) and Jagdpanzer VI Jagdtiger Ausf.B. None of the pre-series vehicles saw any combat with the Italian units and were issued to Panzer Ausbildung Abteilung South (training unit of Army Group C).

After the fall of axis forces in North Africa on 13 May 1943 preparations for planned Operation Husky, the invasion of Sicily began. On 10 July 1943, the allied landings took place and by 17 August 1943 allied forces had reached Messina. Sicily provided the allies with a first foothold in Europe, although the majority of German and Italian defenders were evacuated along with their equipment to the Italian mainland. On 3 September 1943 the Allies crossed the Strait of Messina and invaded the Italian mainland. The Italian campaign, with its prolonged heavy fighting, did not have a significant impact on the course of war other than the fact that it tied up a large number of German troops. The campaign ended on 2 May 1945 when the last German units in Northern Italy surrendered.

During the Italian campaign allied forces used a variety of armoured fighting vehicles, but it appears that only a small number were captured by the Germans. This can be explained by the fact that during the course of the campaign Germans were mainly on the defensive or were skilfully retreating.

THE WESTERN FRONT

The best indication of the allied view of the qualities of German armour and armoured formations generally comes from the US army handbook. As a document actually designed for those going into the field, we have an excellent view of the German forces through contemporary eyes.

It is interesting to note that the main lessons from the development of the German tank forces were already becoming apparent when this remarkably well-informed piece was being written in 1945:

'The story of German armored vehicle development is concerned principally with tanks, which have undergone considerable change since the beginning of the war. German tanks have shown, in the course of 5 years of war, a gradual change from the Blitzkrieg concept of battle to greater emphasis on defensive, or at least offensive-defensive, operations for which the latest German tank, the King Tiger, heavily armed and armored but relatively slow and unmaneuverable, was most suitable.

German tank development began in 1934, ostensibly at the same time as the rest of the rearmament program, but there is no doubt that considerable thought and experimentation had been devoted to the subject before then. By 1939 the Germans had evolved four types of tanks: the Pz. Kpfw. I, II, III, and IV, with which the Blitzkrieg campaigns were conducted. There is evidence that larger tanks were being developed in 1939, and specimens of what are assumed to have been a Pz. Kpfw. V and a Pz. Kpfw. VI in an experimental stage were employed in the invasion of Norway. These, however, must have proved unsatisfactory, since they were dropped, and the present Pz. Kpfw. V (Panther) and Pz. Kpfw. VI (Tiger) have no connection with them.

Meanwhile, the Pz. Kpfw. I and II gradually became obsolescent, first being relegated to reconnaissance roles and then finally disappearing in 1943 from the Table of Equipment of the Panzer regiment. The heavier tanks, Pz. Kpfw. III and IV, which had proven satisfactory under fire, were modified to meet new conditions by thicker armor and more effective guns.

In 1942, the Pz. Kpfw. VI, or Tiger, appeared in Russia, and later in Africa. The Tiger was designed in the direct German tradition, and simply was armed more heavily and armored more thickly than its predecessors. It appeared out of its proper order in the line of succession, for the Pz. Kpfw. V, or Panther, did not appear until nearly a year later. The Panther was somewhat of a surprise, since it marked a departure from the conventional lines of German design, and in the arrangement of its armor showed strong signs of Russian influence. Its great success [Pz. Kpfw. is the German abbreviation for Panzerkampfwagen, meaning armored fighting vehicle or tank] in combat undoubtedly gave rise to the decision to redesign the Tiger, which to some extent had fallen short of expectations. The new version is the Königstiger or King Tiger.

A Panzer II advances deeper into Russia during the early phase of the campaign. By 1944 these tanks were obsolete but some were still in service in a policing role.

OBSOLETE TANKS

GENERAL. The Pz. Kpfw. I, Pz. Kpfw. II, and Pz. Kpfw. III, although obsolete, are discussed here since they still may be met occasionally in the field.

LIGHT TANK (Pz. Kpfw. 1). (1) General. This was the first tank to be standardized by the Germans, and the first ones were produced in 1934. Three models (A, B, and C) and a commander's version (based on model B) have been identified, but model C never has been encountered in action. The hull of the Pz. Kpfw. I was used as a self-propelled mount for several types of artillery weapons, but it no longer will be met even in this role.

LIGHT TANK (Pz. Kpfw. 11). (1) General. This tank is manned by three men: a commander, who acts as the gunner; a radio operator; and a driver. A large number of models of this tank were produced before it became obsolete. In a very much modified form it has reappeared as the Luchs (Lynx) reconnaissance tank in Western Europe. The original experimental models of Pz. Kpfw. II were produced between 1934 and 1936; it finally was abandoned as a fighting vehicle in

1943. A flame-throwing version, Pz. Kpfw. II (F), also has become obsolete and probably will not be met again. Model F, not the flame-thrower tank, was the latest model encountered. The modified hull of the Pz. Kpfw. II is still in use as a self-propelled gun carriage, notably in the case of the 15 cm, s.I.G. 33 and the 10 cm, le. F.H. 18.(2) Specifications.

MEDIUM TANK (Pz. Kpfw. 111). (1) General. This tank has appeared in many models but has retained basic characteristics throughout. The latest models to appear are armed with the long-barreled 5 cm Kw.K. 39 (L/60), which in 1942 displaced the shorter 5 cm Kw.K. (L/42). The original main armament, discarded late in 1940, was a 37-mm gun. The Pz. Kpfw. III now is obsolete and rarely encountered. The excellent hull and suspension have been utilized as the carriage for self-propelled guns, and it is in this form that the vehicle remains in production. The Pz. Kpfw. III has been encountered armed with the short 7.5 cm Kw.K. (the original armament of the Pz. Kpfw. IV), and also as a commander's vehicle, as a flame-throwing tank, as a wrecker tank, as an armored ammunition carrier, and as an armored observation post."

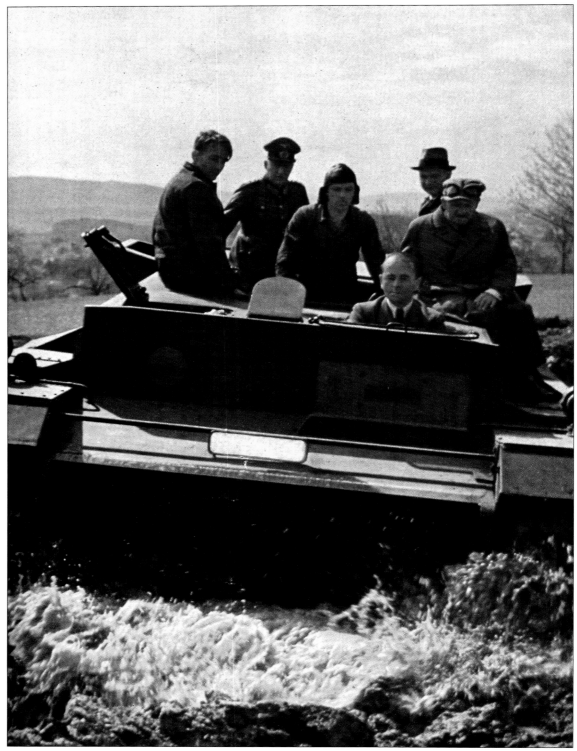

Albert Speer and a group of technicians are seen here driving the chassis of the Tiger E Series. The Tiger proved itself to be well adapted to the strains of the Russian front; the wide tracks made it well-suited for driving through mud as Speer is in the process of demonstrating.

ANTI-AIRCRAFT TANKS

By 1944, the allied airforces in the west enjoyed almost total air superiority. In Russia the airforce had recovered from its early defeats and was now almost as effective as the British and Americans. Vehicle losses reached catastrophic proportions as the fighter-bombers roared over the front looking for targets.

Now the real priority was for anti-aircraft protection which could move with the tanks and give some cover against the relentless attacks of the allied fighter-bombers. It was in this role that more Panzer IV conversions were made. These self-propelled anti-aircraft guns were produced in three forms. Firstly, there was the Möbelwagen (the troops nickname meant furniture van, because of its resemblance to a peacetime removal truck). Interestingly, the same nickname had earlier been used for the Tiger in response to its uncompromising flat-sided construction. The Möbelwagen was followed by two later machines, the Wirbelwind or Whirlwind, and Ostwind or East Wind.

In the case of the Möbelwagen, this was very much a wartime contingency measure, rather than a purpose-designed vehicle.

As damaged Panzer IVs were brought back for repair from the Eastern front, they were converted to an anti-aircraft role by the simple expedient of taking off the turret and replacing it with a 20mm flak gun which was protected, when in transit, by four collapsible sides, which were lowered when the flak gun was in action.

To say this was an unsuccessful design was an understatement, as the 20cm was no longer an effective anti-aircraft gun. Of even greater concern was the fact that the sides of the Möbelwagen had to be lowered to allow the gun to fire. This left the crew with no protection whatsoever, and defeated the whole purpose of mounting the gun on a tank chassis in the first place. The front line troops were quick to point out that, in action, the same result could have been achieved by placing an anti-aircraft gun on the back of a truck.

Miraculously, 240 conversions had been made before this glaring design flaw came to light. Effectively, 240 precious tanks had been wasted. A measure of effectiveness was achieved by increasing the size of gun from 20mm to 37mm, but the Möbelwagen was deemed a failure. It was obvious that what was required was an anti-aircraft vehicle that gave the crew the benefits of armour protection while they were in action.

The immediate solution was the Wirbelwind. It used the Panzer IV chassis and four 20mm flak guns in a quad arrangement, now mounted on a fully rotating turret which gave the crew some measure of protection.

Even mounted in groups of four, the 20mm flak gun was still ineffectual against the heavily armoured allied aircraft, so the Wirbelwind was discontinued after 100 had been built.

The successor to the Wirbelwind was the Ostwind. It carried the more effective 37mm flak gun, in a fully rotating covered turret, but the end of the war was now in sight and only 43 machines were made to combat an allied airforce which was flying 20,000 aircraft in the skies over Germany.

Despite the revolutionary quality of many of the machines produced for Hitler's armies, they could never hope to match the sheer weight of numbers ranged against them.

This virtually complete air supremacy was put to extremely good use during the battle for Normandy. Allied bombers could reduce German beach defences, and cut German lines of communication, thus paralysing the build up of German forces opposite the amphibious and airborne landed British and American forces. And of course tactical air support could create absolute havoc to any German unit in Normandy foolish enough to try to move its strength by day. Newsreels of the period show German vehicles covered in branches in an attempt to disguise any vehicle movements from the air. The crew constantly scanned the horizon for the first signs of the British fighter-bombers, which made any movement on the ground an extremely hazardous undertaking.

MEDIUM TANKS IN NORMANDY

The US handbook, as always, gave a good assessment of the armour types which the allies were liable to meet on the ground in Normandy. By now the allied intelligence network had a clear picture of the main machines in operation by the Wehrmacht forces and was able to produce a highly prescient insight into the Panzer forces in the field under very short timescales. This extract gives an assessment of the Medium and Heavy Tanks in service against the Allies during the 1944-45 period:

Operational Status of Tigers on the Eastern and Western Fron[t]

	1st Sep 1942	1st Oct 1942	1st Nov 1942	1st Dec 1942	1st Jan 1943	1st Feb 1943	1st Mar 1943	1st Apr 1943	1st May 1943	1st Jun 1943	1st Jul 1943	1st Aug 1943	1st Sep 1943	1st Oct 1943	1st Nov 1943	1st D[ec] 19[43]
Tigers issued in the month	4	3	0	2	0	39	34	0	40	27	18	50	43	66	27	4
Operational Tigers	2	4	4	6	6	15	30	20	90	110	125	40	45	40	75	8
Tigers in need of repair	2	2	2	2	2	21	37	39	12	19	22	139	145	186	146	18
Total writeoffs	0	1	0	0	0	11	3	5	0	0	0	18	32	30	32	2

Legend:

- TIGERS ISSUED IN THE MONTH
- OPERATIONAL TIGERS
- TIGERS IN NEED OF REPAIR
- TOTAL WRITEOFFS

1st September 1942 - 5th April 1945

5	80	82	74	43	36	106	171	71	115	9	139	141	32	47	51
5	115	130	130	122	285	215	150	105	267	185	267	330	233	140	95
-3	143	154	120	146	61	93	132	117	79	127	141	136	93	120	78
4	57	52	110	62	0	76	147	179	28	46	35	29	86	146	122

1st	1st	1st	1st	1st	1st	1st	1st	1st	1st	1st	1st	1st	15th	15th	5th
n	Feb	Mar	Apr	May	Jun	Jul	Aug	Sep	Oct	Nov	Dec	Jan	Jan	Mar	Apr
44	1944	1944	1944	1944	1944	1944	1944	1944	1944	1944	1944	1945	1945	1945	1945

155

A Marder tank-destroyer moving past the flaming wreckage of a Russian village. The Marder was very much a stop-gap solution but it was widely used on the Eastern Front.

'Pz. Kpfw. IV. (1) General. Of the four tank types with which the Germans started the war, only the Pz. Kpfw. IV survives in service, although its role has been changed and it now carries a main armament which resembles the original gun only in caliber. It was armed originally with a short-barreled 75-mm gun (7.5 cm Kw.K. (L/24)) and a machine gun mounted coaxially in the turret. In later models a hull machine gun was added. With this short, low-velocity gun the tank was primarily a close-support weapon. In 1942 it was re-armed with a long-barreled, high velocity gun, the 7.5 cm Kw.K. 40 (L/43), and thus changed its role from a close-support vehicle to a fighting tank and displaced the Pz. Kpfw. III as the main armament of the Panzer regiment. At the present time the Pz. Kpfw. IV is only a stop-gap for the Panther. If enough Panther tanks become available, the disappearance of the Pz. Kpfw. IV may be expected.

The latest version of this tank to appear is the Model H, which differs from the Model G, of which details are given, only in its 75-mm gun being 48 calibers long instead of 43. There is no change in the ballistic characteristics.

This tank also has appeared in a commander's model, as an observation-post tank, as an ammunition tank, and as an armored antiaircraft vehicle. The hull and suspension also have been employed for self-propelled guns.

HEAVY TANKS

Pz. Kpfw. PANTHER. (1) General. In this tank, probably the most successful they have produced,

the Germans have departed from their customary lines and sought inspiration in the design of the Russian T-34. The tank weighs about 50 short tons, and the effectiveness of its armor is enhanced by the fact that most of the plates are sloping. It has powerful armament, and has a high-powered engine which gives it a maximum speed of about 30 miles per hour. Internally the Panther is arranged in the standard German manner, with the driver's compartment in front, the fighting compartment in the center section, and the engine at the rear.

The Panther's design employs the double torsion-bar suspension. There are eight double, interleaved, large Christie-type bogie wheels. Each set of bogie wheels is mounted on a radius arm on the projecting end of a torsion bar which is coupled in series to a second one lying parallel to it. This ingenious device has the effect of doubling the length of the torsion bars.

The Panther first was met in action on the Russian front in the summer of 1943. Originally designated Pz. Kpfw. V, its nickname, Panther, was adopted as its official nomenclature in February 1944. The latest version to appear is the Model G. The principal reasons for the success of the Panther are its relatively high speed, maneuverability, dangerous armament, and good protection. Variants of the Panther tank which have been identified are the commander's version, the wrecker tank (Bergepanther), and the self-propelled gun Jagdpanther, which consists of the 8.8 cm Pak 43/3 or 4 on the Panther chassis.

Pz. Kpfw. TIGER, MODEL B (KING TIGER). (1) General. This tank is a development of the Tiger along the lines of the Panther and with a new main armament, the 8.8 cm Kw.K. 43 (L/71). The armor is as thick as that of the Tiger - in some parts thicker - and the improved design and the slope given to the majority of the plates (as in the Panther) give the tank vastly improved protection.

The King Tiger is a tank designed essentially for defensive warfare or for breaking through strong lines of defense. It is unsuitable for rapid maneuver and highly mobile warfare because of its great weight and low speed. To accommodate the gun the turret has been made unusually long in proportion to the total length of the tank. When 'buttoned up' the tank is extremely blind, and this is one of its weakest points.

Since the King Tiger first appeared in August 1944 in Normandy, modifications have been made *in the turret to eliminate the excessive plate-bending involved in the original construction. The King Tiger virtually is invulnerable to frontal attack, but the flanks, which are less well protected, can be penetrated by Allied anti-tank weapons at most normal combat ranges."*

After the war Fritz Bayerlein and the commander of the Panzer Lehr Division recorded the effects of the allied air attacks. General Bayerlein, like all the other divisional commanders on the ground, knew that in the face of allied air superiority it was almost suicidal to move during the day. Nonetheless, in their desire to rush as many troops into battle as quickly as possible the German High Command proved to be stubbornly inflexible, as Bayerlein bitterly recalled:

"At 2 o'clock in the morning of 6 June I was alerted that the invasion fleet was coming across the Channel. I was told to begin moving north that afternoon at 5 o'clock. Well this was too early. Air attacks had been severe in the daylight and everyone knew that everything that could fly would support the invasion. My request for a delay until twilight was refused. So we moved as ordered and immediately came under allied air attack. I lost 20 or 30 vehicles by nightfall. At daylight next morning, the commander of the 7th Army gave me a direct order to proceed and there was nothing else I could do, so the vehicles moved off as ordered. By the end of the day I had lost 40 trucks and 90 others. Five of my tanks were knocked out and 84 half tracks, prime movers and self-propelled guns. These were serious losses for a division not yet in action".

THE CHAIN OF COMMAND

On the German side, the allied air superiority was just one of a number of serious disadvantages which had to be overcome if they were to conduct a successful campaign in the West. Chief among these was the confusion and disorganisation which prevailed in the chain of command. As Supreme Commander, Adolf Hitler constantly dabbled in every aspect of the forces at his command and he had a habit of reserving particularly powerful formations for his personal control.

The situation in France was an especially complicated one. The nominal commander-in-chief was Von Runstedt, who controlled Army Group B, responsible for northern France and

Belgium, and Army Group G, which was responsible for southern France, but Rommel, in command of Army Group B, enjoyed the favour of Hitler and in practice could not be overruled by his superiors. To further compound matters three of the Panzer divisions operating within Rommel's area of influence were allocated to a separate formation known as Panzer Group West. This powerful grouping was designated as an Army Reserve and could only be deployed on the express authority of Hitler himself. This complicated and divisive policy was a result of Hitler's mistrust of the generals, and there is a great deal of evidence to suggest that the 'divide and rule' policy was a deliberate stratagem on Hitler's part.

By 1944 the flaws which affected the High Command were also reflected in the declining quality of the men in the ranks. The steady war of attrition in Russia meant that the Wehrmacht had to accept lower and lower standards of physical fitness for new recruits. Men who would previously have been refused for the armed services had to be called into action. One famous example is 'the stomach battalion' which was filled with middle aged men who had stomach complaints, and therefore required a special diet.

At the other end of the spectrum from the ageing warriors of the stomach battalion, the German Army also had to allow the deployment of the 12th SS Panzer Division, better known as the Hitler Youth Division. This division was led by experienced officers drawn from the famous SS Leibstandarte Division, and the ranks were filled almost entirely by teenagers. The average age of the division was just 18. Although the Hitler Youth Division fought with enormous courage and ferocity in the coming battle, the mere fact that it was now necessary to deploy divisions composed of schoolboys shows the desperation of the German army.

The overwhelming demands of a war on three fronts posed hosts of additional problems for the German logistics and supply system. Allied fighters and fighter-bombers had not restricted their attacks to the troops on the ground, they also carried out a massive air and interdiction campaign against the German supply lines. Roads and railway lines were mercilessly targeted, which meant that supplies of essential fuel and ammunition stocks could not reach the hard-pressed front line. By this stage of the war,

Germany was under constant attack by allied bomber formations and fuel was already in very short supply. In Normandy, in many cases, German tanks which were needed urgently to resist the invasion could not move through lack of fuel.

To offset the many disadvantages which faced the German troops fighting on the ground in Normandy, they did enjoy some real advantages over the allies. Many of the Panzer divisions which would be used to fight the allies had a strong core of battle hardened, experienced troops, who had already seen four years of brutal warfare. This gave them the mental toughness which would serve them in great stead during the coming battle.

The German forces also enjoyed a very real superiority in the quality of their tank forces. Not only were the crews hugely experienced thanks to their years on the Russian front, but the tanks themselves were far better than those used by the allies. In particular the Tiger, Panther and the new King Tiger tanks could all engage allied tanks at much longer ranges than those at which the allies could fight back. The superior armour of the tanks also gave the Germans a marked advantage in battle. Time and time again, allied tank soldiers described that disheartening experience of seeing their own shells bounce off the armour of the German tanks. This disparity in quality was to have a very real impact on the coming battles.

WITTMANN MOVES WEST

Wittmann also took advantage of this brief pause from the fighting, while he recovered, to marry his sweetheart, Hildegard Burmeister. Once again, it was an unmistakably Nazi event. After the wedding ceremony, performed by the civil magistrate, Wittmann accepted a gift copy of *Mein Kampf*, a speech was then given by SS-Sturmbannfuhrer Pein, who declared that the philosophy of life of the Teutons still had meaning in their lives.

Wittmann's period of calm was to prove short-lived. On 6 June 1944 the allies landed in Normandy. It was here that he would gain lasting fame.

The actual events of the D-Day landings themselves have little impact on our story, save to say that most of the allied objectives were achieved on that crucial first day with one major exception - the capture of Caen.

The only German armoured formation to be engaged against the allies on 6 June was the 21st Panzer Division. As we have seen, this was not the famous formation which had fought so tenaciously under Rommel in North Africa. Now once again under his command, this reconstituted formation consisted of a tiny cadre of staff who had somehow escaped the North African debacle bolstered by a large number of inexperienced recruits.

The 21st Panzer Division fielded Panzer IVs as its main battle tanks, but it was also forced to use a number of captured French tanks which had been taken in 1940. Not surprisingly this was a less than fearsome adversary. Nonetheless, the 21st Panzer Division did enjoy some success on D-Day and actually managed to reach the Channel coast before being forced to withdraw by the arrival of superior allied forces.

The city of Caen, which should have been in allied hands on D-Day plus one, was to remain in German hands until 18 July, six weeks after the beginning of the battle. The reasons for the successful defence at Caen lay in the extremely difficult nature of the Bocage country in which the campaign was fought. The Bocage was a closely packed area of narrow lanes and high banked hedgerows enclosing small fields and sunken lanes. It proved to be ideal defensive terrain where anti-tank guns and machine-gun nests could be concealed until the last possible moment.

The allies had the advantage in numbers of tanks, but in the claustrophobic world of the Bocage, anti-tank teams could get close enough to the tanks to attack them at murderously close range.

Faced with their inability to take the remaining D-Day objective the British High Command had no alternative to fighting in the Bocage. As casualties steadily mounted, the airfield at Carpiquet on the outskirts of Caen became a vital target. It was tenaciously defended by the youngsters of the Hitler Youth Division against a series of assaults by larger British forces.

These youngsters were disdainful of the traditions of the established SS Divisions of the German army and for their divisional symbol they adopted a German runic symbol, but arrogantly placed it over the key symbol of the veteran SS Leibstandarte Division, in a challenge to the experienced members of the most senior SS Division, who now knew that they had a younger rival for the mantle of the Third Reich's leading

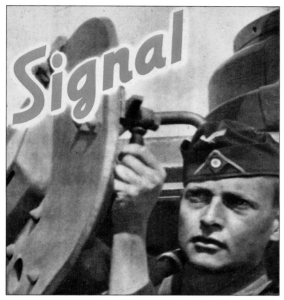

The gun-loader of a Panzer IV closes the turret side hatch in preparation for moving into battle. These side hatches were recognised as a major design flaw which compromised the effectiveness of the turret armour.

fighting formation. The Hitler Youth Division performed very well in battle but the High Command must have taken a dim view of their habit of painting their girlfriend's names on their tanks in preference to the approved divisional numbering. Under incredibly difficult circumstances, the Hitler Youth Division fought so well that their commanders had little choice but to turn a blind eye to this breach of regulations.

VILLERS-BOCAGE

In an attempt to outflank these stubborn defenders at Carpiquet, Montgomery dispatched his highly experienced 7th Armoured Division, the 'Desert Rats', to make a broad sweep south of Caen, which was scheduled to begin on 12 June. The attack was aimed at the small town of Villers-Bocage and it was here that one of the most famous tank actions of the war would be fought. The allied spearhead was halted and almost single-handedly destroyed in a fierce battle through the streets and fields surrounding Villers-Bocage by German Tiger tanks of the 101st heavy battalion, led by the famous Michael Wittmann.

On the morning of 13 June 1944 Wittmann was near Villers-Bocage when he surprised a squadron

of the County of London Yeomanry. The unsuspecting British troops had stopped for breakfast, when Wittmann's Tiger roared up. In no time the lightning reflexes of Wittmann and Bobby Woll had claimed twelve half-tracks, three light tanks and six medium tanks. Wittmann then dashed back and gathered three other Tigers and a Panzer IV.

At eight o'clock a lookout reported to SS-Obersturmfuhrer Wittmann that a large column of enemy tanks was advancing on the Caen-Villers-Bocage road. Wittmann, who was in cover with his Tiger south of the road, saw a British armoured battalion followed by an English armoured troop carrier battalion advancing for Villers-Bocage.

The situation called for immediate action. Wittmann was unable to get the order to his other tanks, who had moved off. Instead, he immediately drove at the English column with his single tank, firing on the move. This rapid intervention initially split the column. For 80 metres Wittmann destroyed four Sherman Firefly tanks, positioned his Tiger next to the column and drove ten to thirty metres beside it firing in his direction of travel, along the column. He succeeded in knocking out 12 enemy tanks in a very short time. The accompanying battalion, in armoured troop carriers, was almost completely wiped out. The following German tanks and infantry company took about one hundred and thirty prisoners, but Wittmann drove on, in advance of his company, into the town of Villers-Bocage.

Just before the Hotel du Bras d'Or he destroyed another Sherman, and then found himself facing several enemy tanks at the exit from the town, the Jeanne d'Arc Square. He subsequently turned his Tiger around and drove back down the main street. As it passed the Huet-Godefroy clothing store, the Tiger was hit by a shell fired by an anti-tank gun, which wrecked one of the drive sprockets.

TANKS IN BUILT-UP AREAS

Wittmann should have known better than to take a tank into the streets of the town. Despite the myriad dangers, the tank was the Queen of the battlefield in the wide-open spaces of North Africa and Russia. In the first four months of the war, the Germans discovered that there was one environment in which tanks should never be deployed - the built-up areas of towns and cities. There, they became especially vulnerable to lurking infantry and anti-tank guns.

The Germans learned this lesson as early as the Polish campaign of 1939, in the battle for Warsaw, but despite all of their previous experiences, these mistakes were repeated at Stalingrad, Kursk and in Normandy. Some commanders continued to commit tanks in towns right up to 1945.

In 1944 destroyed German tanks littered the streets of Villers-Bocage. They were destroyed by concealed British anti-tank guns when they grew too confident and rolled into the town after a period of conspicuous success in the open fields around the town.

OPERATION EPSOM

During the last three weeks of June, as British casualties climbed, Montgomery knew that something had to be done to break the stalemate around Caen. His answer was Operation Epsom, which was launched on 26 June 1944. It began with a massive allied artillery bombardment which pounded the enemy defences around the airfield. On the receiving end were units from three Panzer divisions, the Hitler Youth Division who were still holding out around Carpiquet airfield, the 21st Division, and the elite Panzer Lehr Division. Despite the incredible bombardments these three divisions held their ground and the 15th Scottish infantry division was badly mauled in the fighting. The Epsom offensive ground to a halt less than four miles from the British start line. But there was even worse to come. Anticipating German reinforcements, Lieutenant General Sir Miles Dempsey, Commander of the British Second Army, withdrew from even the small gains which had been achieved.

Operation Epsom was abandoned with Caen still in German hands, and with its failure Montgomery decided that it was now time to take a sledgehammer to Caen, which was to be attacked and captured in a frontal assault, codenamed Operation Charnwood, scheduled for 8 July. Until the allies could break out past Caen, the beachhead would continue to be jammed with men and supplies, unable to move inland and highly vulnerable to counter-attack.

More importantly, the British had yet to capture an airfield. Charnwood was meant to provide a quick and brutal solution to the problems, but the sheer scale of the operation and the overwhelming level of back-up support available to Montgomery

actually worked against the British forces.

To soften up the German defenders, no less than 467 British and Canadian bombers were allocated to attack the town prior to the offensive. This total disregard for the lives of their civilian allies caused 10,000 civilian casualties. More importantly, it created a wilderness of rubble similar to that which had appeared after the allied bombing at Monte Cassino in 1943. The huge bomb craters and acres of rubble produced a ready-made series of impenetrable defences. For the men who had seen action in Russia and Italy, the ruins of Caen provided a heaven-sent opportunity for men who knew from bitter experience exactly how to defend ruined cities.

Once again the attack had to be called off in the face of huge British casualties, but this time there was at least one glimmer of consolation: the Royal Winnipeg Rifles had finally succeeded in capturing the airstrip at Carpiquet and wresting the Garrison from the Hitler Youth Division.

Despite this moderate success, Montgomery was now the recipient of some worrying news from London. The enormous casualty rate around Caen was draining away the British replacements and if the loss rate continued at its present level replacements would run out at the end of July.

It was against this background that Montgomery decided to try one last offensive. Designed to capture the territory south of Caen, it was codenamed Operation Goodwood and scheduled

With the allied domination of the air, a number of attempts were made to produce decoys - in this case a wooden model of a Panther tank has been constructed.

for 17 July. Operation Goodwood was a massive tank attack involving all four British and Canadian Corps in Normandy. There were so many troops involved that there was a day's delay while all the necessary men and vehicles were brought into position. But hopes ran high that the war of attrition had finally turned in the British favour.

Goodwood began with an overwhelming air, naval and artillery bombardment, designed to blast a path for 750 tanks to advance towards the high ground south of Caen. Once again their opponents were to be men of the Ist SS Panzer Corps, many of whom had been in action since 8 June. In the steady war of attrition the SS Corps had been reduced to a strength of just 100 tanks but they could still command the deep defensive positions of the Bocage and they were backed up with the deadly 88mm anti-tank guns. The opening allied barrage was so intensive it was described by some German veterans as the biggest and most intense artillery bombardment they had ever witnessed, even in Russia. There are accounts of Tiger tanks being thrown into the air. Under this intense storm of steel men went mad and had to be committed to mental hospitals, and there are at least two documented cases of German soldiers who committed suicide rather than endure the bombardment any longer.

Despite massive preparations which were made, Goodwood was an even greater failure than the previous offensives. Although the southern sector of Caen was cleared of the enemy, the allies lost 200 tanks in a single day as they tried to cross the Orne. Fighting for Caen continued until 20 July but once again the operation had to be postponed, with part of the city still in German hands.

Despite all the British had done, Operation Cobra - the breakout from Normandy -still faced some tough fighting before the American forces were finally able to break out of the Bocage and sweep southwards into open country. As the American offensive began to gather pace, the British forces took advantage of the confusion in the German ranks to form the northern pincer in this huge encircling movement, designed to trap the German forces in Normandy in a huge pocket centred on the town of Falaise.

As always the 1st SS Panzer Corps continued to resist every step of the way and they inflicted a severe reverse on the 1st Polish Armoured Division on 9 August when the Poles lost 150 tanks. Losses

on this scale would have been catastrophic for the German forces, but to the allies, with their resources, they appeared to be little more than an inconvenience. In the face of continued resistance the British forces kept up the drive southwards and by 20 August they had linked up with the American forces to close a ring around Falaise.

Although 40,000 German troops had managed to escape before the pocket was closed, 60,000 remained trapped inside along with the bulk of the German armour. It was now that the allied airforce swept in for the kill. Led by squadron after squadron of rocket firing Typhoons, they pounded the densely packed columns of German troops as they struggled to free themselves from the allied trap. The scene of carnage in the retreating columns is almost impossible to describe. 10,000 Germans died in the incessant air attacks; 50,000 more were taken prisoner.

These men represented the remains of 40 German divisions which had been destroyed in the battle for Normandy. Four-fifths of the German army who had been committed to the campaign in Normandy had been destroyed. Montgomery had won his battle and exactly as planned the allies were on the River Seine by D-Day plus 90.

PANZERS IN THE FIELD

As the war continued each surviving tank in the German Panzer Divisions became an increasingly valuable asset. As battlefield losses rose, the war-ravaged German factories which were being pounded day and night by allied bombers could no longer keep increasing the supply of war vehicles to match those destroyed.

However, provided it wasn't actually blown apart, or completely gutted by fire, a battle-damaged tank could actually be repaired and brought back into service.

For the allies, with their limitless supplies of men and material, this was a less pressing issue, but for the Germans it was a vital matter. It was a source of great frustration to many German tank crews that Hitler himself placed a priority on the production of new tanks over the supply of replacement parts and engines. In many cases, old tanks could easily have been brought back into service at the front line with a regular supply of spare parts and engines, which would have been easier and more efficient.

Panzerkampfwagen VI (B) Sd.Kfz. 182

The Tiger II Ausf B was known as the King Tiger ("Konigstiger" / VK 4503 (H)) and is recognized as the most powerful combat tank of the war. It resembled the Panther more than the Tiger I and had a long barrelled 88mm gun which could destroy a Sherman Tank at a range of 2000 metres. Like the Tiger I, the Tiger II suffered from poor mobility from its excessive weight and high fuel consumption.

Production of the King Tiger began in January 1944 after Hitler had passed the wooden mock-ups presented to him the previous October. The crew of five were protected by a thick sloping body of armour which very few weapons could hope to defeat. The King Tiger was compared favourably with the Russian T-34/85 and JS-II and had a reputation as a superior war machine. From November 1944 a number of Tiger II's were converted to command tanks mounted with additional radio equipment. This was designated as the Befehlswagen Tiger II Ausf B.

Armour - Tiger II Ausf B.
Armour Type; Homogenous rolled/welded nickel-steel
Hull Front: 100-150mm
Hull Sides: 80mm
Hull Rear: 80mm
Hull Top: 40mm
Hull Bottom: 25-40mm
Turret Front: 180mm
Turret Sides: 80mm
Turret Rear: 80mm
Turret Top: 40mm

Armament - Tiger II Ausf B
Main Armament: 8.8cm L/71 KwK43
Secondary Armament: 2 x 7.92mm MG34
Ancillary Armament: Grenade/bomb Launcher

The first time that the King Tiger went into combat was in May 1944 near Minsk, followed by Poland in July. It also saw battle on both the Western and Eastern Fronts and was an effective combat weapon. The problems with mobility presented by its huge weight, and the vast amount of precious production resources consumed by each King Tiger ultimately outweighed the advantages of the mark.

Tiger IIs take shelter under trees to avoid being seen by allied aircraft during the fighting in the Normandy campaign.

Model:	Pz.Kpfw. VI Tiger II Ausf B
Crew	5
Hull Length	7.25m
Length (gun forward)	10.43m
Width	3.72m
Overall Height	3.72m
Gross Weight	68.5 tons
Ground Pressure	0.78kg/cm²
Fording Capacity	1.6m
Maximum Gradient	36 degrees
Maximum Trench Width	2.5m
Maximum Vertical Obstacle	0.85m
Suspension Type	Torsion Bar

Engine:	
Powerplant	Maybach HL230 P30 V-12 water-cooled petrol
Capacity	231 (5 gallons)
Output	700bhp/515kW at 3000rpm
Power/Weight Ratio	10bhp/tonne
Fuel Capacity	8601 (189 gallons)
Range (Road)	170km (105 miles)
Range (Crosscountry)	120km (70 miles)
Maximum Speed	38km/h (24 mph)

Panzerkampfwagen VI (B)
Sd.Kfz. 182

Tank Numbering

German tanks usually carried a three figure identification number painted on the turret.

Regimental staffs usually used the letter R in place of the letter 0, so R01 would be the regimental commander. Battalion staffs used the number of the unit in Roman numerals, therefore I01 would be the commander of the 1st battalion.

The first number specified the company, the second number specified the platoon number and the third number specified the number of the tank within the four tank section or (Zug). Using this system tank number 414 would be the fourth tank in the first Zug of the fourth company.

Headquarters command tanks in companies were identified by the prefix 0 followed by a designated number from 1-9.

Company command tanks were generally identified by the number 0 in place of the platoon number and a standard number which identifies the officer's place in the hierarchy. For example, number 004 for the HQ Leader and 005 for the Company Commander.

THE WESTERN FRONT 1944-1945

The King Tiger was only available in very limited numbers during the fighting in Normandy. This picture, taken in the late summer of 1944, shows one of the four machines which made it into the fighting.

> "The breakthrough along the entire front was to be carried out by the infantry divisions. The armour was then to exploit the shock effect of the assault and drive through the gaps. It was to head due west into the enemy rear. It was to by-pass strongly held villages and not worry about exposed flanks. These tactics had frequently been employed with success in the East."
>
> *General Hasso Von Manteuffel, on the Ardennes offensive*

By 17 September 1944 the allies had liberated France, Belgium and Luxembourg and had reached Dutch and German borders by 1 September 1944. On 17 September 1944 they launched an ill-fated operation to gain a bridgehead across the lower Rhine, while outflanking the defences of the West Wall. Codenamed Market-Garden, this operation ended on 25 September as a partial failure because intelligence reports of the German strength in the area were ignored. The 9th and 10th SS Panzer Divisions therefore shared the dubious honour of contributing to Germany's last clear-cut victory in arms during the Second World War. Although unsuccessful, Operation Market-Garden provided allies with an important salient for the upcoming drive into Germany. On 16 December 1944 the Germans launched their Ardennes offensive, designed to split the allied armies and to capture the port city of Antwerp; although this offensive enjoyed some success at the early stage it was contained, and on 28 January 1945 the focus switched to the last battles in the East.

CAPTURED ALLIED TANKS

The allied forces at this time were equipped with a variety of American, British and Canadian made armoured fighting vehicles, and the Germans captured relatively few of them, mainly as a result of local counterattacks. By this point Germans were either on the defensive or retreating eastwards.

The American M4 Sherman medium tank (and its variants) was the most numerous allied tank following D-Day and the Germans knew it from North Africa, Italy and Russia. The M4 Sherman tank was designated by the Germans as Panzerkampfwagen M4 748(a); they captured a few vehicles which were then grouped into captured tank platoons and units in the west. These formations included the famous 21st Panzer Division, which was continually engaged against the allies until early 1945, as well as the 25th Panzer Grenadier Division. The 10th SS Panzer Division 'Frundsberg', which was also engaged against the allies until early 1945, had at least ten captured Sherman tanks, the 5th Fallschirmjäger Division and Panzer Brigade 150 were also known to have used some captured Sherman tanks. SS Panzer Division 'Frundsberg' captured 12 Sherman tanks in the Upper Alsace (Western Germany) on 17 January 1945 and operated them against the Russians until 7 May 1945, when they were destroyed by their crews in the Schmiedeberg (now Kowary, Southern Poland). In addition to those units, there were a number of unrecorded tanks pressed into service by German units. SS-Obersturmbannführer Otto Skorzeny's Panzer Brigade 150 was to be equipped with ten Sherman tanks for the Ardennes offensive. When it was organised in November 1944, in practice only two unserviceable Sherman tanks were available along with two troop carriers, five to ten scout cars and some fifteen to thirty trucks. The 5th Fallschirmjäger Division on the other hand utilised some six captured Sherman tanks as late as January 1945, following the Ardennes offensive. In July 1944 Schwere Panzer Abteilung 503 captured two British Sherman tanks near Colombelles. Schwere Panzerjäger Abteilung 654 is known also to have used a captured Sherman tank as a recovery vehicle in late 1944 and early 1945. During the fighting in Normandy, 1st SS Panzer Corps comprising the 1st SS Panzer Division 'Leibstandarte Adolf Hitler', the 12th SS Panzer Division 'Hitlerjugend' and the Panzer Lehr Division managed to capture a number of Allied tanks including at least one Sherman Firefly. This variant was armed with a British 17 pound gun mounted in a modified turret and was designated as Sherman VC (V -base variant and C -17 pound gun) Firefly. There are a number of photographs taken by Germans of captured Fireflies being examined and tested but it is unknown if any were pressed into service, and if so it can only have been for a short period of time. A few Fireflies from 7th British Tank Division were captured following the engagement by the most successful and famous tank commander of World War II - SS Hauptsturmführer Michael Wittmann, at Villers-Bocage.

In addition, German units captured a few M10 Wolverine tank destroyers in late 1944. At least one was captured by the 6th Panzer Division in Belgium in November 1944 and a few more were taken during the Ardennes offensive. They were temporarily pressed into service, their brief service lives limited to only a few days by the shortage of ammunition and fuel. They were designated by the Germans as Jagdpanzer M10(a).

A few M5 Stuart Light Tanks were also captured by the German units and temporarily engaged in 1944 under the designation of Panzerkampfwagen M3 740(a).

THE BRITISH TANKS

The British Cruiser Tank M.VIII Cromwell (A27M) was one of the most important tanks in British service during the campaign in the west. Its variants were armed with a 6 pound gun (75mm gun) and the 95mm Howitzer and were operated by a crew of five. Only a few Cromwells were captured by the Germans and were designated as Kreuzer Panzerkampfwagen Mk.VIII(e). It appears that at least two machines from the 7th British Tank Division were captured following the engagement at Villers-Bocage, including a Cromwell VI (armed with a 95mm Howitzer) and a Cromwell with the 75mm gun. There is photographic evidence of them being either examined or tested, but if any were used it could only have been for a short time.

THE ARDENNES OFFENSIVE

After the German failure at Kursk, even Hitler at last began to realise that it was now impossible to inflict a serious defeat on the Russians. Despite all the evidence to the contrary, Hitler believed that a well executed offensive in the West could defeat the western allies and free up much needed forces for the East, to at least try and halt the Russian advances. With his planned western offensive, he anticipated he could force the allies to sue for peace from a stalemate position, but even Hitler must have known this was to be the last chance for the Panzers.

One thing the Panzer Divisions did have on their side was experience, and before they were swept away, the small groups of Tigers performed heroically. Michael Wittmann alone was responsible for a huge number of allied tank kills. By June 1944 Wittmann and his Tiger had been responsible for taking out more than 130 Russian

tanks when he was transferred to the Western Front.

Even with the skills of men like these, the Tigers were still being destroyed as fast as they were being delivered, and Wittmann himself fell in action in August 1944, his machine totally destroyed. Such losses were simply unsustainable.

In 1944, despite the pressures of allied bombing raids, some twenty thousand German armoured fighting vehicles were manufactured. But battlefield losses were running at some 23,000 machines, so the number of German tanks available in 1944 at the front line actually fell.

During 1944, on average, there were never more than 100 Tigers available for action at any given time on the whole of the Russian Front. The remaining machines were either under short or long-term repair. It was this tiny force which forged a legend.

On the Western Front the allies by now enjoyed total air supremacy and the allied airforce was able to rove at will, destroying German aircraft on the ground.

The high rate of attrition on their armoured force caused the Germans to cast around desperately for

The tank hunter version of the King Tiger was due to be in action at the start of Operation Wacht am Rhein but to Hitler's dismay transport difficulties delayed the appearance of the machines in which he had a pathetically high expectation.

The Jagpanzer IV utilised the excellent chassis of the Panzer IV and combined that reliability with an excellent 75mm gun and well sloped thick frontal armour to produce a highly efficient fighting vehicle.

a solution. One successful expedient was to dispense with the turret of the new Panther tanks to produce turretless vehicles with less flexibility but heavier firepower. They were also easier and quicker to manufacture; three could be made for every two tanks.

These tank killers were known by the German name Jagdpanther. By this stage of the war German armour was fighting almost exclusively defensive battles for which the Jagdpanthers were perfectly suited. They could lie in wait, firing from fixed positions.

As with the turretless tanks, there was also a steady increase in size and armament in the tank hunters, which evolved from the simple Marder I, based on the Panzer I, to the ultimate tank killing machine, the Jagdtiger, based on the upgraded Tiger II. Massive armour and a superb high calibre gun made these machines deadly. But, once again, the design and engineering effort took valuable resources away from producing simpler designs in the volume the Germans needed.

PREPARING THE ASSAULT

By a small miracle of logistics the hard-pressed Germans of the Third Reich somehow managed to scrape together the men and machines for one last great offensive. In the middle of December 1944 Hitler launched his surprise winter offensive in the Ardennes region of Belgium. For this offensive 250,000 men and over one thousand tanks and armoured vehicles had somehow been assembled. After the destructive battles through France in the summer, this force represented the very last reserves of manpower. Hitler placed all of his hopes on this offensive, the last great offensive in the west during the Second World War.

The plan for this attack was fairly straightforward. The Ardennes region had provided a successful launch pad for the Blitzkreig campaigns of 1940. Once again Hitler planned to push a strong, armoured-led thrust through the allied held positions and on to Antwerp. This would split the two main allied armies and, he hoped, force them to accept defeat or evacuate back to England as they had done in 1940.

Unlike 1940, however, the Germans were fighting an army who were used to their tactics. This time the allies had better equipped forces that they could call upon to meet any threat. The terrain and supply problems did not favour the Germans this time either. The German Generals could see the shortcomings of the offensive, but at this late stage in the war few of them dared to question Hitler's authority for fear of their lives.

The Germans had been busy developing new tanks and assault gun designs during this period. In 1944, during the battle, the allies captured the powerful monster known as the Sturmmoser or Sturm Tiger. The troops who knocked out this giant adversary must have breathed a huge sigh of relief because this devastating machine was so powerfully armed it had outgrown mere artillery power and was equipped with a rocket launcher of ferocious attacking force.

It was designed to attack even the strongest fortification. Due to the range limitations of its rocket launcher, the Sturm Tiger had to get very close to its target to fire its payload, but it was so heavily armoured that it was nearly impervious to any anti-tank gun on the battlefield. The Sturm Tiger's role was to rumble right up to infantry bunkers or strong points and fire the rocket almost at point blank range. Obviously, the chances of survival for its target were slim indeed.

The enormous rockets it carried were so heavy the vehicle needed its own crane to be able to load

The desperate plan for the Ardennes offensive called for the employment of captured American vehicles. With the failure of the forces on the ground to deliver enough machines, Kommando Skorzeny who were to use the captured tanks had to resort to attempting to disguise German tanks as allied vehicles.

the shells. Once loaded, the inside of the tank was so cramped it carried enough rounds for only thirteen shots, but when it did fire, the results were devastating.

The Sturm Tiger was the last in a line of turretless tanks which the German army had produced in increasing quantities since the outbreak of the Second World War, but this highly specialised vehicle was produced so late in the war that only 19 were manufactured before Germany finally surrendered. One of the most significant new designs was the Tiger II B, or King Tiger.

The Tiger II is a remarkable tank by any standards. It mounted a bigger and more powerful gun than the Tiger I and the armour was thicker and sloped, giving it a tremendous advantage. For a tank which came into service in 1944, it looks almost good enough to use today, and was a considerable tribute to the German designers. The trouble was that it was getting near the limit of weight that the engine and transmission could stand and, of course, producing a tank like this under wartime conditions was a tremendous strain, especially when the industry was being heavily bombed. Therefore, in terms of gun power and armour, it outclassed tanks such as the T-34, but was never available in sufficient numbers and

certainly wasn't easy to ship around the country in a hurry and get to trouble spots, so it has to be regarded as a failure in terms of tank design.

The Tiger B was the largest practical tank to see action in the Panzer Division. Already its huge size was giving enormous difficulty in negotiating narrow roads and moving across bridges, few of which could carry its huge weight. It also needed huge stocks of the vital fuel supplies which Germany could no longer provide.

Around 50 vehicles were fitted with Porsche turrets, the remaining 439 Tiger IIs were fitted with the Henschell turret. The first time that King Tigers saw action was during the allied invasion of France in June 1944; around 15 King Tigers were involved in these battles. A full battalion of 45 King Tigers was later sent to the Arnhem area in September 1944, where they helped to ensure that the allied Operation Market-Garden was thwarted. They were next to feature in the coming German offensive in the Ardennes. Like the Tiger I, this tank was better suited to the open country and the majority of them were sent east to battle with the advancing Russians. A full battalion of 45 tanks was earmarked for the assault. The SS 501st heavy tank battalion, which was part of the 6th Panzer Army, was placed with Kampfgruppe Peiper, at the front of the armoured advance.

By late 1944 the assault guns and tank destroyers had become a valuable addition to the German arsenal. The Jagd Tiger was a highly effective tank destroyer but a total of only 70 Tiger II chassis were ever converted to the new design. This was enough to equip two heavy tank destroyer units. One of these, the 653rd, saw action during the Ardennes offensive. This very imposing machine was more suited to the open country and not the closed confines of the Ardennes. Overall, this vehicle was an excellent destroyer of allied tanks, but its introduction was too late in the war and the numbers too few to have any effect on the final outcome.

The manufacture of assault guns was more cost effective and these types increasingly proved their worth on the battlefield. More and more resources were put into developing new designs and the trend was not always to larger machines. One of these new designs was the Hetzer, based on the vehicle chassis of the 38(t).

Another assault gun design used by the Germans during the Ardennes offensive was the JagdPanzer IV Lang. This vehicle was based on the Panzer IV chassis and weighed around twenty-six tons. The crew contained four men. Its main armament was the very potent 75mm L/70 main gun; this was the same gun that was used on the Panther. One MG42 machine gun provided the close quarter support. The armour protection was 80mm thick and the top speed was 24mph. This vehicle had a low silhouette and, together with the very effective main gun, became a very capable killer as the US handbook made clear:

Another view of one of the Panzer IV tanks disguised as an allied vehicle for the Ardennes offensive.

'Jagdpanther, 8.8 cm Pak 4313 OR 43,14 (L/71) ON THE PANTHER CHASSIS. (1) General. This tank destroyer is intended for engaging armored targets at long ranges from stationary positions. A single, heavy, sloping plate protects the front of both hull and superstructure. The gun is mounted centrally in this plate, giving the vehicle the appearance of an assault-gun, with the gun rather high'.

These new tank designs joined the existing German machines including the Panzer IV, Panther and Tiger. On the whole the German tanks were probably superior to those of the allies, who still relied on the Sherman.

'WACHT AM RHEIN'

The Ardennes offensive was given the code name 'Wacht am Rhein' or 'Watch on the Rhine'. Hitler, however, did not fully realise the extent to which the situation in December 1944 was very different to that in May 1940.

For one, the planned route for the new offensive cut straight across the Ardennes. In 1940 the route used had travelled in a south-westerly direction and utilised the road system that generally ran in that direction also. The new route was to the north-west and the Ardennes offered few north-westerly roads. This would seriously restrict movement of the German forces and cause immense delays in the deployment of the vital armoured spearheads.

Another restrictive feature of the planning was the lack of sufficient fuel. To make up for this, the German troops were expected to capture enemy fuel dumps and supplies en route. Even the amount of fuel that was originally requested for the start of the operation could not be fulfilled. The fuel factor on its own was to play a significant part in the eventual failure of the operation. The deployment of the forces was not best suited to ensure success either. The advance towards Antwerp required the forces to swing north-east after the Germans had reached the Meuse river. Given that the allies had strong forces in Belgium and Holland, it was suspected that they would eventually mount a counter-attack into the German left flank. However, the strongest armoured German forces were situated on the right flank and too far removed to meet any potential threat.

The Germans did have some elements in their favour. The weather was bad at this time and it was expected to remain like this for at least a week. The overwhelming allied superiority in the air had inflicted heavy losses on the Germans over the last few months. The much-feared Jabos or rocket-firing planes struck fear into the heart of every German soldier. The poor weather situation prevalent in the middle of December 1944 would keep the allied planes on the ground for the vital opening phases of the attack. This would, with luck, allow the advance to make a good start and reach some of the objectives.

When the attack began, the scale of the unleashed German forces surprised the allied commanders. Some of them had expected a German attack imminently, but not to this extent. Some of the forces that were part of the German attack had been severely mauled during the Normandy battles. The planned area of attack was also being held by allied troops who themselves had only recently been involved in heavy fighting around the Hurtgen forest. Hitler was confident of success and did not allow any alterations to his plans. By 16 December everything was in place. The quiet Ardennes sector was about to erupt with the sounds of battle. The Panzers were once again moving west.

The Germans had assembled an impressive line up of tank forces for the offensive. The powerful 6th Panzer Army were positioned in the north under Obergruppenführer 'Sepp' Dietrich. This force included the 1st SS Panzer Division 'Leibstandarte Adolf Hitler', 2nd SS Panzer Division 'Das Reich', 9th SS Hitler Panzer Division 'Hohenstaufen' and the 12th SS Panzer Divisions. Their task was to advance along the route from their forming-up area near Dahlem in Germany and into Belgium around the town of Losheim. Their objective was to cross the Meuse just below Liège and advance onto Antwerp.

Just to the south of this force was the 5th Panzer Army under the command of Lieutenant General Hasso von Manteuffel. He had the 2nd Panzer, 9th Panzer, 116th Panzer and the Panzer 'Lehr' Divisions together with the 15th Panzer Grenadier Division. Their objective was to move from Prum in Germany and onto Antwerp via Brussels. The 7th Army under General Erich Bradenberger was to take the southernmost route into Luxembourg. This was an infantry-only formation made up from the 5th infantry divisions including a grounded Parachute Division. They were to move from Bitburg in Germany and into the area held by the US 3rd Army, with the objective of tying down these forces. All of these forces were part of Army Group B commanded by Field Marshal Model.

The devastating combination of artillery fire and mastery of the skies meant that there were few hiding places for German tanks in the closing phase of the war.

New recruits are taken through their paces using the turret of a Panzer II for instruction. By this phase of the war training vehicles were in very short supply.

They had very limited reserves, in the shape of the 3rd Panzer Grenadier Division and the 'Führer Begleit' Brigade and the 'Führer' Grenadier Brigade.

This total force had 2,000 artillery pieces, over 1,000 tanks and assault guns and 250,000 men. To have assembled this impressive force after the destructive battles in Normandy and the east was an exceptional feat on its own, but the size masked some real weakness. Each of the Panzer armies relied on Volksgrenadier battalions to provide its infantry support. These men were Germany's equivalent of the British Home Guard. They were scraped together into formations which were intended as a last ditch defensive mechanism; they had no part to play in a full-bloodied offensive.

The storm was about to break on just four Infantry Divisions who were part of the US V Corps under Major General Gerow. Two were positioned opposite the 6th Panzer Army. Facing Manteuffel in the centre were the 28th and 106th Infantry Divisions who were part of Major General Troy Middleton's VIII Corps. In the south facing Brandenberger's men were the 9th Armoured and the 4th Infantry Divisions. All of these American units had recently been involved in heavy fighting and were in the area for a rest. They totalled around

80,000 men, less than 450 tanks and assault guns and around 400 artillery pieces. Although initially outnumbered, the allies had strong forces positioned close by, including Patton's 3rd Army, that could be called upon to back up the defences in this area.

On the morning of 16 December the German artillery opened fire along the entire front line. The object of this was to confuse the enemy, disrupt their lines of communication and open gaps in the lines. Due to the extreme secrecy, the Germans were unable to identify the allied positions in advance. The result was that the German bombardment had limited success. It did sever allied lines of communication, inflict some casualties and provide some confusion, but not to the extent that was hoped by the Germans. In the north, Dietrich's forces advanced towards Elsenborn Ridge. A German parachute drop had been ordered for this area with the objective of capturing a vital road junction in the Baraque Michel. This drop did not go well as the Falschirmjager were scattered over a wide area. They found themselves in amongst the US 1st Infantry Division, so the small force had to find their way back to their own lines. The failure of this small, but significant, action would delay the advance of the SS armour.

Dietrich's men had Obersturmbannführer Jochen Peiper at their head; this SS officer was a seasoned veteran of Russia and Normandy. He had a battalion of 45 King Tigers under his command, but in the opening stages they were not with the lead force. He helped to ensure that the advance got off to a good start towards the Elsenborn Ridge, under the cover of the bad weather. However, the Americans gave a good account of themselves and succeeded in preventing the Germans from taking this vital high ground. Slightly south of here the main body of the 1st SS Panzer Division moved into the gap that had been opened up between the US V and VIII Corps. The route of their advance was towards Honsfield, which they reached on the following day. Various delays had taken place, but by the end of day one progress had been made.

In the 5th Panzer Army's area the advance got off to a good start. They moved against the thinly spread American units and forced through the enemy positions. Some of the American forces slowed the advance and managed to hold some of the bridges in the area. By the end of day one, however, crossings had been made over the river Our and the German Panzers rolled on towards Clervaux. Further south the 7th Army ran into similar difficulties to Dietrich. The ground was favourable to the defender and Brandenberger's men made little headway.

Overall, although difficulties had been encountered, 17 December would see the all-important armour committed in strength. However, the American High Command was starting to react to the German attack, and reinforcements were being rushed to the area to meet the threat. Among these reinforcements were the 7th and 10th Armoured Divisions together with the 82nd and 101st Airborne Divisions. These last two units were ordered to the vital road junction of Bastogne. The German attempt to reach their objective continued. Dietrich in the north was keen to make progress. He moved the 12th SS Panzer Division from their attack on Elsenborn Ridge, and pushed them in behind the 1st SS Panzer Division who were moving towards the Ambleve River. The move actually helped to relieve the pressure on the Americans defending the ridge area, and to set up a defence that the Germans could not breach.

Dietrich had an ace up his sleeve in the shape of the 150th Panzer Brigade. This force was under the command of Otto Skorzeny (probably best known for his dramatic rescue of Mussolini). They were using captured American jeeps and trucks together with German tanks adapted to resemble American tank destroyers. Their task was to infiltrate behind the American lines and race ahead to capture vital crossings and hold them for the main forces. They were also to pass false information to the enemy and generally cause confusion. They did have some successes; the most notable was when they reached the Meuse. They were unable to capitalise on this success as the main body of troops was too far behind. Also, groups of them began to get stopped and arrested by the Americans. The rumours quickly spread that there were Germans driving around posing as friendly forces. Everyone became a suspect and some very high-ranking American officers found themselves in awkward situations. Eisenhower himself was confined to his headquarters in fear of assassination. Although their objectives were not entirely reached, the psychological effect that this unit had was very widespread and out of proportion to the small numbers involved. Most of those that were captured were shot as spies.

Peiper's advance in the north had come across a group of Americans who they took prisoner. They were held in a field near the crossroads at Malmedy and it was here that around eighty of them were shot. The Americans insisted that this was in cold blood, the Germans claimed they were trying to escape. The bodies were found a short time later and the search went out for the culprits. The story spread throughout the American lines and actually helped to instil resistance in the men. Just before this incident, Peiper's men had succeeded in capturing a fuel dump at Bullingen, which had helped the advance to continue. They reached the bridge at Stavelot, but were held up for a number of hours when they came under attack.

The advance into Stavelot resumed the following morning and the town was captured. The advance continued towards Trois Ponts; close to here were the bridges that cross the Salm and Ambleve rivers. These bridges were destroyed by the American defenders as Peiper's men approached, and Peiper was forced to move back towards La Gleize. He tried to advance through to Chenaux, where another bridge crossed the Ambleve, but came under attack from American planes, so set up defences around La Gleize and Stoumont.

With the failure of this advance, the main emphasis was shifted to the 5th Panzer Army's sector. They were having better luck against the US 106th Division. However the US 101st Airborne Division had reached Bastogne and set up all round defences. They offered such stiff resistance that Manteuffel ordered his forces to bypass the town and continue their advance. This created a 'bulge within a bulge' and would provide a very prickly thorn in the Germans' side. On 22 December the Germans went to Bastogne with a white flag and the offer of surrender for the Americans. The garrison commander, General McAuliffe, offered his famous 'nuts' reply. The key town of St.Vith, further north, had fallen to the Germans on the same day. They had been fighting around this town for days, and as in other areas these delays allowed the Americans to build up defences further back. On the 24th Manteuffel's forces reached an area just west of Celles. This was to become the furthest point reached by the Germans during this offensive. Christmas Day 1944 saw the besieged Bastogne coming under increasing pressure from

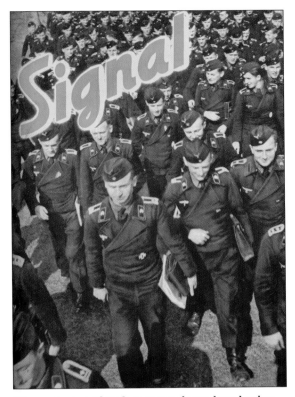

The next wave of tank men are shown here having completed the officer training part of the course. These are the men who would provide the tank commanders for the last two years of the war.

the Germans. They pushed more and more forces into the area in an attempt to eliminate the pocket. Further south, elements of Patton's forces were moving closer and, on Boxing Day, they managed to force an opening through the German lines and into Bastogne. This was the start of the end of Hitler's Ardennes offensive.

Another significant occurrence around this time was the improvement in the weather. This allowed the allies to send sorties against the German positions. At La Gleize, Peiper could see the hopelessness of the situation. His men were receiving a pounding by American artillery and tanks; the Americans fired over 58,000 shells into the area during the battle. This provides a good picture of the punishing fire that Peiper's men would have endured. He ordered that the tanks and half-tracks that had not already been destroyed by allied fire be destroyed by his own men to prevent their use by the enemy. They were out of vital fuel and ammunition. He left some of his men behind to give the impression that they were still fighting and

also to look after the 150 American prisoners they had captured. He took the remaining 800 survivors with him and made for German-held lines, which he managed to reach a few days later. The escape attempt had been dangerous and on more than one occasion his men became involved in firefights with American forces that were moving across Peiper's escape route. Peiper not only left behind some of his men, he also left behind an impressive bag of irreplaceable armoured vehicles that included six King Tigers, 13 Panthers, six Panzer IVs and over fifty other vehicles including around forty-five armoured half-tracks. These losses were hard to take at this stage of the war.

Further south, the corridor into Bastogne was slowly widened. Ferocious battles took place around this area and both sides fought desperately for control. The Americans pushed more and more forces into the Bastogne area including the 4th Armoured Division, the 26th Infantry and the 80th Infantry Divisions. The 'Battle of the Bulge', as the Americans called the battle, was proving a very hard fight for both sides. As the allies were able to push more forces into the area, they slowly succeeded in pushing the Germans back. By 2 January 1945 the front line had been reduced by around fifteen kilometres.

Although the Ardennes offensive is always associated with American forces, British forces also played a vital role. In the early stages of the operation Montgomery had recognised the importance of the river Meuse to the Germans and had placed strong British forces in a defensive position along the northern sector. He was also given command of some of the American forces; this in itself caused a rift between the Allies and in some respects almost helped Hitler to achieve his goal. When the time was right, Montgomery launched a counter-attack into the German lines with the objective of linking with the Americans further south. This objective was finally reached on 4 January at the town of La Roche. This meant that a solid defensive line now existed that the Germans could not hope to penetrate. Also, the river Meuse, vital to German success, was now out of reach.

Hitler still ordered the advance to continue and achieve the original objective, but at this stage it was an increasingly impossible task. However, the intensity of the battle is best described by Patton himself, who on 6 January expressed his very real fears that the war could still be lost by the allies.

The 1st SS Panzer Division were moved down to this area at the end of December to help destroy the Americans. This did nothing to change the final outcome and only added to the German casualty list.

Allied fighters flew sortie after sortie against the Germans and inflicted further aerial destruction on the increasingly pressurised German forces. The Luftwaffe launched their own attacks in the early days of January, when around a thousand planes flew against allied targets. This attack had some notable successes, including the destruction of 300 allied aircraft and the damage to some twenty-five allied airfields. The Germans themselves lost around a hundred planes and, more importantly, experienced pilots. At the time the allies played down this part of the battle. Towards the middle of January some of the German units were withdrawn, including the 1st SS Panzer Division, which put even more pressure on the remaining German forces. Hitler had also launched another smaller offensive called 'Nordwind' at the start of January. It had the objective of destroying the allied positions around the Vosges Mountains. The attacks quickly bogged down against the allied

defenders, but the fighting continued until mid-January. The operation itself achieved nothing of any significance, but it represented a high irreplaceable cost to the Germans in men and machines.

By the end of January the front line was back to where it had been at the start of the German offensive six weeks earlier. The cost to both sides was high; the allies lost around seventy-five thousand men, the Germans suffered around one hundred and twenty thousand casualties and lost a considerable number of irreplaceable tanks. As the allies discovered when they came across the vehicles, a large portion of them had been abandoned because their fuel tanks had run dry. The allies could make their losses good, but the Germans simply could not. The loss of the Ardennes offensive removed any reserves that the Germans possessed and which could have been used in the defence of the Reich. In the east the Russians had launched their new offensive in January 1945. There was nothing available to counter this threat. Hitler's last gamble in the west had failed completely and the end of the Third Reich was in sight.

A Pz.Kpfw VI(B) King Tiger tank knocked-out and abandoned by its crew during the latter stages of the fighting in Normandy.

LAST BATTLES IN THE EAST

An artist's impression of the problems of keeping the Sturmgeschutz re-supplied in action. The limited storage capacity meant that these precious machines had to be constantly re-stocked with ammunition, even under fire.

"There was much we could do but we were not magicians. There needs to be close co-operation between Panzers and the infantry. Often we came under the command of infantry officers who did not understand how Panzers should be handled in action. We lost many machines through carelessness and inexperience... heartbreaking."

Oberst Paul 1946, on the battle for Berlin

After the failure of the Ardennes Offensive the writing was now on the wall for the men of the Panzerwaffe, but there was still more fighting to be done. Despite the deteriorating situation, Hitler now sought to rush his precious Panzer Divisions to Hungary where they were commanded to take part in Operation Spring Awakening to secure the liberation of Budapest and secure the Reich's last supply of oil.

The weight of numbers was now running very strongly against the Panzerwaffe; only the quality of the German armour now separated the two sides. Although they were massively outnumbered, the diminishing ranks of German Panzers managed incredible feats in action.

There was also a number of far-sighted innovations which had to be rushed through to try to stem the tide. Amongst these radical leaps in technology was the introduction of night-vision equipment into the Panther tanks, which actually worked in practice. The inevitable teething problems and production difficulties meant that this development made little practical impact in the full, but the technology was developed for the future.

HERR RUEHS

One veteran of the Panther in action was Herr Ruehs who later recalled his experiences in the closing stages of the war;

"I had originally been a Panzer grenadier but I didn't want to sit outside the tanks anymore, so I trained as a medium-wave radio operator. Before this I was acting as a gun-loader. Our own gun-loader had got out to help tow another tank that had gone off the road and broken down - it had lost its right-hand caterpillar - they were fired at, and he was badly wounded.

We went into action at the railway embankment near the Plattensee. We couldn't get any further unfortunately, although we had ten good, almost new, Panther tanks. The road was occupied by a PAK, and they were able to see us very well so we just couldn't advance any further. We had our first casualty there. As soon as we left the road with our heavy tanks, one was hit and it blew up. They were all killed inside the tank of course.

My best friend was also killed there. He was still a Panzer grenadier, but he didn't want to sit on top of a tank at the rear. He said, "Man, that is too dangerous for me, I am an only son. Let me go to the rear." But he was ordered with his squad - about twenty of them - into the trenches in front of our tanks, and he was killed by a direct hit, together with the other two men in the hole. He died there. I had to identify him later.

We were attacked from the air many times by the Russian planes. I was in a tank of the company Commander - I was told later that we had broken through the enemy lines on such and such an occasion and that later we could read all about it in books - which I have actually - but mostly, in those days, we retreated.

We hadn't had any losses until then. All ten of our company tanks were present, except that we had no more fuel. We positioned ourselves behind a hill - our company Commander was called Werner Scherp, he got the Knight's Cross for this action - within twenty minutes we had destroyed five T-34's with our own tank. Every shell a hit! We could fire quite accurately, that was our advantage. The Russians were numerically superior but our firing

was accurate and they couldn't get us because we only had the turret visible behind the hill. We even had equipment for seeing at night. To keep it short, we used five of the ten tanks as towing vehicles and set off for West Brem. Eventually we had to blow up all ten tanks because we had no more fuel. A very expensive exercise, and very sad too."

TRANSPORT ISSUES

In operations such as Spring Awakening, entire Panzer Divisions had to be moved all the way across Europe. The cumbersome process of loading and transporting an entire Panzer Division for transport from West to East was an enormously complex operation, but it was one which had been carried out a number of times. The standard procedure for moving a Panzer Division by rail had not escaped the all-seeing eyes of allied intelligence, and was published in the US Army handbook of 1945;

'STANDARD TROOP TRAINS. The Germans have found it desirable to use troop trains of a reasonably constant composition. The standard trains found in the Balkans, Italy, and Norway are composed of fewer cars than the base types in Germany, Denmark, and the Netherlands which are described below. All types are designed as far as possible to carry a self-contained unit such as a company or a battalion. Non-standard trains also may be used for troop movements.

K-trains (Kraftfahrzüge or motor vehicle trains) average 51 cars per train and carry approximately 250 soldiers, 20 heavy vehicles (weighing up to 22 short tons per vehicle),and 20 light vehicles, plus other equipment. If lighter equipment is carried, the number of soldiers can be increased.

S-trains (Sonderzüge, or special trains) are made up for the movement of very heavy tanks and self-propelled guns. The number of men carried per train averages 125 ; the number of cars forming the train is between 30 and 35. An S-train usually carries from four to six Tiger tanks or from six to eight Panther tanks, interspersed with lighter equipment.

Sp-trains (Sonderpanzerzüge, or special tank trains) carry approximately 20 medium tanks together with personnel and other equipment. The standard Sp-train is composed of about 33 cars.

I-trains (Infanteriezüge or infantry trains) of about 55 cars per train hold some 350 officers and men, 10 light vehicles, 10 heavy vehicles of a maximum weight of 22 short tons per vehicle, and 70 horses, together with other equipment. If a minimum of equipment is carried, up to 800 troops can be moved. It is possible that the I-trains seldom are used by the Germans at present.'

SOVIET CAPTURED TANKS

In 1943 a new generation of heavy tanks entered production - the Josef Stalin series. The JS-1 was a development of the KV series of heavy tanks with numerous improvements and modifications. The JS-1 was an interim model on the move towards the JS-2 and only 102 were produced in 1943. These early tanks were armed with the same 85mm gun as the T-34/85. Later they were equipped with a 100mm main gun. In 1944 all existing JS-1s were re-armed with 122mm guns and were followed by the JS-2, which was an improved version and was to be the main production model. From 1943 to the end of the war 3,854 JS-2 tanks including rebuilt JS-1 tanks were produced. There is no evidence of JS tanks ever being used by the Germans but knocked out examples were carefully examined

and probably a single JS was provided to German Army Office for examination and testing purposes. The JS-2 was designated by the Germans as Panzerkampfwagen JS-122(r).

As the war progressed the Soviet Army began receiving the SU (Samokhodnaja Ustanovka) and JSU series. The SU-76 and SU-122 both appeared in 1942 in very limited numbers, eventually being followed by SU-85 and the SU-152 in 1943 and the SU-100 in 1944. Both the JSU-122 and the JSU-152 also appeared in 1943 in limited numbers.

The SU-76 and SU-76M assault guns were based on lengthened T-70 light tank chassis mounted with the superstructure open at the top and rear housing a 76.2mm gun. It was operated by a four-man crew and only 26 were produced in 1942, but eventually 12,671 were built by the end of the war. It is known that the Germans captured and pressed a number of SU-76 into service, and they were relatively easy to maintain, because the Panzerwaffe already used T-70 light tanks, and 76.2mm ammunition was widely available. In addition to the SU-76s used by Germans on the Eastern Front at least one saw service during the Ardennes Offensive in December of 1944 with a

Captured Russian T-34 tanks are sent into action with German markings, manned by SS crews.

A Panzer IV being transported to the front on railway carriages. Judging by the excellent state of repair it looks as if this machine has probably come straight from the factory.

Waffen-SS unit. Before the Ardennes offensive, this particular assault gun was in service on the Eastern Front and was transferred along with its unit to the Western Front. The SU-76 was either designated as Panzerjäger SU76(r) or Sturmgeschütz SU-76(r).

The SU-122 assault Howitzer was based on a T-34 with its turret replaced by a fully enclosed armoured superstructure housing a 122mm Howitzer. It was operated by a five-man crew and only 25 were produced in 1942, but eventually 1,148 were produced by 1944, when production switched to SU-85. The Panzerwaffe captured and pressed a number into service. The Germans encountered few problems maintaining the SU-122 because it was based on the T-34 medium tank and 122mm ammunition was also widely available. It was designated by the Germans as Sturmgeschütz SU-122(r) / Stug.122(r). A Single SU-22 was captured by schwere Panzer Abteilung 502 on the Leningrad Front in November 1943 and was also pressed into service.

The SU-85 tank destroyer was basically a modified SU-122 mounted with an 85mm gun and operated by a four-man crew. 2,050 were produced in 1944. In 1945 the SU-85 was replaced by the SU-100 tank destroyer. The SU-100 was an improved version of SU-85 armed with the 100mm

gun. 1,675 SU-100 tank destroyers were produced from 1944 to the end of the war. The SU-85 was designated by the Germans as Jagdpanzer SU85(r) and SU-100 as Jagdpanzer SU-100(r). It is known that the Russian volunteer units (possibly Kaminski Brigade) serving with the German Army used a small number of captured SU-85 tank destroyers.

The SU-152 was based on the KV-1 heavy tank mounted with a fully enclosed armoured superstructure housing a 152mm howitzer. Only 704 were produced in 1943, but the SU-152 proved to be successful when dealing with German Panther and Tiger tanks and it was nicknamed 'the animal killer'. The Germans captured a small number but there is no evidence of them being ever used, although a single example was captured by the Germans on 19 August 1943, following the Battle of Kursk Salient, and was probably handed over to the German Army Office for examination and tests. The captured SU-152 were designated as Sturmpanzer SU-152(r) or Sturmgeschütz SU-1 52(r).

The ISU-122 and ISU-152 were further developments of the SU series but based on the chassis of the IS heavy tank series. The ISU-152 was armed with a 152mm howitzer and the ISU-122 was armed with a 122mm gun mounted in fully enclosed armored superstructure. Four thousand and seventy-five were produced from 1943 to the end of the war. None was pressed into service and possibly a few captured examples were handed over to the German Army Office for examination and tests. ISU-122 was designated as Jagdpanzer JSU-122(r) and ISU-152 as Sturmpanzer JSU-1 52(r).

THE BATTLE FOR BERLIN

In February 1945 the last battle of the Second World War was drawing to a terrifying conclusion. This, the most titanic of all conflicts, was certainly not about to end with a whimper. Although all hope of victory was long gone, the bitter fighting in the battle for Berlin would witness the frantic death throes of a desperate regime.

This was Hitler's long promised 'Götterdämmerung' - the Twilight of the Gods. Those Gods would witness the agony of a city sacrificed to make a dramatic exit for one man.

Herr Ollech was one soldier who vividly recalled

the collapsing German morale after the death of the Führer:

"We slept beside one another, we ate together, we were out there together in this misery, together we learned that Hitler had shot himself, that our 'all powerful father' was gone, we felt that we had been left behind, absolutely abandoned, he had deserted us, and what now..."

The tides of war were running inexorably against Germany. Hitler's thousand year Reich was already on its knees and it seemed there was a very real prospect of an end to the conflict before the end of the year.

From the skies over Germany the Third Reich was experiencing destruction on a scale never before experienced by any nation at war. Hundreds of thousands of German civilians had perished in a series of raids which devastated German cities, among them the old port of Hamburg. In the wake of a heavy allied bombing raid Hamburg was swept by such intense firestorms that tornadoes were formed which sucked living people into the flames.

On land, too, the noose around Germany was tightening. In the west the allies had at last established the long awaited second front, but it was in the east, in the cauldron of the Russian Front, that the events of the Second World War would be decided.

By October 1944 the German army Group North besieging Leningrad had been driven back and was now trapped in the Kurland Bridgehead.

Following the success of Operation Bagration, the great offensive against Army Group Centre, Russian armies were already on the border of Poland.

In the southern sector an unremitting pattern of defeat and retreat had seen the German forces driven back from Kharkov to the Balkans.

Faced with disaster on this scale the logical scenario would have been a German capitulation. In fact, the surviving German armies continued to offer dogged resistance to the very last days of the war.

The effect of the military defeats of 1944 on Hitler was catastrophic. He began to hide himself away in his headquarters, embarrassed to face up to the hollowness of his earlier boasts. He found the psychological blows too great to rationalise. He was now unwilling to be seen in the newsreel footage, where once he had held centre stage. Those newsreels from the end of the war produce a picture of a broken, prematurely aged man. All

The chassis of the 38(t) was also used to produce the Hetzer, an excellent tank-hunter design which packed a good punch from its 75mm gun, but produced a small silhouette which made it a difficult target to hit.

traces of the confident leader have disappeared and his uncertain demeanour and hunched shoulders tell more of a story than words can. This was the man who was supposed to lead Germany through her greatest trial.

Ranged against the crumbling German armies was the immense strength of the Red Army and the revitalised Russian airforce.

By now the German army was massively outnumbered and the best estimates are that they possessed one tank for every sixteen which the Russians could put into battle. It has been estimated that against the one million men Hitler could deploy, some five million Russians could be deployed for the battle of Berlin.

While the Western allies concentrated on the strategic bombing campaign against German cities the huge Russian bomber force was deployed against military targets on the ground. By late 1944 wave after wave of fighter-bombers flying overhead made it very difficult for German forces to move on the ground. The Russian airforce was used as a prelude to all of the major offensives on the ground and it played a major part in achieving those victories.

The final assault on Germany itself began at the southern end of the front on 12 January 1945, when the massed tanks and infantry of the first Ukrainian front under Marshal Koniev moved against the German lines. The advance of this front swept through Poland and saw the Russian armies on the border with Czechoslovakia by the end of March.

To their north, the first Belorussian front under Zukhov swept aside the newly formed German Army Group A and, by the end of March, Zukhov's troops were positioned at Kustrin, only 50 miles from Hitler's capital.

Further north still, the last remnants of Army Group Centre were trapped in a huge pocket around Königsberg by the combined forces of the second and third Belorussian fronts advancing from the north of Warsaw and Lithuania.

The rag-bag of forces fighting under SS Commander Himmler known as Army Group Vistula were also thrown back by the advancing Red Army.

The enormous sacrifice made by men fighting in what were obviously lost causes was justified by both the men and their commanders on the grounds that the continued resistance against the Soviet

Happy Russian infantrymen inspect the results of their anti-tank expertise during the closing battles in the East.

A Panther is dug into the streets of Berlin to provide a fixed defensive position.

thrusts had allowed thousands of refugees to escape from the terror of the Red Army advance.

As they advanced into Germany, the Red Army had the opportunity to demonstrate that the forces of barbarism could be replaced by humanity. They chose instead to behave in a manner which aped the vile excesses of the regime against which they fought. With the blessing, and participation of, their officers, the men of the Soviet forces in Germany embarked on an unrestrained orgy of looting, murder and mass rape which, given all that had occurred in Russia, was to an extent predictable.

"The civilians were in the cellars, scared to death, old people, women and children. They only left the cellars to fetch water and maintain a minimum of hygiene; it was like that in the rest of Germany and also in Berlin. Scarcely anything to eat and in constant fear. Sadly, the Red Army made the mistake of turning fear into reality and raped the German women; sadly, those things happened which are incomprehensible now as they were then; if one really intends to forge a new future, then I don't quite understand it."

In the face of Red Army retribution the will to resist remained and in many cases German resistance actually began to increase; there were even successful counter-attacks which revealed to the Germans the level of the horrors that awaited them. Footage taken at a German town recaptured from the Russians shows evidence of atrocities committed while the town was briefly in Russian hands.

All that remained for the ordinary German citizen was to wait for the Red Army to regroup and gather its huge strength for the final assault on Berlin.

The grim joke began to do the rounds of war torn streets of Berlin - 'Enjoy the war while you can because the peace will be terrible'.

Faced with a doomsday scenario, organised German resistance continued and the final Soviet drive for Berlin could not begin in earnest until 16 April 1945.

Even if they had wanted to, Berliners simply could not hoist the white flag and surrender. Despite his pathetic condition, Hitler was still in control of Berlin, the SS and the Gestapo still functioned and he still gave the orders for the defence. And what Hitler demanded he got. Berlin was ultimately a battle which was fought virtually to the last bullet and almost to the last gasp. The German forces, which were still in the field, were determined to fight to the very end, so the closing battles of the war were as hotly contested as anything which had gone before. Fifty-five years on from the events of the battle Herr Ollech recalled the fighting on the outskirts of Berlin:

"We were sent into action in the north-east of Berlin, and suddenly, as a young man - and you can see photos of me - I had to shoot at human beings in order to preserve my own life. You do not consciously experience that process, you only experience it in retrospect. Death does not only strike your comrades, it strikes the enemy too. And for that reason I can only say that war is like diarrhoea. It is truly the lowest rung of humanity. And when your comrades fall beside you, and you are 17 years old, and are directly confronted, directly confronted with the events of war, it causes a change in your mentality."

Although they faced a number of insurmountable difficulties in supply and material the German forces fighting to defend Berlin prepared to do their duty with great courage and thoroughness. The east side of Berlin was strongly fortified with three separate lines of anti-tank defences. In the city itself every street was to be made a strong point. Hitler had hoped to turn Berlin into a fortress. Ringed around the city were three structures which harked back to the medieval castles of old. These were the flak towers, three huge concrete castles with walls so thick that not even the heaviest artillery shells could penetrate. The first was located just off the Brunnen Strasse in the north of the city and was known as the Humboldthain Tower. The second was just to the east of the city centre on Landsberger Allee and the

One of the best all-round fighting vehicles of the war was the Jagdpanther. With well-shaped armour and the excellent 88mm main armament this machine was much feared by allied tank crews.

third was in the south-west of the city centre at the Berlin Zoo. Built in 1945, their real purpose was to serve as anti-aircraft gun platforms to protect the city against the frequent allied bombing raids. Each of the enormous gun towers had a satellite tower a short distance away for the artillery observers to control the anti-aircraft fire. Now, with the Soviet forces beginning to encroach on Berlin itself, they were to become a vital part of the defence ring hastily thrown up around the city. These defences were designed to protect the heart of the Nazi regime located in a bunker close to the Chancellery building on Wilhelm Strasse. Nearby were the city landmarks of the Brandenburg Gate on the Unter Den Linden and the Reichstag on Königsplatz. All of these sites were to see savage fighting in the coming battle, and the makeshift defences would take an enormous toll from the Soviet forces - 333,000 casualties before they finally clawed their way into the Reichstag.

There were still substantial Wehrmacht elements who fought to the bitter end, but they were now augmented by the men of the Volkssturm battalions; these were scratch formations composed of old men and young boys who were now literally fighting to defend their own homes and families; this was to prove a forlorn hope.

Before they were swept aside, the men of the Volkssturm had become highly proficient in the use of the Panzerfaust, which was an anti-tank weapon of deadly effectiveness at short range.

One additional obstacle which the Russians would have had to overcome were the wrecks of their own tanks, which frequently formed a convenient barricade across many of the streets, where they had come to grief against these hand held rockets which made the humble infantryman the equal of the mighty T-34.

The German tank formations had been largely destroyed but in the rubble-strewn streets of German towns and cities tankhunting teams could get to close quarters, and the Panzerfausts claimed hundreds of Russian tanks destroyed at close range by desperate men fighting in their own city. But there were other occasions where the Volkssturm proved less than resolute, as Herr Ollech recalled:

"We spent that night there and the next morning, the weather was dry. We discovered that the infantry units, in the shape of the Volkssturm which was supposed to be in front of us and whom we had seen the day before, had vanished. That, of course, scared the wits out of us and then we got the order to retreat with our unit into the town proper, because the Red Army, primarily the infantry, but also the tanks, had already gone around us and broken through into the suburbs. If we hadn't changed positions, they would have had us encircled."

Hitler had by now become mesmerised by the arrows on the situation map in the bunker; reduced to clutching at straws, he began to believe once again that the flags on the map represented real military forces. In particular Hitler began to believe that Steiner's 11th army could somehow link-up with the surviving German forces north of Berlin and strike a decisive blow against the Russians. In reality the grand sounding title of army was illusory. The rag-bag of forces at Steiner's disposal could only be described as an army in the deranged mind of Adolf Hitler; in fact, the depleted forces available to the German commanders still fighting on the outskirts of the city had no real prospect of halting the Soviet advance, never mind any question of reversing the tide.

The battered German defenders had managed to mount a spirited defence on the Seelow heights to the east of Berlin, but the Soviet juggernaut in the form of devastating massed artillery attacks made the position untenable.

With the last natural obstacle against a Russian advance neutralised the Soviets could now advance on the city itself.

"The news came that the Soviets were advancing along this road which only became understandable in retrospect; they could see with the naked eye whether or not mines had been laid.

It was an asphalt road so they could see exactly that it had not been laid with mines; as the road was free of mines they advanced. Along it came four T-34s, two Shermans and an assault tank. The road had a small bend and, before the first tank had reached this bend, it was fired at and everything blew apart. We had an artillery gun, the 88mm which had a velocity of 1,200 metres per second, the only gun in the world from which the shell left the barrel at such speed. That meant that the discharge and impact, especially at a distance of 200, perhaps 300, metres, was so short, that you thought that discharge and impact was the same sound. These tanks were soon all destroyed and the Red Army infantry that sat on the rear of the tanks had already dispersed. The tanks glowed throughout that night and if there was ammunition inside it exploded. We spent the night there; we felt like big-game hunters. You know, a hunter is happy when he has killed the game."

Despite the best efforts of hard-pressed men like Herr Ollech, the noose was tightening. Against this gloomy scenario, Hitler hung on to the hope of relief by General Hienrici with the 9th army, but Hienrici was no fool and he knew a lost cause when he saw one. In order to prevent needless bloodshed in a final pointless gesture Hienrici moved his army away from the beleaguered city leaving Hitler to fume in his lair.

Matters took a further turn for the worse when Steiner's 11th army was brushed aside to allow the Russians to complete the encirclement of Berlin. By 22 April Russian troops were fighting on the streets of the German capital; both sides knew the insanity was surely about to end. But in the unconquered portions of the city the street warfare in Berlin raged on as bitterly as ever.

Any prospect of a wholesale evacuation for the Führer and his entourage had now disappeared and a radio broadcast on 22 April announced that the Führer would stay in his capital to the very last.

The cumulative effect of years of allied bombing and the devastation caused by the heavy Russian artillery barrage had created a wilderness of rubble full of ready-made strong points, which naturally favoured the defender. Throughout the city fierce streetfighting continued to rage unabated, as the Red Army fought bitterly all the way to the Reichstag.

The final Russian assault on Berlin began on 26 April; it was preceded by very heavy air attacks and, as always, a thunderous artillery barrage. It

Even in the closing months of the war work continued on tank development programms. Despite the lessons of the Tiger II research was still carried out into the super heavy Maus.

was now that the battles for the flak towers began. Among the last defenders was Herr Ollech, who had retreated with the survivors of his unit to the Humboldthain flak tower, which housed 30,000 terrified civilians in addition to the military garrison.

"We retreated and retreated, and we finally ended up in a flak tower. There were three of them in Berlin, and we got ourselves over to one of them. Our commander was a Colonel Schäfer - and the Soviet Army fired at the tower with their tanks. You could hear the tanks firing at the tower, and it went 'clack-clack' as if someone was knocking on a door. The Red Army discovered that they were not going to get anywhere like that; shooting at it with a 76mm wouldn't achieve anything. So, over a period of days, they brought up 15 cm howitzers and they could fire directly at the tower; so they let loose with direct fire from the 15cm. That still only managed to make tiny holes in the concrete. There were windows which were closed from the outside with heavy steel doors, I imagine that they weighed tons, and the Russians at last succeeded in hitting the upper hinge of one of the doors which burst and one of these broke off, twisted off the other one and hurtled downwards; and that was the only hole that existed. They then brought up a light artillery piece. A tank attack at night followed; they knew that we were lying in relays in the surrounding trenches. We had never experienced that before, tanks at night, and that was the most serious, perhaps the most awful experience, because they attacked and we sought cover, had to lay down on our fallen comrades. We fought off the attack, and the next morning we were able to see the burnt out tanks and the Russian corpses hanging over the edges of their trenches, their machine guns dragged halfway in. They were on wheels which you could hear when they were crossing a street because they rattled 'rat-a-tat' over the street, they dragged it behind them; that was fought off."

While Herr Ollech and his colleagues were fighting their desperate battles, Hitler remained in his bunker. On the night of 28 April, with the Russian forces grinding ever closer to his headquarters, he married his mistress, Eva Braun. After the wedding meal he retired to write his last will and testament. He defiantly reaffirmed his belief in Liebensraum and indulged in one last vitriolic attack on the Jewish race. On the afternoon of 30 April, having made his farewells,

he poisoned his wife and his dog and shot himself.

On the same evening that Hitler committed suicide, the last battle was raging for the Reichstag. The indomitable defenders had bricked up the windows and doors and now made a desperate last stand which had to be overcome room by room. With the Germans inside still resisting. Sergeants Yagorov and Kantariya planted the Victory Banner of the Soviet flag on the Reichstag at 10.50pm. It symbolised the triumph of the Soviet Union over Nazi Germany but it still remained a symbolic act.

Despite all of the enormous difficulties under which they now laboured, the logistical services of the German armed forces continued to produce minor miracles of supply, which allowed some fairly formidable tank formations to enter the final battle for Berlin. Among them was the 503rd heavy tank battalion equipped with the mighty King Tiger tank.

These impressive machines fought alongside the 11th SS division 'Nordland' and, even more remarkably, a battalion of French volunteers which had formed a part of the 'Charlemagne' division. On 25 April there were still 300 men available for combat in the French volunteer battalion. Together these two formations played a key role in the defence of the government buildings in the centre of Berlin. In many respects the Frenchmen had nothing to lose and there was even less at stake for their German masters.

The SS, in particular, knew that they could expect no mercy from the Red Army which had long since adopted the practice of shooting SS prisoners out of hand. Perhaps it was this knowledge which kept

One of the most bizarre ideas to emerge from the drawing boards of German tank designers was this curious machine, knows variously as the Grille, Cricket or Grasshopper. The idea was that the machine would use its tracks to move into action then detach the turret to form a mobile pillbox.

Despite the rapidly deteriorating situation, the German tank designers continued to develop the next generation of tanks including the master, this E-series prototype for a super-heavy tank to rival the Maus.

many formations at their post during the dark days of the battles for Berlin, but as late as 26 April the commander of the 503rd heavy tank battalion was able to report that he still had six tanks ready for active service in the defence of the routes leading to the centre of Berlin. Even more remarkably, they also had stocks of fuel and a plentiful supply of ammunition, including the bulky 88mm ammunition for the massive high-velocity guns which were carried in the turrets of these formidable machines.

Backed up by the Panzerfausts of the French and Norwegian volunteers, this small battle group claimed dozens of Russian tanks during the bitter streetfighting which marked the very last days of the Third Reich.

Incredibly, even the back-up and repair services of the remaining German tank battalions continued to function and, by 1 May, five days after Hitler's death, the number of tanks available to the 503rd heavy tank battalion had actually increased, and there were now 11 tanks ready for action in the bitter street battles which continued as the diehards fought to maintain their shrinking perimeter.

In his memoirs, Marshal Koniev admitted that the Soviet Army had lost 800 tanks in the fighting for Berlin. In many respects this last nut was the toughest that the Red Army had to crack.

The Russians had announced that they would capture Berlin on 1 May but the beleaguered defenders took perverse pride in the fact that by the morning of 2 May there was still fierce resistance in some sectors of the city. Although the official surrender took place on the afternoon of 2 May, a number of German units nonetheless attempted to break out of the Soviet sector and make their way towards the Western allies with the result that Berlin was not finally pacified until 3 May.

After the surrender the city authorities estimated that there had been something like ninety thousand instances of rape in the last few days before the surrender of the city. For the ordinary citizens of Berlin there could be no prospect of relief.

Although military discipline would soon be restored, it was obvious that one barbarous and inhuman regime had been swapped for another. As East Germans, three generations of Berliners would pay a heavy price for loyalty to the man who did not possess the personal courage to face the music.

187

Divisions	Recruiting District	Divisional Elements	Combat History
1st PANZER	IX (KASSEL) FORMED OCT. 1935	1st PANZER REGT 1st PANZER GRENADIER REGT 113th PANZER GRENADIER REGT 75th PANZER ARTILLERY REGT 1st PANZER ARTILLERY SECTION	POLAND 1939 BELGIUM 1940 FRANCE 1940 RUSSIA 1941-43 (LENINGRAD, MOSCOW) BALKANS 1943 RUSSIA 1944 (ZHITOMIR, CHERKASSY RELIEF, HUBES POCKET) HUNGARY & AUSTRIA 1945
2nd PANZER	XVII (VIENNA) FORMED OCT. 1935	3rd PANZER REGT 2nd PANZER GRENADIER REGT 304th PANZER GRENADIER REGT 74th PANZER ARTILLERY REGT 2nd PANZER RECONNAISSANCE SECTION	POLAND 1939 FRANCE 1940 BALKANS 1941 RUSSIA 1942-43 (RSHEV, KURSK, KIEV) FRANCE 1944 (FALAISE, ARDENNES) GERMANY 1945
3rd PANZER	III (BERLIN) FORMED OCT. 1935	6th PANZER REGT 3rd PANZER GRENADIER REGT 394th PANZER GRENADIER REGT 75th PANZER ARTILLERY REGT 3rd PANZER RECONNAISSANCE SECTION	POLAND 1939 FRANCE 1940 RUSSIA 1941-43 SMOLENSK, KIEV, TULA, KURSK, KHARKOV, CHERKASSY RELIEF) POLAND 1944 HUNGARY/AUSTRIA 1945
4th PANZER	XIII (NUREMBERG) FORMED NOV. 1938	35th PANZER REGT 12th PANZER GRENADIER REGT 38th PANZER GRENADIER REGT 103rd PANZER ARTILLERY REGT 4th PANZER RECONNAISSANCE SECTION	POLAND 1939 FRANCE 1940 RUSSIA 1941-44 (CAUCASUS, KURSK, LATVIA) GERMANY 1945
5th PANZER	VIII (BRESLAU) FORMED NOV. 1938	31st PANZER REGT 13th PANZER GRENADIER REGT 14th PANZER GRENADIER REGT 116th PANZER ARTILLERY REGT 5th PANZER RECONNAISSANCE SECTION	FRANCE 1940 BALKANS 1941 RUSSIA 1941-44 (KURSK, DNIEPER, LATVIA) EAST PRUSSIA 1944-45
6th PANZER	VI (MUNSTER) FORMED OCT. 1939	11th PANZER REGT 4th PANZER GRENADIER REGT 114th PANZER GRENADIER REGT 76th PANZER ARTILLERY REGT 6th PANZER RECONNAISSANCE SECTION	RUSSIA 1941-44 FRANCE 1944 HUNGARY & AUSTRIA 1944-45
7th PANZER	IX (KASSEL) FORMED OCT. 1939	25th PANZER REGT 6th PANZER GRENADIER REGT 7th PANZER GRENADIER REGT 78th PANZER ARTILLERY REGT 7th PANZER RECONNAISSANCE SECTION	FRANCE 1940 RUSSIA 1941-42 (KALININ, RSHEV) SOUTHERN RUSSIA 1942-44 (KHARKOV, KURSK, KIEV, ZHITOMIR, HUBES POCKET) BALTIC COAST & PRUSSIA 1944-45

Divisions	Recruiting District	Divisional Elements	Combat History
8th PANZER	III (BERLIN) FORMED OCT. 1939	10th PANZER REGT 8th PANZER GRENADIER REGT 28th PANZER GRENADIER REGT 80th PANZER ARTILLERY REGT 8th PANZER RECONNAISSANCE SECTION	FRANCE 1940 YUGOSLAVIA 1941 NORTHERN RUSSIA 1941-43 (LENINGRAD, KHOLM, OREL, KIEV) SOUTHERN RUSSIA 1943-44 HUNGARY & YUGOSLAVIA 1944-45
9th PANZER	XVII (VIENNA) FORMED AUG. 1940	33rd PANZER REGT 10th PANZER GRENADIER REGT 11th PANZER GRENADIER REGT 102nd PANZER ARTILLERY REGT 9th PANZER RECONNAISSANCE SECTION	NETHERLANDS & FRANCE 1940 BALKANS 1941 RUSSIA 1941-44
10th PANZER	V (STUTTGART) FORMED APRIL 1939	7th PANZER REGT 69th PANZER GRENADIER REGT 86th PANZER GRENADIER REGT 90th PANZER ARTILLERY REGT 10th PANZER RECONNAISSANCE SECTION	POLAND 1939 FRANCE 1940 RUSSIA 1941-42 TUNISIA 1943 (KASSERINE, MEDENINE, TUNISIA)
11th PANZER	VIII (BRESLAU) FORMED AUG. 1940	15th PANZER REGT 110th PANZER GRENADIER REGT 111th PANZER GRENADIER REGT 119th PANZER ARTILLERY REGT 11th PANZER RECONNAISSANCE SECTION	BALKANS 1941 RUSSIA 1941-44 (MOSCOW, KHARKOV, KURSK, CHERKASSY, HUBES POCKET) NORTH WEST EUROPE 1944-45 (ARDENNES, REMAGEN)
12th PANZER	II (STETTIN) FORMED OCT. 1940	29th PANZER REGT 5th PANZER GRENADIER REGT 25th PANZER GRENADIER REGT 2nd PANZER ARTILLERY REGT 12th PANZER RECONNAISSANCE SECTION	RUSSIA 1941-44 (SMOLENSK, LENINGRAD, OREL & MIDDLE DNEPR)
13th PANZER	XI (HANNOVER) FORMED OCT. 1940	4th PANZER REGT 66th PANZER GRENADIER REGT 93rd PANZER GRENADIER REGT 13th PANZER ARTILLERY REGT 13th PANZER RECONNAISSANCE SECTION	RUSSIA 1941-44 (KIEV, CAUCASUS, KUBAN) RUMANIA 1944 HUNGARY 1944-45
14th PANZER	IV (DRESDEN) FORMED AUG. 1940	36th PANZER REGT 103rd PANZER GRENADIER REGT 108th PANZER REGT 4th PANZER ARTILLERY REGT 14th PANZER RECONNAISSANCE SECTION	YUGOSLAVIA 1941 SOUTHERN RUSSIA 1941-42 RUSSIA 1943-45 (DNEPR BEND, UKRAINE, KURLAND)

Divisions	Recruiting District	Divisional Elements	Combat History
15th DIVISION	(DARMSTADT / LANDAU) DEUTSCHES AFRIKA KORPS FORMED AUG. 1940	8th PANZER REGT 104th PANZER GRENADIER REGT 115th PANZER GRENADIER REGT 33rd PANZER ARTILLERY REGT 15th PANZER RECONNAISSANCE SECTION	NORTH AFRICA 1941
16th PANZER	VI (MUNSTER) FORMED AUG. 1940	2nd PANZER REGT 64th PANZER GRENADIER REGT 79th PANZER GRENADIER REGT 16th PANZER ARTILLERY REGT 16th PANZER RECONNAISSANCE SECTION	SOUTHERN RUSSIA 1941-42 ITALY 1943 (SALERNO, NAPLES) RUSSIA 1943-45
17th PANZER	VII (MUNICH) FORMED OCT. 1940	39th PANZER REGT 40th PANZER GRENADIER REGT 63rd PANZER GRENADIER REGT 27th PANZER ARTILLERY REGT 17th PANZER RECONNAISSANCE SECTION	RUSSIA 1941-45 (SMOLENSK, KIEV, STALINGRAD (RELIEF), KHARKOV, CHERKASSY, HUBES POCKET)
18th PANZER	IV (DRESDEN) FORMED OCT. 1940	18th PANZER REGT 52nd PANZER GRENADIER REGT 101st PANZER GRENADIER REGT 88th PANZER ARTILLERY REGT 8th PANZER RECONNAISSANCE SECTION	RUSSIA 1941-43 LITHUANIA 1944
19th PANZER	XI (HANNOVER) FORMED OCT. 1940	27th PANZER REGT 73rd PANZER GRENADIER REGT 74th PANZER GRENADIER REGT 19th PANZER ARTILLERY REGT 19th PANZER RECONNAISSANCE SECTION	RUSSIA 1941-44 (MINSK, SMOLENSK, VELIKI LUKI, MOSCOW, KHARKOV, KURSK) ·EAST PRUSSIA 1944
20th PANZER	XI (HANNOVER) FORMED OCT. 1940	21st PANZER REGT 59th PANZER GRENADIER REGT 112th PANZER GRENADIER REGT 92nd PANZER ARTILLERY REGT 20th PANZER RECONNAISSANCE SECTION	RUSSIA 1941-44 (MOSCOW, KURSK) ROMANIA 1944 EAST PRUSSIA 1944 HUNGARY 1944
21st PANZER	FORMED FEB. 1941 IN NORTH AFRICA (FROM 5th LIGHT AFRIKAN DISTRICT)	22nd PANZER REGT 125th PANZER GRENADIER REGT 192nd PANZER GRENADIER REGT 155th PANZER ARTILLERY REGT 21st PANZER RECONNAISSANCE SECTION	NORTH AFRICA 1941 FRANCE 1943-44 GERMANY 1945

Divisions	Recruiting District	Divisional Elements	Combat History
22nd PANZER	XII (WIESBADEN) FORMED OCT. 1941	204th PANZER REGT 129th PANZER GRENADIER REGT 140th PANZER GRENADIER REGT 140th PANZER ARTILLERY REGT 140th PANZER RECONNAISSANCE SECTION	RUSSIAN FRONT 1942 (STALINGRAD)
23rd PANZER	XII (STUTTGART) FORMED OCT. 1941 IN FRANCE FROM AROUND PARIS	23rd PANZER REGT 126th PANZER GRENADIER REGT 128th PANZER GRENADIER REGT 128th PANZER ARTILLERY REGT 23rd PANZER RECONNAISSANCE SECTION	RUSSIA 1942-44 (KHARKOV, CAUCASUS, STALINGRAD, DNEPR BEND) POLAND & HUNGARY 1944
24th PANZER	I (KONIGSBERG) FORMED FEB. 1942	24th PANZER REGT 21st PANZER GRENADIER REGT 26th PANZER GRENADIER REGT 89th PANZER ARTILLERY REGT 24th PANZER RECONNAISSANCE SECTION	RUSSIA 1941 (STALINGRAD) POLAND 1944 HUNGARY 1944 EAST PRUSSIA 1945
25th PANZER	VI (MUNSTER) FORMED FEB. 1942 FROM OCCUPATION UNITS IN NORWAY	9th PANZER REGT 146th PANZER REGT 147th PANZER REGT 91st PANZER ARTILLERY REGT 25th PANZER RECONNAISSANCE SECTION	FRANCE 1943 SOUTHERN RUSSIA 1943 (KIEV) WARSAW 1944 GERMANY 1945
26th PANZER	III (BERLIN) FORMED OCT. 1942	26th PANZER REGT 9th PANZER GRENADIER REGT 67th PANZER GRENADIER REGT 93rd PANZER ARTILLERY REGT 26th PANZER RECONNAISSANCE SECTION	ITALY 1943 (ANZIO, CASSINO) ADRIATIC COAST 1944
27th PANZER	FORMED 1942	140th PANZER GRENADIER REGT 127th PANZER ARTILLERY REGT	RUSSIA 1942
116th PANZER	VI (MUNSTER) FORMED APRIL 1944 IN FRANCE	16th PANZER REGT 60th PANZER GRENADIER REGT 156th PANZER GRENADIER REGT 146th PANZER ARTILLERY REGT 116th PANZER RECONNAISSANCE SECTION	ARDENNES 1944-45
PANZER-LEHR	FORMED IN FRANCE IN 1944	103rd PANZER LEHR REGT 901st PANZER GRENADIER REGT 902nd PANZER GRENADIER REGT 130th PANZER ARTILLERY LEHR REGT 130th PANZER RECONNAISSANCE LEHR REGT	FRANCE 1944 HUNGARY 1944 GERMANY 1944

Divisions	Recruiting District	Divisional Elements	Combat History
1st FELD-HERRNHALLE PANZER (FHH1)	FORMED SEPT. 1944 IN HUNGARY	HAD NO ESTABLISHED DIVISIONAL STRENGTH	BUDAPEST 1945
3rd PANZER GRENADIER	BASED ON III (BERLIN) FORMED OCT. 1934	8th PANZER GRENADIER REGT 28th PANZER GRENADIER REGT 103rd PANZER BATTALION 3rd ARTILLERY REGT 103rd PANZER RECONNAISSANCE SECTION	EASTERN FRONT 1941 STALINGRAD 1943
10th PANZER GRENADIER	BASED ON XIII (NUREMBERG) FORMED OCT. 1934	20th PANZER GRENADIER REGT 41st PANZER GRENADIER REGT 7th PANZER BATTALION 10th ARTILLERY REGT 110th RECONNAISSANCE SECTION	EASTERN FRONT 1941 DEMJANSK 1943 RADOM 1945
14th MOTORIZED INFANTRY DIVISION	FORMED OCT. 1934	11th GRENADIER REGT 53rd GRENADIER REGT 114th PANZER RECONNAISSANCE SECTION	EASTERN FRONT 1941 RSHEV 1943
16th PANZER GRENADIER	BASED ON VI (MUNSTER) FORMED AUG. 1940	60th PANZER GRENADIER REGT 156th PANZER GRENADIER REGT 116th PANZER BATTALION 146th ARTILLERY REGT 116th PANZER RECONNAISSANCE SECTION	YUGOSLAVIA 1941 DON, ROSTOV 1943
18th PANZER GRENADIER	BASED ON VIII (BRESLAU) FORMED OCT. 1934	30th PANZER GRENADIER REGT 51st PANZER GRENADIER REGT 118th PANZER BATTALION 118th ARTILLERY REGT 118th PANZER RECONNAISSANCE SECTION	POLAND 1939 FRANCE 1940 EASTERN FRONT 1941 STARAYA 1943
20th PANZER GRENADIER	BASED ON V (HAMBURG) FORMED OCT. 1934	76th PANZER GRENADIER REGT 90th PANZER GRENADIER REGT 8th PANZER BATTALION 20th ARTILLERY REGT 120th PANZER RECONNAISSANCE SECTION	POLAND 1939 FRANCE 1940 EASTERN FRONT 1941 (MINSK, BIALYSTOK)
25th PANZER GRENADIER	BASED ON V (STUTTGART) FORMED APRIL 1936	35th PANZER GRENADIER REGT 119th PANZER GRENADIER REGT 5th PANZER BATTALION 25th ARTILLERY REGT 126th PANZER RECONNAISSANCE SECTION	FRANCE 1940 GERMANY 1940 EASTERN FRONT 1941 (ZHITOMIR, UMAN, KIEV)

Divisions	Recruiting District	Divisional Elements	Combat History
29th PANZER GRENADIER	BASED ON IX (KASSEL) FORMED OCT. 1936	15th PANZER GRENADIER REGT 71st PANZER GRENADIER REGT 129th PANZER BATTALION 129th ARTILLERY REGT 129th PANZER RECONNAISSANCE SECTION	POLAND 1939 FRANCE 1940 GERMANY 1941 EASTERN FRONT 1941 (MINSK, SMOLENSK, BRYANSK)
36th MOTORIZED INFANTRY	FORMED OCT. 1936	87th GRENADIER REGT 118th GRENADIER REGT 136th PANZER RECONNAISSANCE SECTION	GERMANY 1940 EASTERN FRONT 1941 (PLESKAU, LENINGRAD)
60th MOTORIZED INFANTRY	BASED ON XX (DANZIG) FORMED OCT. 1939	92nd MOTORISED GRENADIER REGT 120th MOTORISED GRENADIER REGT 160th PANZER BATTALION 160th ARTILLERY REGT 160th PANZER RECONNAISSANCE SECTION	POLAND 1940 RUMANIA 1941 EASTERN FRONT 1941 (ZHITOMIR, UMAN, ROSTOV)

SS Panzer & Panzer Grenadier Division

Divisions	Recruiting District	Divisional Elements	Combat History
1st SS PANZER GRENADIER *"LEIBSTANDARTE ADOLF HITLER"*	FORMED MARCH 1933 FROM HITLER'S BODYGUARD TROOPS	1st SS PANZER GRENADIER REGT 2nd SS PANZER GRENADIER REGT 1st SS PANZER REGT 1st SS PANZER ARTILLERY REGT	POLAND 1939 HOLLAND 1940 BALKANS 1941 ITALY 1943
2nd SS PANZER GRENADIER *"DAS REICH"*	FORMED OCT. 1939	3rd SS PANZER GRENADIER REGT 4th SS PANZER GRENADIER REGT 2nd SS PANZER REGT 2nd SS PANZER ARTILLERY REGT	HOLLAND 1940 BALKANS 1941 RUSSIA 1943
3rd SS PANZER GRENADIER	TOTENKOPF" FORMED NOV. 1939	5th SS PANZER GRENADIER REGT 6th SS PANZER GRENADIER REGT 3rd SS PANZER REGT 3rd SS PANZER ARTILLERY REGT	FRANCE 1940 GERMANY 1941 POLAND 1944
4th SS PANZER GRENADIER *"POLIZEI"*	FORMED SEPT. 1939 (DISBANDED IN 1942)	7th POLIZEI PANZER GRENADIER REGT 8th POLIZEI PANZER GRENADIER REGT 4th SS PANZER BATTALION 4th SS PANZER ARTILLERY REGT	EASTERN FRONT 1941 (DUNABURG, LUGA, LENINGRAD) YUGOSLAVIA 1944
5th SS PANZER GRENADIER *"WIKING"*	FORMED DEC 1940	9th SS PANZER GRENADIER REGT 10th SS PANZER GRENADIER REGT 5th SS PANZER REGT 5th SS PANZER ARTILLERY REGT	EASTERN FRONT 1941 (TARNOPOL, ZHITOMIR, AZOV, ROSTOV) WARSAW 1944

SS Panzer & Panzer Grenadier Division	Recruiting District	Divisional Elements	Combat History
9th SS PANZER GRENADIER "HOHENSTAUFEN"	FORMED MARCH 1943 AT MAILLY-LE-CAMP	19th SS PANZER GRENADIER REGT 20th SS PANZER GRENADIER REGT 9th SS PANZER REGT 9th SS PANZER ARTILLERY REGT	POLAND 1944
10th SS PANZER GRENADIER "FRUNDSBERG"	FORMED FEB. 1943	21st SS PANZER GRENADIER REGT 22nd PANZER GRENADIER REGT 10th SS PANZER REGT 10th SS PANZER ARTILLERY REGT	POLAND 1944
11th SS FREIWILLIGE PANZER GRENADIER "NORDLAND"	FORMED MAY 1943	23rd SS PANZER GRENADIER REGT 24th SS PANZER GRENADIER REGT 11th SS PANZER BATTALION 11th SS PANZER ARTILLERY REGT	EASTERN FRONT 1943 (LENINGRAD)
12th SS PANZER GRENADIER "HITLER JUGEND"	FORMED JULY 1943	25th SS PANZER GRENADIER REGT 26th SS PANZER GRENADIER REGT 12th SS PANZER REGT 12th SS PANZER ARTILLERY REGT	ARDENNES 1944 HUNGARY 1945
16th SS PANZER GRENADIER "REICHS FUHRER"	FORMED MAY 1941	35th SS PANZER GRENADIER REGT 36th SS PANZER GRENADIER REGT 16th SS PANZER BATTALION 16th SS PANZER ARTILLERY REGT	CORSICA 1943 ITALY 1944 HUNGARY 1945
17th SS PANZER GRENADIER "GOETZ VON BERLICHINGEN"	FORMED OCT. 1943	37th SS PANZER GRENADIER REGT 38th SS PANZER GRENADIER REGT 17th SS PANZER BATTALION 17th SS PANZER ARTILLERY REGT	FRANCE 1944 METZ 1944 FRANCE 1945
18th SS FREIWILLIGE PANZER GRENADIER "HORST WESSEL"	FORMED FEB 1944	39th SS PANZER GRENADIER REGT 40th SS PANZER GRENADIER REGT 18th SS PANZER BATTALION 18th SS PANZER ARTILLERY REGT	HUNGARY 1944
23rd SS FREIWILLIGE PANZER GRENADIER "NEDERLAND"	FORMED JULY 1943	COMPOSITION UNKNOWN	HUNGARY 1943
27th SS FREIWILLIGE PANZER GRENADIER "LANGEMARCK"	FORMED MAY 1943	67th SS PANZER GRENADIER REGT 68th SS PANZER GRENADIER REGT 27th SS PANZER BATTALION	POLAND 1943 RUSSIA 1944 (ZHITOMIR)
28th SS FREIWILLIGE PANZER GRENADIER "WALLONIEN"	FORMED JULY 1943	69th SS PANZER GRENADIER REGT 70th SS PANZER GRENADIER REGT 28th SS PANZER ARTILLERY	RUSSIA 1943 (DNIEPER) GERMANY 1944
38th SS PANZER GRENADIER "NIBELUNGEN"	FORMED MARCH 1945	COMPOSITION UNKNOWN	GERMANY 1945

Numbering the Panzer Divisions

1939	1940	1941	1942	1943	1944	1945
1 PzDiv	1 PzDiv	1 PzDiv	1 PzDiv	1 PzDiv	1 PzDiv	1 PzDiv
2 PzDiv	2 PzDiv	2 PzDiv	2 PzDiv	2 PzDiv	2 PzDiv	2 PzDiv
3 PzDiv	3 PzDiv	3 PzDiv	3 PzDiv	3 PzDiv	3 PzDiv	3 PzDiv
4 PzDiv	4 PzDiv	4 PzDiv	4 PzDiv	4 PzDiv	4 PzDiv	4 PzDiv
5 PzDiv	5 PzDiv	5 PzDiv	5 PzDiv	5 PzDiv	5 PzDiv	5 PzDiv
1 LtDiv	Converted from light to Panzer Division					
2 LtDiv	6 PzDiv — Converted from light to Panzer Division	6 PzDiv	6 PzDiv	6 PzDiv	6 PzDiv	6 PzDiv
3 LtDiv	7 PzDiv — Converted from light to Panzer Division	7 PzDiv	7 PzDiv	7 PzDiv	7 PzDiv	7 PzDiv
4 LtDiv	8 PzDiv — Converted from light to Panzer Division	8 PzDiv	8 PzDiv	8 PzDiv	8 PzDiv	8 PzDiv
	9 PzDiv	9 PzDiv	9 PzDiv	9 PzDiv	9 PzDiv	9 PzDiv
10 PzDiv	10 PzDiv	10 PzDiv	10 PzDiv	10 PzDiv		
		11 PzDiv	11 PzDiv	11 PzDiv	11 PzDiv	11 PzDiv
		12 PzDiv	12 PzDiv	12 PzDiv	12 PzDiv	12 PzDiv
		13 PzDiv	13 PzDiv	13 PzDiv	13 PzDiv	13 PzDiv
		14 PzDiv	14 PzDiv	14 PzDiv	14 PzDiv	14 PzDiv
		15 PzDiv	Became the 15th Grenadier Division			
		16 PzDiv	16 PzDiv	16 PzDiv	16 PzDiv	16 PzDiv
		17 PzDiv	17 PzDiv	17 PzDiv	17 PzDiv	17 PzDiv
	5 LtDiv	18 PzDiv	18 PzDiv	18 PzDiv	Reorganised as an Artillery Division	
		19 PzDiv	19 PzDiv	19 PzDiv	19 PzDiv	19 PzDiv
		20 PzDiv	20 PzDiv	20 PzDiv	20 PzDiv	20 PzDiv
		21 PzDiv	21 PzDiv	21 PzDiv	21 PzDiv	21 PzDiv
			22 PzDiv			
			23 PzDiv	23 PzDiv	23 PzDiv	23 PzDiv
			24 PzDiv	24 PzDiv	24 PzDiv	24 PzDiv
				25 PzDiv	1 PzDiv	1 PzDiv
				26 PzDiv	26 PzDiv	26 PzDiv
				27 PzDiv	27 PzDiv	27 PzDiv
	90 LtDiv	90 LtDiv	90 LtDiv	Converted to Panzer Grenadier Division		
		164 LtDiv	164 LtDiv			
				H Göring	H Göring	H Göring
					FF H1	FF H1
					Norwegan	Norwegan
					116 PzDiv	116 PzDiv
					Pz Lehr	Pz Lehr
Gross Deutschland Pz Gren Division	Gross Deutschland Pz Gren Division	Gross Deutschland Pz Gren Division	Gross Deutschland Pz Gren Division	Gross Deutschland Pz Gren Division	Gross Deutschland Pz Gren Division	Gross Deutschland Pz Gren Division

INDEX

A
Alam el Halfa 114
Allied tanks, captured 119
Amoured Vehicle Nomenclature 75
Auchinlech, General 91

B
Badoglio, Marshall Pietro 148
Bayerlein, General Fritz 157
Beck, General 4
Becker, Major Alfred 71, 76
Berlin 183
Bix, Herman 109
British Expeditionary Force 76
British tanks 53-54, 167-168
-captured 76-77, 94-95
Bzura, Battle of 43

C
Caen 158
Captured tanks 68-69
Char Somua 54
-B1 54
Cromwell Cruiser tank M.VIII 167
Czech tanks 17-18

D
Daimler Benz 2, 6, 36
Darwin, Charles vii
Dempsey, General Sir Miles 160
Dieppe 96
Dietrich, Sepp 16, 173

E
El Alamein, Battle of 94, 115
Estimated German Vehicle Production 82

F
Fessman, General-Colonel Ernst 13
French tanks 54-55
-captured 69-74
Fuller, Major General J. C. 13

G
Gerow, Major General 173
Grant tank, 91, 114
Guderian, General Heinz 13, 16, 17, 24, 34, 53, 62, 74, 105, 129, 138
Gun and Ammunition Nomenclature 30

H
Halder, General 100
Henschel 6
Hienrici, General 185
Hitler, Adolf vi, 2, 13, 40, 45, 62, 69, 104, 129, 157, 168, 175, 184, 186
Hoepner, General 105
Hoth, General 100, 140

K
Kama 2
Kleintraktor 3
Konev, General 139
Koniev, Marshall 187
Krupp 2, 3, 6
Kursk 127, 130, 138

L
Leichttraktor 3
Liddell Hart, Captain Basil 13, 34
Liese, General 4
Lutz, Major General Oswald 6

M
MAN 6
Matilda MkI 53
Mk II 53, 94
`Maus` ix
McAuliffe, General 174
Middleton, Major General Troy 173
Mlawa, Battle of 43
Model, Field Marshall 139
Montgomery, General Sir Bernard 91, 115, 160
Mussolini, Benito 80, 148